Advance Praise for (

This is really wonderful stuff. Thou~ ~~. and unique and insightful and funny. It's unlike anything I've ever read, and it took me back to my childhood. The book creates SO MUCH good will by reminding us why we love movies . . .
— *Scott Teems,* **director of** *That Evening Sun*

Gareth Higgins [has written] a truly original and brilliant book . . . Higgins shows us America in the language we understand best—the movies—with a witty sympathy for his subject that cuts America (and all humans) some forgiving slack. Higgins lets us (as he puts it) "kneel at the altar of the white screen and insist that it answer . . . life's questions" alongside him.
—*Frank Schaeffer,* **New York Times best-selling author of** *Crazy for God* **and** *Sex, Mom, and God*

To paraphrase Tennessee Williams, with Cinematic States Gareth Higgins is the opposite of the autobiographer, who gives you personal history that has the appearance of critical and political analysis. Gareth gives you art and political criticism in the pleasant disguise of autobiography.
—**Monte Hellman, director of** *Two-Lane Blacktop* **and** *Cockfighter*

A great book . . . Leaves you wanting to visit or revisit each movie and each place: personal yet universal, funny yet bittersweet. Let's give it that ultimate critical cliche - here, rarely, fully deserved: it'll make you laugh, it'll make you cry.
—**Nev Pierce, editor-at-large,** *Empire Magazine*

Such a fantastic idea for a book that I'm almost shocked that no writer has thought of it before. But I am so glad Gareth Higgins is the writer who did think of it, and then made the journey that allowed him to set the words down. His combination of movie love, wit, sensitivity, perception, compassion and wisdom make 'Cinematic States' a constant joy to read.

—**Glenn Kenny,** *www.somecamerunning.typepad.com*, **former Chief Critic,** *Premiere magazine*

CINEMATIC STATES

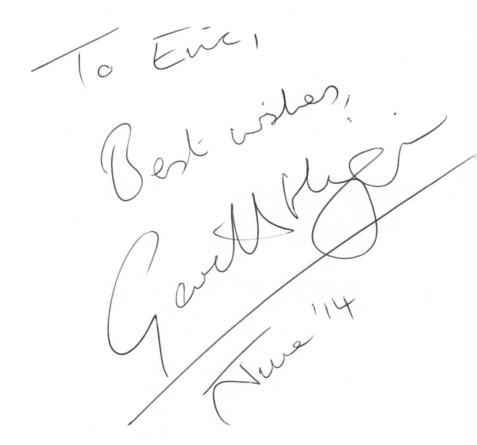

To Eric,

Best wishes,

Gareth Higgins

June '14

CINEMATIC STATES

Stories We Tell, the American Dreamlife, and How to Understand Everything*

*(Mostly. But Not Really. But Sort Of)

Gareth Higgins

Golden   Portland

Burnside Books, a division of Samizdat Publishing Group, LLC
Golden, Colorado.
http://www.burnside-books.com

For information, email info@burnside-books.com.
Burnside books may be purchased with bulk discounts for educational, business, or sales promotional use.

ebook ISBN: 978-1-938633-34-8
paperback ISBN: 978-1-938633-17-1

Cover Design: Jarrod Joplin
Creative team: Caleb Seeling and Jordan Green

Contents

FOR

John O'Donohue
and
Walter Wink

Who teach me how to see things.

You have to be a stranger to the landscape to regard it as a view.
—Geoff Dyer, *Yoga for People Who Can't Be Bothered To Do It*

The secret of American cultural imperialism—the only version of American imperialism that really is irresistible, because it works by consent - is its concentration of all the world's artistic and intellectual qualities in their most accessible form. The danger of American cultural imperialism is that it gives Americans a plausible reason for thinking that they can do without the world.
—Clive James, *Cultural Amnesia*

I wish I had your passion, Ray, misdirected as it may be. But it is still a passion.
— Terrence Mann to Ray Kinsella, in *Field of Dreams*

BELFAST ROBOTS

When I was thirteen years old I put a poster on my bedroom wall of a movie I was then too young to see, but which later came to symbolize the most significant change I have yet experienced. The movie starred Kevin Costner, who was then on the verge of becoming the biggest star of the greatest show on earth; and Susan Sarandon, who not only personified sass, but was the object of inaugural fantasies for many boys my age. The movie also starred Tim Robbins, who not only got to be in some of the more interesting cinematic works of the next two decades, but ended up living with Susan, lucky guy. It was about baseball in small town America and how the game embodies the joys and struggles of ordinary people figuring out what it means to be happy living ordinary lives. It's funny and sexy and represents a world that seems to be dying, a world that could not exist anywhere but in small town America. It's one of the best comedies ever made for adults. I think you'd really enjoy it. The movie is *Bull Durham*. I finally watched it twenty years after I put the poster up. It really did change my life.

But that's not where this story begins.

★

It's 1979—the Carter administration, the end of disco, the Steelers win the Superbowl (whatever that means), Patty Hearst gets out, Ayatollah Khomeni gets in, Israel and Egypt make nice, the Pope goes to Poland, Saddam takes over, the Greensboro massacre takes lives, China starts the one child policy, and Mr. Ed the talking horse goes to paddock heaven.

I'm four years old in Belfast, northern Ireland[1] and, not without precedent in the annals of childhood, I'm playing with my Tonka trucks. My country is falling apart, caught in the long-running civil conflict that will eventually claim nearly 4,000 lives, physically injure 43,000 more, and traumatize everyone else. It is still a couple of years away from the turning point

---

1   Some say "Northern Ireland," some say "the north," some say something else. I spell it with a small 'n', because we still can't agree on what to call my divided home.

that nudges us toward abandoning murder as a political tool and toward something more Celtic-touchy-feely instead.

But I don't know any of that yet. It's just summer and I'm playing with my Tonka trucks. Life seems simple. All I have to do is play, eat, and sleep. The coming September will see me enrolled in this thing called "the big school", in exchange for which sacrifice I'll receive the coveted trophy of a canvas lunch bag, screen-printed with a picture of C3-PO and R2-D2 (although my teacher will chastise my mum for not providing my snacks in bland yet spill-proof Tupperware). I'll meet people in school who may or may not become my friends for life. I'll get excited about the prospect of Christmas. And then I'll spend the rest of my days figuring out what it means to be a person before I join Mr. Ed at the celestial bookies. But, like I said, I don't know any of this. I certainly don't know that one of the most soul-shaping experiences I will ever have is only weeks away.

On December 18, 1979, Walt Disney Pictures will host the premiere of *The Black Hole*, their big new film, their "my-God-it's-full-of-stars" response to *Star Wars*.

It will star Anthony Perkins from *Psycho*, Ernest Borgnine from *The Wild Bunch*, Maximilian Schell from *Judgment at Nuremberg*, and Robert Forster who will end up in Quentin Tarantino's *Jackie Brown*. Timothy Bottoms, who will sort of disappear after emerging here, gets a look in, as will Yvette Mimieux, whose acting career will give way to a vocation in anthropology. Sort of the same thing, I guess.

Perkins, Mimieux, and Borgnine in *The Black Hole*

But four-year-old me won't care about the actors. What will seduce me are the robots. V.I.N.C.E.N.T., Maximilian, and Old B.O.B. will be more lifelike than the human actors (despite the fact that Maximilian can't speak and has no motor functions except to stiffly float and chop things up with his demonic red scissorhands). The good robots will inspire early thoughts of warm fuzzy god-figures, the bad one will teach my heart to fear.

The story takes place in a spaceship on the edge of a Vortex (the kind of Vortex that *earns* its capital "V"). There's a mad scientist, a beautiful woman, an enormous greenhouse, and an android-making machine. The mad scientist puts his crew into this machine to create minions that help him in his attempt to rule the universe. And it all goes terribly wrong.

The Black Hole was in every sense a BIG film. There's an operatic score composed by John Barry[2], there's spectacular sets, there's loud sound effects and even an overture. Dad took my brother and I to see it at the ABC Cinema in the Belfast city centre, the kind of family-run ramshackle movie theater that had a heart precisely *because* it was ramshackle. There was an institutional memory in the building because it had—unlike today's multiplexes—been around long enough for there to be something to remember. The velvety, dark red seats of the ABC were the same color as the walls; the staircase to the theater's entrance transformed the place into a comforting, womb-like chamber. When the lights dimmed, you were immediately enveloped by the movie. At four-years-old, *The Black Hole* conceived my childhood dreams, and they were born in the ABC. It's a parking lot now.

---

2   Barry, along with his first namesake, Williams, would continue to write the music for all the movies I loved as a child. Until I betrayed them, I suppose, at university where I learned how to be pretentious about Cinema. I've discovered since then that you can balance *ET* with *The Exorcist*, *Exotica* and *Eternity and a Day*. You don't have to trade Spielbergian awe for Angelopoulian impenetrability. Just as Rick discovers at the end of *Casablanca*, there is a tension between Being and Becoming that allows you to have both, I don't think you have to choose between 'Popular' and 'Good'.

The Black Hole

After the thrill of witnessing Maximilian overcome by V.I.N.C.E.N.T., androids firing lasers, and spaceships—SPACESHIPS! In Belfast!—I was hooked. I spent more time at the movies in the next three decades than almost anywhere else. I developed a dual identity: One side of me was attached to the land of my birth, with the *craic*—or liveliness—of the northern Irish culture that called a spade a spade, that could laugh at everything even while enmeshed in dark political arts. The other side was colonized by dreams.

Some of these dreams—waking ideas and imaginative spaces where I could guess at a different kind of life—came from friends and family, or even strangers I met along the way. Strangers like the guy who suddenly kissed me in Paris before asking me if I wanted to pay him for sex, or the fella who mugged me in Cape Town and settled for a negotiation because I didn't want to give up all my cash, or the woman who held my hand for a few seconds on the way out of a sports event in Atlanta before she realized

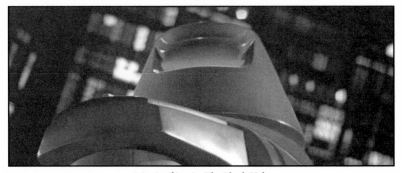

Maximilian in *The Black Hole*

I wasn't her husband. Some dreams came from reading books. But mostly they came from the Book of Life that opened every time the curtain drew back at the ABC, the Curzon Cinema, or the Strand Theatre. Because of the violence that engulfed my community, the limits of *home*—where people were killed because of their voting preferences or religious beliefs or being in the wrong place at the wrong time, where religion *was* politics, and politics *was* violence—were too restrictive for me to accept as the boundaries of being human. Places like northern Ireland struggle to emerge from the lie that being a person is to be merely a receptacle for ideology or a machine for someone else's use. In those moments when our hearts provoke our minds, we all know this lie equates life with death. The movies sparked this for me. I wanted a cinematic life because dreaming was easier than waking reality.

My young life became structured by the works of Steven Spielberg and Martin Scorsese, Ingmar Bergman and Michelangelo Antonioni, Woody Allen and Mike Leigh, and perhaps most extraordinarily by Phil Alden Robinson's film *Field of Dreams*. Robinson seemed to actually believe that listening to the voice in your head and doing the craziest thing imaginable is sometimes the only way to experience life in anything like fullness.

In my overdeveloped teenage cinematic imagination, I visited fields in Iowa, in Provence, and in the North of England. I saw thirty-five year-old untrained farmers plough under their crops in the hope that dead baseball players might visit, and I felt understood because I too have ridiculous dreams. I watched elderly French farmers in *Jean de Florette* destroy their hopes by defining community as themselves alone, and I feared for my own country because that's the way we did things too. I saw an inarticulate little boy in Ken Loach's *Kes* come to life when he gazed at his kestrel soaring above the satanic mills of his broken town, and wept when his brother's inarticulacy manifests as a murderous rage, because I know what it is to be angry enough to want to kill.

Field of Dreams should have kept the name of the book it's based on:

Shoeless Joe. Then perhaps so many of us who judge films by their titles, or who haven't seen it on the grounds of resistance to perceived sentimentality, would be less apt to ignore one of the most emotionally truthful movies ever made. And to those who look down on cinema as a lower art form or because they think it provokes only apathy in people—well, each to their own. Yet *Jean de Florette* is really a Shakespearean tragedy translated to early twentieth century France. And *Kes* proves that Loach's English socialism is as personally compassionate as it is politically committed. You could find a better trilogy of cinematically formative art elsewhere, to be sure. But when I was a child I watched like a child, and I could substitute any number of trios that had emerged into my youthful consciousness: *Back to the Future*, *ET*, and *Superman*; *The Goonies*, *The Golden Child*, and *Koyaanisqatsi*; *Tootsie*, *Cocoon*, and *Le Grand Bleu*; later Tarkovsky's *The Sacrifice*, Pontecorvo's *The Battle of Algiers*, and Kurosawa's *Ikiru*; Kieslowski's *Three Colors*; later still Scorsese's *Shutter Island*, Noe's *Enter the Void*, Reygadas' *Japon*. But these all formed me as much as the farmers and the kid with the bird.

My friend Mark Cousins, who writes about and makes films both cool and rich, says that movies "made" him. They made me too, and they also told me what was possible. When cinema erupted into my four-year-old life with larger-than-life robots, it changed me. I would be forever fastened to a vision of the world that was bigger than my home, bigger than my island, bigger than what school taught me lay within the boundaries of rational expectation. But maybe not bigger than me.

★

THREE DECADES PASS—ACTORS, COWBOYS, SPIES, AND SNAKE OIL SALESMEN SIT in the Oval Office sometimes apparently because they have nothing better to do. Princesses die in car crashes, Iran and Iraq fight each other before they fight *with* each other, and a blood-borne immune system deficiency decimates the gay community before becoming more of an equal opportunity health crisis. Jim Henson leaves this earth for Muppet heaven, OJ Simpson hides in a slow-moving SUV, and a scraggly-bearded guy in a dark blue robe says we should kill an Anglicized Indian writer. Almost everyone famous plays music to End Famine/Free Nelson Mandela/Save the Planet at one charity concert or another, and no one makes my feet move more than Stevie Wonder.

Meanwhile, I become compelled that *being human* is the biggest thing of all. It is the one thing we're never going to get over, no matter how hard we try. It collapses all boundaries of gender, nationality, politics, ethnicity, and taste. The Law at its best—enshrining human rights—says so. Art—making books and music and paintings that are ultimately about love or the lack of it—and Faith—the making and breaking of it—say so too. Religion—well, if you can assume that the times and places in which religious people destroy life are anomalies, or at least not the ideal manifestation of their mystical beliefs—says that human beings are "a little lower than the angels." So, maybe we can assert that being human is bigger than a city, bigger than a country, bigger even than movies.

This theory—that being human is the biggest thing of all and that movies can help us become better at it—takes up my intellectual and imaginative space and I suppose you could say I am Quite Pleased With Myself for it, when another magnificent rupture rips apart the stable life I thought I had.

CEAVING BELFAST

"Do you ever go abroad on holiday?"
"No, we always go to America."
— Paul Durcan

I N THE AUTUMN OF 2007 I FOLLOWED MY HEART AND FOUND MYSELF MOVING to Durham, North Carolina—a city that felt alien to me, in a state in which I felt lost, in a country I didn't understand.

Being me, which is to say sometimes morose and frequently happiest in a darkened room watching light dance on a white fabric screen, I was not initially troubled at the prospect of moving to the country where movies had emerged as the dominant art form. Being near theaters that might show something more varied than the aesthetic desert of Belfast's multiplexes was an alluring prospect. But what I thought I knew about the American South made me nervous. I had experienced the massive urbanscapes of New York, Philadelphia, and Los Angeles enough times to fall in love with the *potential* while being overwhelmed by the *actual*. I'd also spent a large portion of my adult life trying to find a financially viable route to move to Nashville, Tennessee—not because of its music, mind you, but because of its soul. And Durham seemed like it could move me closer to mine.

I was moving to follow my heart. It was unquestionably the right thing to do, because the person and the relationship were, quite simply, the greatest gifts, but it didn't feel like the right *place*. It wasn't Nashville. It wasn't New York. It *definitely* wasn't L.A. All I knew about it was from the *Bull Durham* poster I put on my wall when I was thirteen-years-old—that it was the setting of the story and that Kevin Costner, Susan Sarandon, and Tim Robbins had starred in the movie. I liked Kevin Costner, mostly because he played the thirty-five-year-old farmer in *Field of Dreams* and that made him, among other things, *my* kind of thirty-five-year-old farmer. Also, baseball was an American game that I could get used to.[3] And I had a thing for Susan Sarandon. Don't we all? So, knowing the power of movies to open my horizons, and in an effort to reduce my fears that moving to Durham would

---

3   I'd been to a few baseball games, been shouted at by the crowd for blocking their view of a Mexican wave, eaten a hot dog or two, and wondered why it took so long for a few guys to hit a ball with a stick and run round in circles until a guy dressed like Hannibal Lecter told them who won. It's fun.

represent both a beginning and an end of my dreams, I sat down to watch
Bull Durham a few months before participating in that noble Irish tradition:
escaping to America.

Bull Durham

It went just fine for the first hour. Ron Shelton's film is a witty re-
vamping of Aristophanes' ancient Greek drama *Lysistrata* (wherein women
control men through sexuality) transplanted to a minor league baseball
team's struggle for achievement amidst the Americana of the 80s. Sarandon's
character Annie is the axis on which the players turn; Costner's the washed-
up old star looking for one last shot (with the magnificent name of Crash
Davis); Robbins is the dumb brunette with a killer arm—excitable off the
field and a genius on it. Durham's the town whose infrastructure evokes
the creaky nuts and bolts on one of Buster Keaton's imminently crashing
trains. The dialogue is pepper-hot and reminds me of the best screwball
comedies of the 1930s:

"You'll never make it to the Bigs with fungus on your shower shoes."

"I have been known on occasion to howl at the moon—and if you don't
understand that now, you will." (He was right.)

So it was going along just fine. I liked these characters and it was easy to settle into the familiar vision of America as a place where the men hang out in bars, play pool, and speak in mythic terms about the meaning of life while the women want stability in exchange for sex. Comedy montages are accompanied by a bemused harmonica and a community's well-being is defined by the annual outcome of its socially-constructed competition with a neighboring town.

The film's depiction of Durham didn't make it look attractive in the sense that old towns often are, but there were some agreeable bridges and houses that were easy on the eye. And, at the risk of overstating the case, Susan Sarandon was there. There's an effortlessness to her presence. She's the kind of actor who knows she's beautiful, but doesn't let it get in the way of her intelligence or interest in you. At least that's the way she was in my fantasy of her while watching the film. I was so beguiled by the image of her character that I didn't quite hear it the first time.

Those eight little words she says that defined the next phase of my life—maybe even the rest of it.

Eight words, spoken to Robbins' character as he prepares to move to a bigger city and wild opportunity. Eight words that prepared the soil for the foundation of the second-third of whatever it is I'm doing here on earth:

"When somebody leaves Durham, they don't come back."

She said it with a smile, a gentle knee-jerk riposte to a naive promise of return, as if it's the most obvious thing in the world for a long-term Durham resident to say to a fly-by-night ball player on his way to the major leagues. She said it first in 1988, when I was thirteen, and I'm sure she didn't say it for me. But on a film set in North Carolina, a woman I've never met and probably never will (especially if she reads this—though I'm really more admirer than stalker. Honestly Susan. Desperately.), recited lines that traveled for two decades before they found their home in my heart.

"When somebody leaves Durham, they don't come back."

Bull Durham ends with the cracks in the path of true love filled by laughter and sex, which if I'm honest, frequently seems to occur in real life too. But that night, as I sleeplessly thought about what it would mean to uproot *me*, that is, my sense of meaning, to shut down a house I had made into my cave, to make some friendships transatlantic and to allow other friendships to become extinct, to reduce the number of times I would ever see my birth family again, and to give up my (probably misguided, but nonetheless urgent) ambition of being taken seriously in my home town, Susan Sarandon's words replayed themselves over and over.

The movies had always promised me the moon and the stars, but now the country whose movies were seared into my consciousness felt uncomfortably similar to the launch pad in the 1978 adventure thriller *Capricorn One*, where the shuttle never takes off and the actors inside find themselves victims of a vast government conspiracy to defraud the public and frighten the Russians. Moving to Durham was, as they say in screenwriting class, an "inciting incident." But what would it incite?

ᑎORTH CAROLINA

Mexican Satanists and an Unfingerprintable Cat

MOVED TO DURHAM. AND KEVIN AND SUSAN WERE RIGHT ABOUT ONE THING. I have howled at the moon.

But sometimes people who leave can't wait to come back.

★

I LIVED A FEW MINUTES' STROLL FROM THE BILLIARDS HALL WHERE THE BALL players in *Bull Durham* let off steam, but the challenges of urban crime and my misguided perceptions left me scared to walk in the neighborhood so I never visited it. After a few months of hoping things would change of their own accord I found myself at a neighborhood public safety meeting. The meeting was an opportunity for community leaders and residents to share their concerns and examples of best practice, and it seemed like a good idea.

The meeting started well, with an encouraging turn out of around a hundred and fifty people, some of whom were wearing T-shirts with the neighborhood group's logo embroidered over the heart. These neighborhood groups inspire loyalty, I thought to myself, relieved by the prospect of a solution to what had seemed an intractable problem. The meeting was chaired by a man sporting the biggest mustache I'd ever seen. It was the kind of thick thatch you could build a house in, almost as wide as it was long. This facial hair took discipline and commitment to produce—he looked like Tom Selleck's fantasy of Burt Reynolds. And when the chairman opened his mouth, the provenance of his mustache became clear. He was not a police officer, though he talked like a cop; he wore the t-shirt like a flak jacket; he held the wireless mic as if it were a security baton; he paced the room with the kind of authority that only people who chair neighborhood public safety meetings embody. He was not a cop. He was not a real detective. He was Magnum 2.0.

As I scour my conscience, inquiring if my memory of this meeting is not actually a trauma-induced fantasy, I cannot say that I am certain of the details one way or the other. But I do know that two things occurred that night that will stay with me. The first was that a clearly distressed woman addressed the meeting in sorrowful and anxious tones. She said that a "homicide" had occurred at her house when her cat was nailed to the pavement in cruciform style. She said the police had not been able to determine the identity of the culprits. She had her suspicions, but she could not be sure whether it was "Satanists or the Mexicans who live next door" because it had been impossible to gather appropriate forensic evidence. At this point, of course, Magnum took back the microphone from her and helpfully informed the audience that, "It is, of course, very difficult to take fingerprints from a cat. Even a live one."

Before we had the opportunity to absorb this startling fact, the meeting moved on to other business, and the second life-searing moment of the evening occurred.

I decided to address the group, in an effort at expressing my discomfort and need for neighborhood support. I had rarely felt so small in my life, at least not since the day I saw Hulk Hogan on a train in Norway. Magnum looked into my eyes with compassion as he retrieved the mic from me and I sat down, tremors possessing my hands and feet. Would I be saved? Would I be left to live in peace? Would my belief in America—previously one of the most constant, sturdy things in my life, now reduced through the stresses of immigration to looking like nothing so much as a rickety half-ton bridge—survive the two-ton load currently being driven back and forth over it? Would Magnum offer to move in with me? Would the Mexican Satanists invite me to one of their parties?

Alas, Magnum did not want to be my roommate and I saw no identifiable Satanists of any ethnicity. And I know it wasn't the worst thing anyone has had to deal with—very much a First World, middle-class problem. The war on drugs in the United States more often seems like a war on poor people who (mostly) aren't white, despite higher rates of illegal drug use among young white middle class people than young black people. My presence in this neighborhood was not exactly invited, and I didn't know how to build the relationships necessary to help address such problems without recourse to the simplistic invocation of law and order, which of course means more guns. I wish it had been different, but while I was nowhere near being the greatest victim of this particular neighborhood plot, there were still bruises. It was enough to make me reconsider everything about the country I was trying to adopt and, I suppose, be adopted by. The crowned turquoise statue at America's most famous port invites the tired and weary to a life of opportunity. The fake Texan who spoke for the nation at that time was still talking about freedom as if it was his to give, as if you find it as easily as stumbling over trash on a street corner. But I felt like a prisoner in my neighborhood. I was being stripped of my confidence, of any ability to see beyond the front door that I hated opening. No matter what the ghost of Woody Guthrie might have wanted me to believe, this land did not feel like my land, even in the most enlightened ways of interpreting that statement. There was pain and struggle in my neighborhood, and the truth was, I just didn't feel able to deal with it. Emigrating was a gift, but it wasn't easy.

It was, however, easy to indulge a melodramatic inner monologue that told me my American Dream was ending before it had a chance to begin. Such grandiosity suits writers and movie buffs alike, I guess; and while the distress I felt at how growing up in a society where violence undergirded our self-obsession had not prepared me for the experience of moving to another one, I was still privileged enough to be able to reconfigure the journey I had been on into the one that produced this book. I didn't have the time or money to explore much beyond the boundaries of my new city, so once I moved to another house I decided to stay put and explore my adopted country through the lens of its most evocative art form. In the spirit of whoever it was that suggested small problems were best solved by making them bigger, I'd watch at least one movie from each of the fifty states (and the District of Columbia—I guess you could call this my commitment to interpretation despite no representation). Movies about people who hurt each other, about people who love and want to be ordinary, about people who dream of miracles, about what it means to be human. Movies about America. I would explore whether the American Dream was really the American Lie, and if Lie it was, could I still make a home in it?

It occurred to me that if I was to take this journey seriously, I would have to lay aside my tendency toward a kind of writing that either apes or succeeds at pretentiousness (and I'm not sure which is worse). For these purposes, I wasn't especially interested in the *craft* of film-making. I wanted to know what the movies said about the place I was now living. It would be a travelogue rather than an art review. If I wanted to enter the myth of America in real life, I would have to take the movies as seriously as they were willing to take me. If they asked for my suspended disbelief, I'd give it to them; if they wanted me to trust them, I'd pretend the movies were true and allow for the possibility that cinematic truth could be as true as any other kind. I'd travel in my mind to the Grand Canyon, to the Golden Gate Bridge, to Little Italy, and a diner in the Midwest. I'd think about gunfighters, astronauts, writers, lovers, and cops. I'd watch people dance, shoot, lust, and pray their way to finding themselves. It would be my grand tour of these cinematic states: to see for myself the soul of America. And maybe I'd find a place to fit in. Maybe.

There was no obvious way to proceed, so I decided to take the states one by one in alphabetical order, picking a movie for each (or more if it seemed right) that was at least partly set there. I'd choose movies that seemed, to these outsider's eyes, to evoke something archetypal about the state, but of course the evaluation of the credibility of those choices is up to the reader. Because my first trip to the US, on the cusp of adulthood in 1993, was spent in New Jersey, I'd save that state for last. Thus I'd start in Alabama, stop in

Wyoming, and add a postscript in Jersey. I'd try to write what I saw, making a kind of touristic sketchbook out of the cinematic images and what I gleaned from a quick look at other sources of information. And so what follows is the record of my journey through these cinematic states, the dreaming of their authors, the meaning of these movies, and the unfolding of how I learned to stop worrying and love America.

ALABAMA

BELONGING

For a moment she rediscovered the purpose of her life. She was here on earth to grasp the meaning of its wild enchantment and to call each thing by its right name, or, if this were not within her power, to give birth out of love for life to successors who would do it in her place.
—Boris Pasternak, *Dr. Zhivago*

TO KILL A MOCKINGBIRD. 1962. Directed by Robert Mulligan, Written by Horton Foote, from Harper Lee's novel. Small town Alabama lawyer and lone father Atticus Finch teaches his children not to be afraid while defending an innocent man. The town is hot, the tension is hotter, there is no monster on the porch.

FORREST GUMP. 1994. Directed by Robert Zemeckis, Written by Eric Roth, from Winston Groom's novel. A simple man sees most of post-war U.S. history through a guileless lens. Forrest wants people to be good, and hasn't learned enough cynicism to avoid forgiving them when they're not. The son he has with his flower child wife Jenny—embodying two sides of the country's character—may represent the best hope America has

$\int$OMEWHERE BETWEEN LYNYRD SKYNYRD'S SCREENED PORCH AND NEIL YOUNG'S pot stash lies a mythical land. A place referred to in polite company as "the Deep South," where people keep their memories in boxes, where the evenings are feather light and the days wet hot, a poor state whose slim pickings were once ripped off the backs of slaves, where the topography is described as "general plain with gentle descent," a strange place whose people might tell you there's a *reason* why a meteorite chose Elmore County to dig in its heels and leave one of the largest craters on earth.

"Alabama" means "herb gatherers" or "clearers of the thicket." I imagine ancient sharecroppers picking cotton while gravity flings an enormous rock over their heads, thicket-clearing. The Wetumpka crater is five miles wide, large enough to lay all the theological text books in the world side-by-side many times over. Not that good Alabamians need to learn any more theology (last time anyone checked, 59 percent of the religious folk there said they had a "full understanding of their faith and needed no further learning," thank you very much, sir).

Alabama. When you don't know what Alabama is, you might think it's a theme park. The name sounds just right for a place where you can bounce all day long.

I have a personal connection to Alabama through Tallulah Bankhead, a queen of the radio talk-show/"It" girl/serious actor hybrid of the '30s and '40s—a kind of Oprangelina of her day. My maternal grandmother's cousin, a poor woman looking for work, fled to the US a few generations before I did. Somehow she met Alabama Tallulah. For several years, Ms. Bankhead benefited from my relative's services as dresser, valet, servant, and go-between. My grandmother's cousin once brought Tallulah her tiara in a paper bag during a party where Tallulah felt under-dressed. Then my grandmother's cousin went home to her tiny apartment in a tough part of the city. And that, they might say, was that.

What I know about Alabama from the movies is that it's a place where the best new myths collide with the worst old ones. Everyone thinks the same thing when they think about Alabama. You're thinking it right now, so I probably needn't belabor the point. Me? Well, I never met a person of color until I was fourteen. Her name was Lucy, the niece by marriage of a family friend. Growing up in northern Ireland, where a rabbi could be asked if he came from the Protestant or Catholic sect of Judaism, where until recently the largest non-white ethnic group out of a population of 1.7 million is the few thousand Chinese, it's fair to say there weren't too many black people around my home town. So Alabama always makes me think about how little I know of the human race. Also, because cinematic Alabama is the place that gave filmic form to the purest archetypal father in the movies, Atticus Finch, it makes me think about fathers and family and community.

To Kill a Mockingbird is widely acclaimed as one of the best literary adaptations in the cinema. Based on Harper Lee's novel of socio-political and community relations, it's one of those stories that meant something to us when we were children because we were innocent then—if we were lucky, we had no responsibilities and hope didn't always rub up against cynicism on its way out of the house. This is what is going on in *To Kill a Mockingbird*—kids learning about the world from their dad, the benign tower, the safety net, the hope, the gravitas, the truly good man. When we are children, we are trying to scale a wall that we don't even know exists, and so we need our parents to create a world in which we can fall safely. Of course, for many of us safety is misinterpreted as building more walls, so we never discover how not holding each other at arm's length isn't just fun, but at the very core of what it means to live the good life.

Mockingbird is about fatherhood, racism, being in community, and what we're losing. The children call their father by his first name, by his right name, and learn to see things for what they are: There is no monster on the porch. When you get older you might realize that this isn't always true, but you might also figure out just what the monster is and that allowing your fear to dominate is a sure way to give it power.

When I was younger, this vision of childhood in American movies didn't do much for me when I was younger except breed envy. The kids in America got to sneak into places where they shouldn't be, like abandoned railway yards or spaceships hidden by a shadowy government agency, whereas I got into trouble once for having a toy gun *in my own backyard* because a surveillance helicopter droning overhead might have mistaken it for the real thing. They went to the prom, which presents itself in archetypal stories of small town USA as the peak event of most people's lives where glamour and romance meet for the first time, whereas we had a disco in a dark nightclub filled with bottles of weak cider obtained through less than upfront means. The neighbors know each other's names in *To Kill a Mockingbird*, while northern Irish kids often needed to be discreet about what their father even did for a living.

Now Belfast and Alabama may both have communities beginning to face what has been wrong in the form of the secrets kept that made everyone feel like one big dysfunctional family. Jim Crow did in Alabama something akin to what sectarianism did in northern Ireland—the Tuskegee airmen suffered because the state divided people into categories of more and less human, which is what Belfast did too. It's what we all do.

Alabama in *To Kill a Mockingbird* defines its community on the basis of who it excludes—it takes the religious fundamentalist's way out of attributing goodness by the things we don't do. Boo Radley, the monster on the porch (there *is* no monster on the porch) is ostracized, which means he tells us more about the community than the popular people do, just as what is unspoken can tell us what a person is really saying.

If, as Neil Young would have it, the Cadillac's got one wheel in the ditch and one on the track, then maybe Alabama just needs to know what it takes to get the other wheel up. It's so often the case that, in literature and life, discovering one extra piece of information is enough to change everything.

If only Romeo knew. Or the farmers in *Jean de Florette*. Or Jephthah—the father in the Hebrew Bible's book of Judges who promises to sacrifice whatever walks through his door as an ostentatious thank you to his false image of God—who end ups up killing his own daughter, too proud to admit that his religious vows should also be subject to human compassion.

But Atticus Finch, like his Alabama brother Forrest Gump, knows exactly this: That political ideology—the will of the crowd—must be subject to mercy, otherwise it may kill us all. Each is a man whose evening activity is to sit on his porch, scratch his chin, and think. Sometimes Atticus has to stand outside a jail to save a man's life; he knows the power of a quiet witness. Sometimes he has to teach his children what not to be afraid of. He considers how children understand things, how they visualize things, where they get their information from, what they should and should not see. There is palpable pathos in Atticus's horror when his son sees a gun. *You can't enter the kingdom of heaven unless you go as a child* is the kind of thing Alabamians have been telling each other for centuries, but Atticus knows the truth is deeper than that—you can't be human, you can't live a fully human life, unless you find the place deep within where your innocence is hiding.

Sure, the film leaves something to be desired in its humiliation of a false witness for being unable to read, its abandonment of a woman whose father responded to her pain by raging at others while denying her compassion, and most of all its inability to say *anything* to a man falsely accused of terrorizing this woman because her culture won't allow him to love her. In these regards, it may simply be putting up its hands and acknowledging a hard truth: that unless a society becomes conscious of how it is structured on the threat of violence it will be incapable of the maturity required to fulfill the pursuit of real happiness. If you threaten violence against anyone who disagrees with you, then no one will be able to tell the truth about history, because history is nothing less than the sum total of our differences. And you can't grow up unless you face your past, unless you let it actually *become* the past. Atticus Finch and Forrest Gump are the kind of honest patriots who, as the theologian Donald Shriver would say, love a country enough to remember its misdeeds. Atticus speaks the way we want God to, and Forrest speaks like my inner child at its most honestly inarticulate. Both of them know that if you want to show leadership in the world of human beings, you shouldn't over-react. When a man strikes you in the face, there is a time to respond with dignified silence.

Alabama has produced some of the most courageous people in American history. Figures like the civil rights leaders Booker T Washington, Ralph Abernethy, Rosa Parks, and Coretta Scott King, as well as athletes like the color line-smashing Joe Louis and Jesse Owens. And we must not forget Helen Keller, the woman who showed how it takes more than eyes to see, or George Washington Carver, the agriculturalist who helped poor people feed themselves. But it's been a hard place to live, this Heart of Dixie. Hard enough that it made Angela Davis kick against its goads, leaving Lionel Richie feeling he had no option but to dance on the ceiling. The groove, alas, may have passed over George Wallace and Fred Dalton Thompson, which may of course prove only that some Alabamians don't find their vocation until *after* they've run for President.

★

FORREST GUMP BEGINS WITH THE IMAGE OF A FEATHER DRIFTING ON A SMALL town breeze, a token that could have fit in Scout's box in *Mockingbird*, but this should not be taken as a sign that the film is weightless. One of the first things Forrest says is a lie that he spends the rest of the film disproving. Because life is not like a box of chocolates, you *do* know what you're going to get, or at least you know that if you keep doing the same things you'll produce the same result. But then again, sometimes we all do things that don't make sense. Like refusing half the population a stake in the society we all share, or refusing to integrate the education system. But we can get where we need to go, eventually, with the help of a good father, if we can find one.

Forrest Gump roots the American journey in the Deep South but manages to trace a map of the whole country. It travels through the brokenness of gender politics, the emergence of rock and roll, the idea of love at first sight and what it can mean, the played-at egalitarianism of the US education system (Forrest, who isn't all that smart, gets to go to college because he can run fast!), the many ways to cook shrimp. It also covers some deeper, darker matters, like why some people are so scarred by the past that they want God to make them into birds so they can fly away. Or what the Vietnam War did to this country (and what all war does to any country), and that we will continue to forge our history in blood until we realize as Forrest does that war is not an adventure, that kindness is not a sign of weakness, that there is a time for nothing more than a self-respecting refusal to speak.

In the end, Forrest marries his childhood sweetheart. The former dissolute-rebel-freedom fighter and the former stupid-genius-innocent passive businessman mingle heart, body, and mind and have a child. The mother dies, the child is beautiful, and Forrest waits for his son's school bus every day sitting on a tree stump, enjoying the beautiful world. He knows what he has, for what he has lost is more precious than gold. Atticus has lost the same thing, and found it too. Two Alabamian men trying to be good fathers, knowing that they have been given stewardship over the most important thing: new life.

You might think that Alabama is far from Belfast, but it's not. Like I've said, I come from a place that also denied the humanity of its neighbors. I was lonely as a child and identify too well with Forrest being chased by the bigger boys. Hell, I even harbored a secret ambition to be a lawyer once. And now, I know and love Southern people whose identification as Southern and rural does not preclude them from embodying characteristics that are among the most urbane and postmodern, working as they do to resist dehumanization, giving confidence to my hope of finding something like a communion of selfless love in a culture obsessed with denying it.

What if Forrest and Atticus didn't know what they had? What if the nation knew that in the incarnation of American love and life it already has a beautiful child? Can we deal with our broken past without becoming trapped in cycles of bitterness? Can we come back to each other? The sun rises and the sun sets and Atticus will be waiting 'til Scout gets to sleep. And Forrest will be waiting for Forrest Jr. to come back from school. There will always be fathers who care about nothing more than their children. Smart or simple, delicate or brick-firm, lawyers or fishermen, fathers come in many guises. The sun will rise and fall on Alabama, and some of these fathers will know that there are things that need to be done to replace the old with something new. They will teach us that an integrated world emerges out of curiosity and open heartedness. They'll know that printing "shit happens" on a bumper sticker will make money, but they might just keep that to themselves. If they want to tell us about Alabama by picking three of its famous sons at random they might choose Nat King Cole, Walker Percy, or Zelda Fitzgerald. Want to challenge your stereotypes? Try those on for size. That seems like a good enough start to me. Maybe they'll show us why the people sing, "Lord, I'm coming home to you."

ALASKA

VULERABILITY

You know, it's funny—Texas always seemed so big. But you know you're in the largest state in the Union when you're anchored down in Anchorage, Alaska.
—Michelle Shocked

THE GOLD RUSH, 1925. Directed and written by Charlie Chaplin. A little tramp finds a little gold and a lot of love. The emergence of an archetype, fully-formed innocence, guilelessness, recognizing that to love always requires the risk of loss.

LIMBO. 1999. Directed and written by John Sayles. A man, a woman, and her daughter bond over a shared sense of regret for the past. They face a crisis and become a family. And who knows what happens next? Juneau, Alaska in *Limbo* looks like a place where all the exiled white people from what Alaskans call "the lower forty-eight" have ended up. A lesbian couple running a restaurant; salmon-processors out of a job from a factory that "the Chinese might buy;" corporate raiders turning the state into a tourist's amusement; singers, sailors, and a slick pool player named "Smiling Jack"—all failing to realize the same thing: that if the story you live by is a bad story, you'll have a bad life.

INTO THE WILD, 2007. Directed and written by Sean Penn. A young man wanders across America, and finds himself too late; the risk of all journeys of self-discovery being that you might find you need other people.

1. Communal warmth

In the winter of 1925, the expert Norwegian musher Gunnar Kaasen saved the people of Nome, Alaska from a diphtheria epidemic by making sure they got the right antitoxin in time. He performed this astonishing feat, as mushers often do, by mushing. Mushing a sled. "Mush, mush," he said to his alpha dog Balto, starting the final leg of a 630 mile relay. He saved thousands of lives. The fact that you have heard of Balto, but not of Gunnar, may be sufficient evidence to signal the decline of Western civilization. If an obsession with trivia is a virus, then Western civilization is dying from the common cold.

Now, it may sound obvious, but in a world where old wisdom gets mislaid at approximately the same rate as arachnid species are being made extinct, perhaps it's worth remembering that when you're dying from the cold you need to be kept warm. (Trust me. I learned this from the movies.) The best way to keep warm is to strip, and hug another naked human being (unless you should find yourself a lone Jedi on the Planet Hoth, in which case look for the nearest Ice-cave Wampa). (I learned this from the movies too.) This fact may save the human race. Because, when you're dying from the cold, an opportunity for real community emerges—your life might ultimately depend on the blood flowing through the veins of a stranger.

There are libraries of philosophical and theological literature devoted to the science of inter-communal relations. My favorite of these is Desmond Tutu's adopted notion of *ubuntu*, which, loosely translated, strongly suggests that not only do the lion and the lamb eventually lie down together, it's likely that neither of them is going to get any sleep until both agree to close their eyes at the same time. They need each other. But, most of the time, they don't know it. So one scares the other, and the other fuels the anger by showing fear. If they are warm enough not to care about the immediate need for a healthy body temperature, one might kill the other. If they are freezing, they might realize they have to cuddle. This phenomenon, known in the scientific literature, I suspect, as the "lion-lamb mutual mastication variable temperature paradox" has exercised minds far greater than mine, but their conclusion is simple: When you're dying from the cold, your body becomes a site of possibility.

2. ALASKA: A SITE OF POSSIBILITY.

Of course, what many of us think we know about Alaska comes from its recent winking governor, but delve a little deeper into the part of your subconscious that contains traces of the frozen Northwest and you'll probably find Sarah Palin accompanied by a touch of Charlie Chaplin. For most of us, all of Chaplin's performances blend into one. It's difficult to tell this little tramp apart from that one, but in *The Gold Rush* he's amiably buffeted by the movement of greed that shifted an entire population to Alaska in the nineteenth century. He gives shelter to a criminal. Helps a little girl. Loses himself. Eats a shoe. Being the largest state, Alaska's the easiest one in which to get lost. Who knows how many people have disappeared into the wild while trying to keep others away from their dream of a pot of yellow glory? Who knows how many of them *wanted* to disappear? This is good news—for Alaska seems so far from anywhere that it might just be the ideal place to start again.

In *Limbo*, Alaska is a place where the key American tradition is invented. So fixated is its common mythology on the history of pioneers that the place could give awards to people for out-pioneering each other. It is filled with stories of how the state was established by "desperate men" seeking their fortune or running away from the law. Once known as "Russian North America," it was supposed to stay with the Czar, but he didn't want to pay the phone bill so he sold it for an amount that might buy you a nice house today. This is a true story: Alaska is American because the Russian Czar refused to collaborate in setting up a communications system that the people who lived there didn't want anyway. The irony of the contemporary world's universal wiring and wifi-ing may not be lost on today's Alaskans—because they don't want to be found. They know it's cold, but they've got fleece jackets. They just want to be left alone.

People are cold, but in *Limbo* they're embarrassed to touch each other, even though that's what they most want to do. Someone sings, "I need you at the dimming of the day," and when you remember that for six months of the Alaskan year, dim's all there is, you get the picture. Instead of human contact, they keep warm by telling stories—of how the state was founded, of how some of its inhabitants live from the regret chiseled into their souls, of how while everyone's from somewhere, they're here trying to hide so they can be nowhere. They're forced to tell stories because there's nothing else to do. Except fish. And even that lends a dimension of identity that urban dwellers lack—they know something about where their food comes from. They are one step less removed than most from the circle of life and what sustains it. In this sense, Alaskans may even understand more of what it means to be human.

To be human is to be, first, a story-teller. You're rooted as an *individual* in the stories about your birth, about your parents' relationship, about your childhood, losing that first tooth, your first day of school, and your first kiss. You're rooted as a *community member* in stories, alas, about whose grandfather killed who and why. The stories get told and re-told until their details are forgotten but the narrative heart still beats. And so it continues, with people living at a distance from each other (or else subject to each other) because of misinformation.

We tell stories because we live in one. We make the stories small because we know the truth is too big to grasp or imagine. Or maybe it's too frightening. And so my story becomes about the neighbors who let a hedge grow too high, or about the girl who broke my heart when I was twenty, or about the job I didn't get, when it's conceivable that the story I find myself in has something more to do with interplanetary alignment, the Industrial Revolution, or the whimsical delight of an entirely benign Infinite Supreme Being.

3. Nudity and Happiness

Limbo, which, for the record, might be the best American film of the 1990s, contains multitudes of stories: It's about how parents, terrified of their children not turning out right, may make things worse in their clunky attempts at fixing them. It shows us the loneliness of having creative urges in a place that values only what you dig out of the ground or pull from the sea. It's a world in which nobody's telling anyone anything, but also where every word matters.

One of the characters in *Limbo*, an anthropomorphized capitalist soul-extractor (you can't really call him a person, so committed is he to commercializing the green earth for his benefit—if you can only be human in respectful relation to others, then he's of another species) says, "History is our future, not our past." Maybe he understands more than I give him credit for. He wants to turn Alaska into a theme park because, as far as he's concerned, that's the only way you can convince people to visit. The British social theorist Eric Hobsbawm recognized a long time ago that tradition has to be invented: For a vision of community to persist, someone needs to make the case that there are transcendent reasons for it to do so. And so Alaska has transformed itself from frozen tundra that few sane humans would visit for pleasure, to the El Dorado of the North, to Sarah Palin's metaphysical hockey rink/Russia-surveillance empire, to becoming the only part of the country where the government actually pays you to live.

Alaska is a frontier. It has been a state for only about half a century, getting in just before they closed the door with Hawaii, which means that although it is the last bastion of what America used to be, it's also one of the places least settled about its future. Alaska is in limbo—a condition of unknowable outcome. Christopher McCandless, the central figure in the book and film *Into the Wild* sought his soul there, believing that solitude could produce a distilled, pure version of the pioneer spirit. But as he lay dying, his journal shows that he realized what seasoned Alaskans must already have known: that happiness is only real when it's shared. It's understandable to want to believe you can find contentment alone. It's counter-intuitive to take your clothes off and be held by someone who isn't a lover. It's antithetical to our fantasies of Alaska to imagine it as one big nudist colony. But the truth about Alaska is that, in spite of its bluster and enormity, it is the most vulnerable place in America. If you're going to make it there, among its three million lakes, its trillions of mosquitoes, and its sixth wealthiest but least religious people, you need to be prepared to get naked with strangers.

ARIZONA

DISTANCES

The Grand Canyon is carven deep by the master hand; it is the gulf of silence,
widened in the desert; it is all time inscribing the naked rock;
it is the book of earth.
—Donald Culross Peattie

3:10 TO YUMA, 1957. Directed by Delmer Daves. Written by Halsted Welles, from Elmore Leonard's short story. Amidst a drought, a man finds dignity by embracing his shadow side. Meanwhile, Superman's adopted dad finds his humanity by embracing compassion. It starts to rain.

RAISING ARIZONA, 1987. Directed and written by Joel and Ethan Coen. Great lovers build a life, make a family, and defeat evil. Yoda's on the jammies.

PSYCHO, 1960. Directed by Alfred Hitchcock. Written by Joseph Stefano, from Robert Bloch's novel. Mommy's Boy is rude to houseguests. The psychology is trite, the drama over-egged, the music screeching into caricature. But for a movie about killing, it's so full of life.

GRAND CANYON, 1958. Directed by James Algar. Disney nature documentary originally screened with the first release of the animated *Sleeping Beauty*. On the surface, perhaps the most beautiful film I've ever seen. There's no trick photography, just a long look at the environs and creatures of the Grand Canyon. There are no people—we may presume this is how it looked a million years ago, and will again a million years from now. Watching induces humility.

ⒶRIZONA PRODUCES MOST OF THE COPPER MINED IN AMERICA, SO THERE wouldn't be air conditioning without it. This fact alone may stand for why Arizona matters, but it's also the home of an even greater gift to the nation. It has one of the best preserved meteorite craters on earth, a physical representation of the country's history and prejudice embedded there. *Psycho*, which starts in Arizona, is like a meteorite crater on the face of cinema: full of overacting, caricatured people, and most of all the quiet absurdity of deciding that cross-dressing and mommy issues do a killer make. Hitchcock was experimenting with the creation of an archetype—and Norman Bates is a kind of hybrid Greek dramatic anti-hero and late modern neurotic; a man with such an obsessive desire to be pure—to return to the source—that he actually becomes his own parent. The funny thing is, we're supposed to like him.

Raising Arizona, which wanders its delighted way through the suburbs and the plains and the mobile home sites and the soul of a man, invites us to identify with a guy who would kidnap someone else's baby (and wear pantyhose on his head to steal diapers) because he can't think of another solution to his wife's sorrow. And *3:10 to Yuma* confronts the audience with a more interesting moral dilemma than most—when the hero proves incapable of saving himself, and the bad guy has to step in to do it for him, we get one of those moments that portrays what we all know to be true but the movies don't usually like to show us: that sometimes good people are apt for cruelty, and sometimes people perceived as evil can still connect with their hearts. These are paradoxical movies—good guy saved by bad guy, child kidnapper revealed as superheroic, multiple murderer turned into sad sack in the corner. Their protagonists are contrarian, like Arizona itself, which stands out from the crowd by producing people like John McCain (who always seemed uncomfortable with the concept of team), Alice Cooper (a golf-playing fake rat-decapitating conservative Christian heavy metal star), and Frank Lloyd Wright (whose straight edges sometimes mask astonishing poetic architectural intent), and also voting for more female governors than any other state (and by refusing to observe Daylight Savings Time).

It's a vast place, whose topography doesn't lend itself to human survival, so it makes sense that Arizona gives life to stories in which people will do otherwise crazy things just to get water, as Van Heflin does in *3:10 to Yuma*. He is being slowly emasculated by just standing by and watching—he's scared, and the vulnerability is palpable. Yuma captures what it means to be an ordinary man faced with fear in a cultural environment where empathy remains in its primitive stage. Life is taken so cheaply in *3:10 to Yuma*, and yet we're attracted to the rogue who takes it, and not just because he has the face of Glenn Ford (a face that belongs on a banknote to be sure). But it's not because of his roguery that we like him either, and certainly not for his killing. It's because, unlike Heflin's poor farmer, he's not afraid to ask for what he wants. The poor farmer is trapped in an honor system where pride stops him asking for help—his "reputation" matters more than whether or not he starves. He's got enough desperation to be willing to take on a life-threatening task because the reward will allow for six months crop irrigation in the midst of drought, but if his community had been attentive to the hospitality traditions of Arizona's Navajo population, he might never have had to leave home to get water. Of course, neither would he have been living on an isolated farm, nor enshrining a nuclear family, nor been laboring under the amusing misapprehension that a human being can actually "own" land. The psychologist Steven Pinker writes of the concept of honor that it is a "strange commodity that exists because everyone believes that everyone else believes that it exists." Arizona, in *3:10 to Yuma,* depends on this plainly inaccurate belief. The making of America included an attempt at the refutation of cultures that had served people well for centuries; yet *3:10 to Yuma* ends with a turning back to older, better ways: two guys deciding to save each other because the nobility of ordinary human decency trumps self-interest. Of course there are things worth forgetting about the past, traditions that don't serve the common good, patterns of behavior from which we must evolve to survive and thrive and love. I think we can safely assume that the normalization of killing for entertainment, so taken for granted in *Psycho* and *3:10 to Yuma* will eventually be seen as one of them.

But that's not all there is. In a place so vast, how could it be? A year after Glenn Ford discovered empathy on the Yuma train, and just a couple before Norman Bates let his mother shadow get the better of him, another Arizona film came along that could have shown them a better way. The Disney nature short *Grand Canyon* is the antidote to nationalistic plunder: a film about how the serenity and grandeur of the Arizona landscape cannot but humble the human audience. It smashes the lie of unrestricted individualistic selfhood into so many grains of sand, swept away by the Colorado River that still grinds inexorably deeper the bottom of the gorge. *Grand Canyon* revels in Arizona's physical beauty, but also serves as a reminder that if we continue to have fun with psychos, the rocks will outlast us, and the earth might just be grateful.

ARKANSAS

ON ITS OWN TERMS

THELMA AND LOUISE, 1991. Directed by Ridley Scott, written by Callie Khouri. Two girlfriends escape from Arkansas by driving across the country. They complain about men the whole way, with good reason.

SLING BLADE, 1996. Directed and written by Billy Bob Thornton. Karl serves a murder sentence in a prison hospital, but is released before he wants to leave. He saves some people, then kills a bad guy in order to be sent back to the only place he feels safe.

THE NATIVE AMERICAN SCHOLAR JOE GONE ONCE TOLD A FRIEND OF MINE that 48% of Americans have a diagnosable mental illness. It's true, apparently; even after researchers nuanced the indicators and covered their asses with control groups and cultural sensitivity, nearly half of the people here need to see a shrink, take Prozac, or spend some time working on their brain plasticity. Presumably, a disproportionate number of these folk make their living in Hollywood—the creative arts have depended on the psychological fringes ever since Hogeye the Cave Painter unleashed his pre-emptive zoetrope pre-historical pre-montages upon the good folk of ancient Arkansas. As with so many other innovations (New Coke, electric cars, my writing career), wisdom ended up being a minority sport.

Movies about Arkansas share a common denominator and ancestor—President Bill Clinton came from Hope, and that's what Arkansas-based cinema wants to give 'em. But maybe not too much. The two most archetypal Clinton-era Arkansas films are sparing in their dosage. The arc of Arkansas stories moves from the abandonment of its people to the cruelty of nature or other men, to an attempted and failed escape, to finally accepting with resignation the inability to do so. Inasmuch as Stanley Kubrick believed that *The Shining* was an optimistic film because it asserted the possibility of life after death, despite the potential for that life to encounter horrifying shades, there is I suppose a certain kind of hope in recognizing your limitations. If depression derives mostly from unmet expectations, then Arkansas' acceptance could do a soul some good.

Sling Blade starts with a guy trying not to be released from prison and ends with him killing someone partly so he can go back; *Thelma and Louise* begins with two women in the glass-ceilinged cage of chauvinist society escaping to the open road, but discovering that even the open road has to end somewhere. Both of these films have moments where men stare into or just past the camera, and they seem to ask, "What are you going to do about *me*?" They are half-made people, never having been permitted access to, nor perhaps even offered, what could make them complete.

Both films are about compassion and where it is lacking, about folk who have nowhere to stay, the mingling of Southern hospitality and redneck humility with the inability to healthily deal with anger, and about how some people think that killing is the only appropriate outlet for their rage.

The characters in *Thelma and Louise* and *Sling Blade* are always looking toward the hills, as if Arkansas exists only as a place from which people want to flee. Of course, where they want to flee to is money—money is the path to happiness, or the path to freedom, or at least the path to not dying in the parts of America that have forgotten to care about the vulnerable—in this case, the developmentally disabled and the targets of gender discrimination. These films depict a perfect rhythm between the inspiration to escape and the inevitability of a justice system that is as brutal as it is labyrinthine.

There is a moment when the car *Thelma and Louise* are driving—a turquoise romance—is framed in total isolation on the road, and you feel that anything could happen. They could be caught, or they could escape. Hell, aliens could use a tractor beam to abduct them. But one certainty overrides everything else: Their lives are not their own. In these Arkansas movies, the forces of the South wind blow people back from whence they came—Karl is going back to jail, *Thelma and Louise* are going to die. We may be left with a sour taste because they seem to imply that the rejection of patriarchy can only end with the destruction of its opponents. Karl's choice to kill a man so he can be returned to the only place where he feels he knows himself breaks the moral spine of an otherwise perfect film. What remains is the notion that life itself is sometimes so harsh that people would rather die, or kill, than go back to an Arkansas that only provides a lot of eggs and emotional entrapment. But I suppose the American myth upon which these stories are built reminds us that at least all three—Thelma, Louise, and Karl—submit to inevitability on their own terms.

CALIFORNIA

A DREAM CORRUPTED

You may think you know what you're dealing with, but believe me, you don't.
—John Huston as Noah Cross in *Chinatown*

CHINATOWN, 1974. Directed by Roman Polanski, written by Robert Towne. Private eye Jake Gittes investigates an adulterous affair which turns into a murder and becomes a citywide scandal. The more he knows, the less he understands. Nobody is happy. Jack Nicholson and Faye Dunaway twist sex into an avoidance of death (temporary, probably). Jack discovers the sorrow at the heart of a city built on lies (permanent, perhaps).

℞E-ENTERING *CHINATOWN*, SO EASILY CAUGHT UP IN ITS DEVILISH PLOT, MASsive visual scope, and mythic structure, I remembered how cinema had fueled my hopes as a teenager and how I first fell for America—the magical teenage rebellion of Marty McFly in *Back to the Future*, the Abrahamic vision of Roy Neary in *Close Encounters of the Third Kind*, the day from which Ferris Bueller would almost certainly never recover. I remembered that, although my taste in cinema had been broadened over the years and that I was as likely to find solace in Russian sci-fi mystics or Swedish existentialism as I would in tales spun by Burbank bungalows, I was now living in the land of The Movies. If I was to make it here, I needed to understand the heart of the myth-making machine. It seems to me that we derive our vision of the future from our interpretation of the past, tilling the soil of our historic experiences until they flatten into paths that can be easily repeated. If Los Angeles is where movies are born, then surely that city plays a central role in forming our identity. Hidden somewhere in LA County, therefore, is nothing less than the sanctuary of cinematic memory.

★

MEMORY, OF COURSE, IS IN A PROFOUND SENSE *WHO WE ARE*, BUT IT'S NOT SO MUCH *what* has happened to you as *how* you remember it. What I remember about landing at LAX is that the first thing you notice is how flat things are in Los Angeles. The sunlight is filtered so that the ground's color spectrum is somewhere between white and yellow, and despite the cluster of skyscrapers in the center of this center-less city, most everything is small. Restaurants and cafes are tiny, the Santa Monica pier is not much more than a few pretzel stands and a Ferris wheel, Venice Beach has a patch of grass in the middle that doesn't really deserve to be called a park, and I've never been in an LA apartment much larger than a McDonalds rest room. Perhaps the small scale of the buildings makes space for the freeways—roads that are at once the most inaccurately named structures in the world and among the most frightening places on earth.

Chinatown knows why: The city was founded on greed and blood and monstrous fathering. Its corporate children are the enervated offspring of a dream that in the 1930s, the time of its setting, had only recently been daily enacted through Wild West sidewalk violence, saloon rape, and gap-toothed men lusting for gold. Searching for the Frontier. The glass-half-empty part of me is tempted to comment on the timelessness of social static (which is just a high-falutin' way of saying that the more things change, the more they stay the same), but the world presented in *Chinatown* is, of course, not the whole world. The California of JJ Gittes exists simultaneously with the North Carolina of Crash Davis: Ultimately, they're both about how you have to take the rough with the smooth. So, then, the fact that no one gets killed in *Bull Durham* means that North Carolina has the benefit of a head start toward seeming like the right America for me.

Early in *Chinatown*, a city bureaucrat lays out a plan to build a "dirt bank terminus dam," which, other than being a magnificent name for a mid-90s garage band, is a good metaphor for Southern California itself, or at least the industry for which it is best known. Movies, as Hollywood would often have it, are as much about what you *don't* get to see as what you do—the moguls decide what you want and they force feed it to you. In the 1970s, said moguls decided that what you wanted was smart stories about political dissent and the spiraling cynicism to which a Presidential impeachment gave a home. *Chinatown* is the masterpiece of this period—I've seen it at least fifteen times. Fifteen times with any great film might be enough to make one complacent about its riches, but it's not the case with *Chinatown*. I could go on watching it forever. I see new things in it with every viewing:

Politics.
Sex.
Violence.

The American Dream.
Cars.
Venetian blinds.
Celebrity.
Sunshine.
Fish.

Throw in a bit of religion and you'd have the Great American Novel. And if you were willing to risk hyberbole, you might even say that you had America itself. Since overstatement and I may be rather too intimately acquainted, I'll leave that notion in the realm of the hypothetical.

Chinatown stakes its claim by opening on the hands of a crying man holding voyeuristic photographs. Of course it does: This film is about the very concept of going to the movies, of *watching*. It snoops through a labyrinth of sorrow in which the only thing anyone considers important is their social status, where everyone lies to everyone else, where everything is sinister all the time. The suggestion that the city at the center of the film industry might have been built on corruption must have seemed like a good joke to the people making *Chinatown* in 1974, when the occupant of the Oval Office was still secretly recording his conversations. As with Watergate, everyone in *Chinatown* is implicated, but no one takes responsibility. We're all semi-passive observers; we know something is rotten in Denmark, but we can't rouse ourselves to action. The best known line in the film begins with the words, "Forget it, Jake," and there may be no better key to understanding this movie because its primary purpose is to take a long hard look at what America is hiding: what are the *disappeared* elements of America's memory of itself?

I'm aware that in asking this, the monstrous enemy at the heart of *Chinatown*, John Huston's Noah Cross, would respond, while looking at his fingernails, "Do you know the expression, 'Let sleeping dogs lie?'" He'd mean it more as a threat than a piece of advice, telling me that some people believe American politics has too many dark secrets unsafe to tell, so let's not threaten national security by bringing them into the light, shall we? *Chinatown's* California, its America, is menacing: sex is used for control and not intimacy; and people die for the same reasons they died in the Wild West—because they threatened somebody's business. Someone once said that the best way to face a problem that appears insoluble is to make it bigger. *Chinatown* illustrates: Jake Gittes, the detective protagonist, is hamstrung by thinking he's only dealing with someone else's marital indiscretion, but what's really reeling him in is the future of the country.

A technical hitch once reduced me to watching it with the sound off, and strangely enough, this painted film works in silence too. Indeed, *Chinatown* has a surprising amount of near-silence. Unlike the big picture vision many people have of America, the truth is found in the gaps. The gaps are what the movies (at least) should fill.

Chinatown suggests simply this: that the country has a shameful past, but that its protagonists do not feel the shame. Everyone's lonely, everyone's lying, and the only thing about which they care is money or their own brokenness. Money makes everyone forget morality. The last line of the movie tells JJ Gittes that the kind of awfulness he has just witnessed is par for the course in *Chinatown;* and it isn't going to change. It might also be trying to tell viewers that this is Hollywood and we'll never understand it. Or it might be trying to tell *us* that this is America and we don't belong. All of this seems so far away from me—the building of a city, the killing of a truth-teller; but it's also near, because it's about love and faith and mortgages and tuna fish, greed and need and why people do the things they do. What they are thirsty for is what you and I are thirsty for, and that, of course, is the water of life—companionship and shelter and a sense of home mingled with the desire to be *seen*. When Jake's photo is in the paper, his barber tells him, "You're practically a movie star." Twenty-five years after *Chinatown*, *The Matrix* showed us that nothing much has changed, when in one of its more delicious flourishes the turncoat known as Cipher insists that in his new, virtual life he wants to be "someone Important. Like an actor."

That's what the country has been built on. This is the myth of the frontier. This is why America needs a good therapist. In its shadow, it wants to be seen by others, but it can't bear to look at itself. We both do, of course, me and America, and after watching *Chinatown* again I knew I had to head for the hills, to find someone wise enough to bring me back to earth.

COLORADO

THERAPY

He who makes a beast of himself gets rid of the pain of being a man.
—Dr. Johnson

**THE SHINING. 1980. Directed by Stanley Kubrick; Written by Kubrick &
Diane Johnson.** A writer goes slowly mad in an isolated hotel due to an extreme
case of writer's block and self-loathing. He eventually tries to kill his family.
They escape. He never could. Jack Nicholson and Shelley Duvall are not exactly
an ideal couple, and while the idea of five months' solitude might appeal to the
writer in each of us, when all you've got for company is a typewriter, a meat
freezer, and a tricycle, it can wear a bit thin, to say the least.

**CITIZEN KANE. 1942. Directed by Orson Welles; Written by Welles and
Herman J Mankiewicz.** A man becomes powerful in every respect other than
over his own soul. Sets with ceilings, cuts between one thing to another thing
that looks the same as the first thing but turns out to be something entirely
different thirty years later, naturalistic performances, huge fireplaces, a tug of
war between parents over a child that involves the child coming into and out
of focus, incisive political satire, depth-of-field photography the likes of which
had never been seen before, overseen by a bloke who was 25 at the time...There
are reasons many people think this is the greatest film ever made.

COLORADO HAS NO NATURAL BORDERS, WHICH, AMONG OTHER THINGS, MEANS you can stand in four states at once, letting the dust of Arizona, New Mexico, and Utah also mingle with your sandals. No natural borders, which among other things, means that the extreme conservatism of the Religious Right can be headquartered in Colorado Springs to coexist alongside the hippie havens of Boulder, Manitou Springs, and La Junta—the birthplace of Ken Kesey, the Merry Prankster and advocate for ecstatic human freedom. No natural borders, which among other things, means that Allen Ginsberg (a one-time resident) and Karl Rove (born in Denver) could have run into each other—and oh how different the world might be today if Rove had become a beat poet, or Ginsberg a political strategist.

No natural borders, which means, I suppose, that you could be there without even knowing it. Maybe, like Jack Nicholson's possibly spectral character in *The Shining*—the quintessential Colorado movie—you've always been there. Or, like Orson Welles' *Citizen Kane*—a film the Argentine writer José Luis Borges describes as a "metaphysical detective story," one whose purpose was to find out nothing less than the meaning of a man's life—maybe all you're trying to do is to get back to Colorado, where you remember feeling innocent and playful and not yet corroded by cynicism. Maybe this geoellipsoidal rectangle with no natural borders is the real America.

Now to be real, to be authentic, you have to be *established*, and one way of being established, of course, is to be *old*. Colorado certainly looks ancient enough—the Rocky Mountains weren't built in a day. There have been Native Americans in Colorado for over 13,000 years. Some of them are apparently buried under the Stanley Hotel, which Stanley Kubrick dressed up as the Overlook in *The Shining* and turned into a reason not to take romantic weekend vacations there. Some of them presumably own—although they might of course challenge the notion that a human being can own *anything*—the Colorado Lode, the mine that granted Charles Foster Kane his fortune but stole his soul.

Like other iconic films, there's a sense in which there's nothing left to discover or ponder in *Citizen Kane* and *The Shining*—our culture is saturated with references to "Rosebud" and "Heeeeeerreeee's Johnny!" to the point they have become two of those films most of us think we know well, even if we haven't seen them.

It's a shame, because *The Shining* and *Citizen Kane* are, not to understate it, Quite Something. They look beautiful—the images are framed like paintings. In *The Shining*, the agenda captions manage to make words like "Monday," "Thursday," and "One Month Later" seem sinister. In both, the performances feel so authentic it's like watching a real man—or a real family—disintegrate in front of your eyes. *Citizen Kane* and *The Shining* could easily be seen as yet further dehumanizing artifacts in a culture in which media slices of loss, brokenness, and lack of mercy or compassion constantly threaten to push our lives into overdrive. These films are supposed to scare you. They push you into confronting stories of selfish ambition, murder (of real people and of a man's soul), sorrow, and abuse. They have horrifying endings and are sometimes unpleasant to watch. Yet three things occur to me: For a start, they are serious metaphors for what happens when addiction, self-loathing, and selfish ambition do meet the balm of community and therapy; second, if watched through the lens of Kubrick's assertion that *The Shining* is "an optimistic film," it might lead to reflection on the amazing possibility that there is an unseen world in which human souls are finding their way to rest. As for *Kane*, it may serve as a salutary lesson—a kind of slap in the face that might be enough to make an audience member change their path in life.

These films, two of the most serious American horror movies, represent Colorado as a place where, as Jack's wife Wendy says, "The air feels different." Altitude sickness may be one reason a man would go mad and try to kill his family, as Jack does, or why a mother would for all practical purposes sell her son to a lawyer, as happens to Charles Foster Kane. The air feels different, the mountains are astonishing, and the rivers are cold and beautiful. It's a place where you can ask yourself just what it means to be human: "What is my place in the universe?"

Of course it's impossible to know for sure, but the natural wonders of Colorado may be the reason both Welles and Kubrick decided to use the state as the setting in which to explore one of humanity's most fundamental questions: How do you deal with regret? Kane is a rich, powerful man who has everything except freedom from self-hatred. Jack has failed at parenting, marriage, and writing and he can't let anyone else in to help him build the kind of community that could make for a whole life. These characters inhabit such a large space in the public consciousness that it's not hard to imagine either of them being elected governor. In some respects they are caricatures of themselves, just like some of the religious zealots who seem to populate the Colorado Springs non-profit sector.

What if the businessman who eats everything in his path (Kane), the father who fights for recognition (Jack), and an evangelist for Puritanism— perhaps representing three dimensions of the American male archetype— actually *met* and had to figure out a point of connection? Even better, what if the godfathers of conservative Christian culture tried to bend their psychological and counseling powers to minister to Jack Torrance and Charles Foster Kane?

SUBJECT 1: *A man, rotund, three piece suit, pocket watch—the whole deal, plus extravagant mustache. He is Charles Foster Kane, 70, newspaper magnate, born in Colorado, heir to the Colorado Lode, failed political candidate, currently lives secluded in huge hilltop mansion. Three marriages. Frequently exhales the word "Rosebud," which appears to indicate lost innocence. Instructed to attend therapy because of reckless selfishness and emotional destruction.*

SUBJECT 2: *A man, skinny, 5-day stubble, purple cardigan over plaid shirt and jeans. Tired. He is Jack Torrance, 39, high-eyebrowed "writer" from Denver, married to Winifred, one highly imaginative son, Danny, handy with an ax. At therapy for court-mandated anger management sessions.*

COUNSELLOR: *A man, not a stranger to a good meal, business suit, conservative glasses, nothing flashy. In charge. He is Rev. Jerry Fisher, 68, political activist and cofounder of Family First, based in Colorado Springs, married to the same woman for a hundred years, huge kin network, dedicated to the preservation of the American patriarchal unit. Believes nothing matters as much as discipline. Won't like it if you disagree with him.*

JF: So, last week we were discussing your sense of failure and deep inner discontent. Let's pick up with your memories of growing up in Colorado.

CFK: I'm not interested in that sentimental nonsense. I'm a newspaper man—I want the facts, not poetry.

JF: But Mr. Kane, we're here to examine your consciousness—the human soul does not begin and end with scientific objectivity. You can't make a life without aesthetics. You can't be human without art. Have you ever read the delightful novels of Laura Ingalls Wilder?

CFK: Look, I came to you because I'm feeling a bit depressed. My third wife doesn't like me, and I can't stand the sight of her. My staff resent me and the few men who I considered friends abandoned ship at the first sign of deep water. Sure, you'll have to put up with a dip in circulation from time to time, but the people will always want gossip. That's what I provide. Gossip. Facts. Gossip. All the same to me. Did I ever tell you about the time I met the Maharajah? We were walking beside the Taj Mahal . . .

JF: Mr. Kane, may I remind you that I charge by the hour. If you want to waste our time, that's fine, but it's on your dime.

CFK: Ah! Poetry! De-lightful. Did they teach you any more rhyming couplets in headshrinker's school?

JF: I can only help you if you're prepared to help yourself. I'm a man of the Bible, so let's go back to the Beginning. Who is this Rosebud?

CFK: Rosebud? It's the answer . . . It's what I lost . . . It's what gave me meaning, protected me, put a shroud between me and that bastard father of mine. Sometimes I think it was the only friend I ever had.

[Jack Torrance arrives.]

JT: Sorry I'm late. Got held up in the snow. The kid wanted me to chase him round a hedge labyrinth, the little bastard.

JF: That's okay, Jack, but next time maybe you could leave a little earlier—we're on a schedule here. The end time matters as much as the beginning. You can't expect to raise healthy children without some structure. Do you believe in discipline?

JT: Sure, whatever you say, Doc.

JF: Charles was just telling us about Rosebud.

JT: That your wife's name?

CFK: I do object to this vulgar man joining us.

JF: There but for the grace of God go any of us. I don't like the vulgarity either, but even our Lord spent time among reprobates. We're here to see what you guys can learn from each other. And, if I'm honest, I thought Mr. Kane might like to make a donation. But let's talk about Rosebud.

JT: Sounds a bit fruity to me. Hey Doc, did I tell ya about a job offer I got? This hotel up in the hills is looking for a caretaker for the winter. It's a great place—beautiful mountains, great spacious zone, lovely building. If it was any more Coloradan it'd be a cliché. We sure do like to do things big up here, don't we? Heading up there next month, so I'll be out of town till April.

CFK: The Overlook Hotel?

JT: You know it?

CFK: Know it? I *own* it. Mother told me it would be a good investment. Make sure you keep the fire in the lobby going and don't ever go into the meat refrigerator without someone on the other side of the door. And, while you're at it, best stay out of room 237. Bad memories.

JT: Thanks, Charlie. You know, you're not such a bad deal. Kooky. But not bad. What's this Rosebud thing anyway?

CFK: Rosebud? It's the greatest metaphor for lost innocence in the history of art. It's a Pandora's Box of untold regret. It's a comforting blanket which I can almost feel when I picture it. If I'd never let it go I wouldn't be where I am today. But, then again, if I'd never let it go, I wouldn't be where I am today either.

JT: Whaddya mean?

CFK: I'm rich, but I'm not happy. I could imagine myself, in some far distant spark of memory, inheriting the opposite. I could be happy, but not rich. It's Rosebud's fault.

JT: Sorry to hear of your troubles, man. Not sure I understand the rudiments, but I get the spirit. I'm a bit lost myself.

JF: Good, Jack. Not that it's good that you're lost (although I specialize in lost souls), but that you might have something to say about it.

JT: Well, I suppose I just feel that my wife doesn't understand me. I've been trying to write this book for a while and she keeps interrupting. She doesn't realize that an artist needs space to create.

CFK: Couldn't have said it better myself. You know, Jack, the more you can get rid of the distractions in your life, the better for all concerned.

JT: Thanks, buddy, I'll take it under advisement. Anyway, like I was saying, I just need space. I gotta get the book out of the way. And the kid, Danny, he's . . . well, he's a bit on the girly side, if I'm honest. Too close to his mother.

JF: When you spare the rod, you spoil the child.

JT: I know, I know. I keep trying to get him to play catch, or take some interest in the vast range of adventure sports we have up here, but all he wants to do is ride his fuckin' tricycle.

JF: Biking's a sport. In fact, this very week on my radio show I'm interviewing a man who just biked across Africa to tell the natives about Jesus.

JT: Not this kind of bike, my friend. It's a goddamn plastic tricycle with goddamn annoying wheels. Can't get the sound out of my head. Anyway, I'm hoping the hotel gig'll clean things up—get my head straight. I'll crank out a book and—who knows?—maybe I'll find some of that, whaddya call it?—"success" that ol' Charlie boy here got for himself. Friend, I cannot for the life of me figure out why you seem so sad. You got yourself a big house, a nice lady, all the cash you can smoke . . . What's the problem?

CFK: I am aching inside.

JF: Would you like an Advil?

CFK: It's not that kind of ache.

JF: How about an antacid?

CFK: I'm afraid, Dr Fisher, my pain is such that no pill can heal. I am existentially lost. I look out at the wide open spaces of Colorado and where you might see the potential for freedom, I see only my own inner prison. I know it may sound like a silly thing for a man of my stature to say, but I want my mommy, and there's nothing you can do about that.

JT: Sheesh, Charlie, you're in a bad way. Wanna come up to the hotel for a little retreat? I have a rubber ball we can throw at the wall together. And there's an open bar—all season long.

CFK: I don't think that would help. Too much time to think.

JF: To think about what?

CFK: About the state of things. About the state of this state which gave me life and whose natural resources took it from me. About how there are 70,000 new Coloradans born each year, born to the kind of possibility I see when I look at mountains. Or at least I used to see. About how the Religious Right spends about a hundred and fifty million dollars a year on such notable social concerns as abstinence education that prevents neither disease nor unplanned pregnancy, and the prevention of gay marriage which has no negative impact on the straight kind, while the poverty rates are increasing as is the prevalence of homophobia-related suicide.

JT: Like I said, Charlie, you're in a bad way. I'm just trying to find a way to get over the mistakes I made in the past and make something of my life. At least to write a halfway decent book and kill my demons.

CFK: Hmmm, I thought there was a touch of the satanic about you. I mean, no offense. It's mostly your eyebrows. Have they always looked like that?

JT: Have you always been so fat?

JF: Gentlemen, gentlemen please, come on, let's keep it civil.

JT: You mean the way your organization talks about people with whom they disagree?

JF: We have a lot to learn too, but that's not what we're here for. We're trying to help you see the error of your ways. It's the only way to save you.

CFK: You've got your work cut out for you, doctor.

JT: Hey, I gotta get going soon—there's a blizzard forecast for tonight.

CFK: Me too. I'm buying a country later.

JF: Alright, gentlemen. Any final thoughts before next week?

JT: All I can say is that I'm happy to be a resident of this state. You know, even the darkest shadow can only be seen because of how hard the sun's shining on it.

CFK: Call yourself a writer?

JF: Mr. Kane, please stick to the topic at hand. I must insist.

CFK: Alright, alright.

JT: I'm just saying, to be an artist, it's a tough gig. To be an *American* artist—maybe that's tougher still. The competition's so good. Look at our state for starters—you got David Fincher who made that amazing movie about masculinity in *Fight Club*, he was born in Denver. There's Dalton Trumbo, the blacklisted writer; Glenn Miller played his trombone all over Boulder, and that's just three.

CFK: You're right. And Coloradans haven't done too badly in politics either—John Kerry was born here (and I know a thing or two about stolen elections). Golda Meir grew up in Denver, for God's sake.

JT: True enough. So yeah, we got some good writers and directors and politicos. Colorado's a pretty sophisticated state, when you think about it. And here was me, thinking everything's bleak and awful just because I'm plagued by nightmares that I might kill my family and freeze to death in the open air. You know, sometimes I'm faced with nothing but a typewriter and no sense of what comes next. It's not so much the art of war as the war of art. I have all this darkness inside me and I feel isolated from everybody else. Maybe that's what being a writer is.

CFK: Jack, Jack, you're getting all morbid on us. Listen, this fellow I know once said of a man brought low by over-reaching, "The trouble was that his greatness drove him down to nothingness because he was careless." You have to find something to do with your darkness. Write it out of your system, run up a mountain and exorcise it through exercise, or put it in an abandoned hotel room and lock the door when you leave. Just don't take it out on your family.

JT: Sometimes I think I'm cursed. Cursed by my dream of being a writer. Bruno Bettelheim says somewhere that we are afraid of what we hope for—because if we get it, we won't know what to do with it and our lives will have to change to make space for it.

JF: Who's Bruno Bettelheim?

CFK: Listen, Jack, I know what he means. I faked an alien invasion once, made the audience so scared that they wanted to kill me afterward. That's the definition of getting what you want, but not what you expect.

JT: I thought that was when the greyhound finally catches the electric rabbit, wins the race, and gets electrocuted.

CFK: Ha. All I'm saying is, if you want to make God laugh, tell him your plans. And if you want to fail as a writer, conceive of writing as the most romantic path a man can tread. That's a sure way to keep it a dream. We

Coloradans have something we don't really value: a landscape that suggests limitless possibility. It can devour you—like I think it's already done to me—or it can make you live in wonder. Don't write because you want to make money. Write because you've got something to say. Money will turn you into a giant. Just remember that giants aren't exactly reputed for the lack of destruction that follows them.

When I was young, I wanted to be famous, to be powerful. I used the media as an instrument of my will. I broke men with ink. I thought I'd be a king, but I'm a two-bit hustler. I'm bloated and broken. I live in a fairytale castle, but I'm an ogre. Someday someone'll probably make a great movie about me. You could tell the story of a whole social era through my life. But I'll tell you this—they won't understand me if all they do is tell the story of the newspapers and the politics and the wives and the floor shows. The art. The money. The power. You can only truly understand a man if you know what he's missing.

The floor shows . . . Isn't that what we're all doing? Stumble-dancing in a discount cabaret, lit low to hide the blemishes, thinking we're still entitled to our fantasies of what might have been?

JF: I'm afraid our time's up. Shall we pray together?

CFK: I try to be a Christian, but I don't pray, really. I don't want to bore God.

JT: Now I'm depressed. Look, Charlie, you're not such a bad guy. Come up to the Overlook and we'll get drunk together. I might even read you some of the new book.

CFK: No thanks, Jack. That's not what I want.

JF: What do you want?

CFK: Me? I just want my sled back.

CONNECTICUT

COMMERCE

THE ICE STORM, 1997. Directed by Ang Lee, written by James Schamus, from Ricky Moody's novel. Key parties, coffee percolators, EST, long hair, nascent feminism, suburban angst, parents not knowing how to raise their children, and everyone's suspicious of everyone else in the not-living-up-to-its-name town of New Canaan. Happy times in the Constitution State.

HE ICE STORM BEGINS WITH IMAGES OF 1970S COMIC BOOKS AND THE HOPE that something exciting could happen. It ends with a man weeping as he fails to find the strength to tell his son about the death of another child. The faux artistocracy of big houses belonging to the people with the highest per capita income in America in one of the smallest states mingles with the coldness of a New England winter. We're in what the social commentator Rick Perlstein calls Nixonland. Adults are running around acting like children—they're the first generation that doesn't know what it wants to be when it grows up because they're the first generation to ask that question. The legacy of the sixties appears to be a deadening of the ability to relate to other people as individual selves. Self-help voices try to cover the deadness with incessant television droning, wanting to convince us more of the fear that there is something wrong with us than of the promise that we can do something about it. The new religion did not heal the nation, and families hurt, says *The Ice Storm*. Suburbia is a disease and when we invest ourselves in things we lose our souls. People bore each other to death with stories about nothing and there may be no possibility for real love—just terrible need. Life consists of the commute and the return, the lie and the repressed hope.

Yipp-ee-kay-yay, then.

Connecticut looks beautiful on the outside, and I must say that I have sincerely enjoyed the couple of visits I've paid there (particularly great omelets, too—I'm not sure why). But there's something underneath that troubles me. Maybe it's the fact that George W Bush was born and raised there, which means that a case could be made for Greenwich as a kind of "fake Texas." It's not for nothing that this state also gave birth to PT Barnum. *The Ice Storm* asks us to look long and hard at ourselves to see what we're afraid of. It suggests that fear to be the worry that we may never be able to grow up, that life is simply too big for us to face or make sense of.

Jack Kerouac wrote of his aspiration to reveal the unity in all human angst, saying, "I want to fish as deep down as possible into my own subconscious in the belief that once that far down, everyone will understand because they are the same that far down." If only we could hear him. The good people of New Canaan could put their town's name into practice if they were patient enough to look up from the privatized lives the last President gave them and see a most reassuring thing: When everyone is asking the same question, no one is alone.

Delaware

Wounds

FIGHT CLUB, 1999. Directed by David Fincher, written by Jim Uhls, from the novel by Chuck Pahlaniuk. Shirtless guys kick the crap out of each other because they think they've nothing better to do. It's a really strange time in their lives.

¶'VE ONLY BEEN IN A COUPLE OF "REAL" FIGHTS. I WAS A TIMID KID, OFTEN lonely, not confrontational, but chunky, and therefore perceived to be strong. Once another kid at school tormented me a step too far; I remember becoming almost possessed by rage, half picking him up, and pushing him backwards into a desk. His anger at my violence was transcended by his shock that I would do anything like this. I remember him actually laughing in surprise and I think he later shook my hand out of respect. I had, in his eyes, become a man. A few years later I was threatened in an Indian kebab shop by a Belfast guy who implied that, as I had had the temerity to say hello to his girlfriend after she greeted me, his social cohort might arrive at my house in the middle of the night to teach me a lesson. They didn't. The reason I know this is that I stayed awake all night in case they did. I sometimes think we're addicted to fighting. The unparalleled interpreter of what ails us, Walter Wink, says the real religion of America is violence. If he's right, then the undercurrent of dread I'm left with invites repentance. Maybe Delaware can help.

The problem is, hardly any movies have been set in Delaware. *Dead Poets Society* was shot there, but the location was standing in for Vermont. Sources will tell you that Terry Gilliam's bleak time travel work *12 Monkeys* spent a day or two filming in the state, but on a return viewing of that extraordinary film, it appears to have been mostly so they could use a bridge to get to Philadelphia. Thankfully, as these things often do, at the point of giving up I bumped into a folk singer from the City of Brotherly Love (no, really) and he told me just what I needed to hear. It turns out that one of the most interesting and troubling recent films is set, fully immersed, wrapped, and ribboned in the First State. It also turns out this film is a key to understanding my generation of guys—a film so universal that it doesn't want to say it's from Delaware, even though it couldn't take place anywhere else.

Fight Club opens by plunging us into Edward Norton's internal organs.

We don't know this at first—to the uninitiated viewer it could be the belly of a whale, the synapses of a computer's brain, or, I suppose, the gut of God. Anyway, it's SOMEONE's insides, and there's only two ways out, so let's get this over with quickly. After a short swim up-bile-stream we find that we're emerging from Ed's small intestine, and Brad Pitt is penetrating his tonsils with a gun. The bland fact that we really are inside a human person, nothing more innocuous or sinister than that, is disappointing. A film opening inside Orca's tummy would have a certain sense of unique drama about it, and this whale belly image would have been philosophically meaningful too given the fact that *Fight Club* is largely about how the political economy is a monster, with men as its teeth. It invites the metaphor of a lumbering seaborne beast consuming every piece of plankton it can sweep into its mouth. The whale, of course, became a kind of fetishized object for environmentalists in the 1970s, the period in which the protagonists of *Fight Club* would have been learning the broken warrior traditions that catechized American boyhood (which by then were abandoning John Wayne for Travis Bickle). Now they're adults, disillusioned by the *thing*-centered, self-help wisdom passed on to them by their Boomer parents, and the protagonists attempt to completely demolish what they learned it is to be a man.

Our hero, Norton's "Jack," identifies himself at first this way: "People are always asking me if I know Tyler Durden." Now, the fact that Jack is suffering from a split personality and happens *to be* Tyler Durden doesn't necessarily mean that he *knows* Tyler Durden. And that's the point—whether or not, and how, we can attain some sense of reconciliation with ourselves. Tyler Durden reminds us that males have mislaid the rituals for becoming adults that served our forebears well until the turn of the last century. And so most grown men are still little boys, caught between a will-you/won't-you nesting instinct, yearning for mommy on one hand and the primitive desire to randomly cut guys and penetrate girls (or whatever combination is preferred) on the other. We're supposed to find a way to integrate all of this, but something has interrupted the flow, leaving the adult men of my generation stunted, acting out ever less-spectacular fantasies on Playstations and in the gym. We buy yin-yang coffee tables from IKEA because someone else has told us it will confer coolness, our work lives have been reduced to hearing and carrying out instructions from an economic superior ("Make these your primary action items"), we fear we may only eke out the barest semblance of an identity.

Jack is so sick of his life as a cog that he can't sleep. He seeks a cure by going to self-help groups, where he ends up crying in the arms of Meat Loaf, whose antibiotically mutated chest is like the teat of God. The Delaware River of mother's milk.

Why Delaware? It's not because of Joe Biden, though I suppose I wouldn't object if it was—he's funny, he says "fuck" and "God love ya" at press conferences, and he loves trains. What's not to like? You need to wait for the end of the movie to figure out why it's set in Delaware—Pahlaniuk's novel, and Fincher/Uhls' film, exercise their respective right to excitable climax by blowing up a few skyscrapers which happen to be the headquarters of today's greatest movie villains: credit card companies. It's a corporate idyll—over half of the publicly traded companies in America are based there. So, if there is such a thing as a reboot button for the economy, it's probably hidden somewhere under a concrete seal in Wilmington, Delaware. The fighting boys have aroused themselves to recognize that they really do have a Great Depression, a Great War. Their lives, deadened by consumerism, will only be resurrected if everything is returned to zero, a fresh start, a blank slate onto which a new community can be drawn. Now, I'm all for an egalitarian distribution of wealth, but the notion that blowing up buildings can redeem the world seems a little too . . . how should I say it? Reaganite?

The irony doesn't end there, for a film so dedicated to exposing the crow-like nature of the postmodern male wallet, *Fight Club* has itself become a fetishized object. Gorgeously packaged "Anniversary Edition" DVDs question whether the owners of its copyright endorse or even understand the film's politics. I once heard Pahlaniuk say publicly that on the same day he was told that Rupert Murdoch hated the movie based on his book, one of Murdoch's sons told a friend that it was his favorite film. It was only a matter of days before Murdoch's company prioritized Chuck's books for production. As Paul Schrader would say, in the battle between hubris and commerce, commerce will always win. And as for the famous moment when Brad Pitt enjoins us to realize that we "are not our fucking khakis," well, given that some of the time it seems that Brad Pitt clearly is his fucking khakis, and gets paid a hell of a lot for his trouble, it's rather difficult to know what to do with that statement.

I also heard Pahlaniuk say that some of those biting, potentially cynical parts of the story arc in *Fight Club* resulted from his personal attempt at self-improvement. Jack sees IKEA catalogues as postmodern porn—Pahlaniuk doesn't own any IKEA furniture, but he told me that the reason for this appearing in the book is not so much to become a coruscating, snide remark about the lives of others, but to satirize himself in order to resist the status quo.

When IKEA opened in Belfast the police were prepared for an outbreak of bad traffic and lined the road for miles with cones to avoid a Swedish flat pack-inspired rush of moderate taste. But, in one of those moments that reminds me why I'm proud to be northern Irish, almost nobody came. We had already had our depression, and our war. Sure, the store was packed by the end of the week, but we still had enough of a sense of proportion not to buy the hype about how getting a set of fluorescent orange dinner plates or randomly-sized frames for black and white photographs before anyone else would make us complete. *Fight Club* says that America is a hustle in which people can be persuaded to fill a house with expensive condiments, even though every dollar spent on groceries is matched by another buck spent at restaurants. It is a country that nearly broke the world's economy because people started to believe their fantasies about money: that it is elastic and will therefore always come back to you.

This movie wants us to cut the foreplay and just ask each other for help. It wants us to notice that gatherings of human beings can be—should be—benign. The fact that the typical American urban soundscape is daily, even hourly, punctuated by police sirens indicates that our appetite for destruction may outdo our yearning for community. Hell, I get lonely enough that there are times I'd settle for a Mexican Satanist Tupperware party just for the company. When Tyler Durden refers to the last conversation he had with his dad, the term "long distance" protrudes like an arrow out the back of its target. This country has pushed its children to live apart from their parents in ways unthinkable anywhere, or anytime, else. The children of this mass migration are left with no ground to stand on, nothing but a mirror into which to stare and ask: When you've been beaten up by yourself and you're lying at the bottom of a staircase looking your shadow side in the eyes, what do you see? What do you fear? What do you want?

"How much can you know about yourself if you've never been in a fight?"

It would be, I think, a mistake to take this film literally. Sure, it looks like it feels good to hit each other consensually with no outcome other than guessing you've grown up a month or two. Sure, "if this is your first night, you have to fight" might not be a bad way to inspire steps for personal growth. Sure, when Jack arises from a basement skirmish he is baptized in blood and "afterwards we all felt saved," and the idea of people, as Trent Reznor and Johnny Cash rasp, hurting themselves to see if they still *feel*, names the decadence of a society that has forgotten what *society* means.

But the belief that you must use violence against others in order to live? Nah. And thinking that's what the film advocates denies *Fight Club* its rightful place as a wise spiritual work. What it's really saying is that being fully human depends on losing *everything* in order to be free to do *anything*, that we are by default caught in an illusory culture that feeds on the soul of humanity. We think we're something that we're not—consumers—rather than what we are—creators. We think that a life dedicated to dancing and fighting (even if our opponent is computer-generated) is worthwhile. We know we're supposed to live better, and none of us is quite sure how we would feel about our lives if we were to die today. Unlike Meat Loaf's Robert Paulson, the character anointed heroic as the fight club moves catastrophically toward self-destruction, society has not given us a name. And it has made us sick.

Fight Club ends, as I've said, with dynamiting debt in an attempted reboot of the economy. Yet mingling pyromania with the spirit of Amish-tinged asceticism produces yet another irony. The country that *Fight Club* wants to speak for knows well what it is to burn buildings. The new millennium, only a dozen and a bit months after *Fight Club*'s release, was inaugurated by a portion of its young men being recruited to burn and die for the vengeful fantasies of emotionally immature other men. I'm sure some of the new recruits were inspired by *Fight Club* to join the military. But I think they misunderstood the movie. The point is not that in order to live your own life, you must fight someone else. The point is that *you are already dead*, that you *cannot come to life on your own*, and that the most important thing you can do *right now* is to stop wasting your time and start the battle-dance with your own shadow.

The story has some room for Zen—people can't join the monastic community that emerges from the fight clubs unless they are prepared to wait; but, of course, Zen has no room for killing. So if you want to learn to channel your anger into something creative, you will have to learn to wait. It may well be the case that, as Jack discovers at the end/beginning of the film, you can think reality into being. If marketers can make you believe that you need a six-pack (abs, beer, guns, socks) then surely you can hypnotize yourself into creating a life bounded only by imagination and not an APR. And of course, credit cards are just another way of denying responsibility, I suppose—buying things we can't afford, to dull the pain of what we lack.

America's dream of itself, in the films we've explored so far, suggests that lack, or the fear of it, is at the heart of the American shadow. That this country's story is the story of the removal of people from the land they knew in exchange for the land of the uncertainty of the people who took over. We still live there today. And we are waiting. Delaware in fact has been waiting a long time. The Dutch colonized it in 1631. It's the second smallest state, but holds the imaginary purse strings for an entire nation. It deserves to be taken seriously, at least for the fact that it could destroy the economy, or wipe the slate clean, if it wanted to. But it has the same problem as California and Texas and Alaska. Its place names—New Castle, Kent County, Sussex, evoking the British Royal Family — sound like it suffers as much as anywhere else in America from a romantic dependence on a distant, detached past to carve its own identity. And maybe like anywhere else in America that likes to speak for the rest of the world, it doesn't know where it's going, because it can't admit where it's been.

ꟼHE ꟽISTRICT OF COLUMBIA

MAGNIFICENT INTENTIONS

It is sometimes called the City of Magnificent Distances, but it might with greater propriety be termed the City of Magnificent Intentions . . . Spacious avenues, that begin in nothing, and lead nowhere; streets, mile-long, that only want houses, roads, and inhabitants; public buildings that need but a public to be complete; and ornaments of great thoroughfares, which only lack great thoroughfares to ornament—are its leading features.
— Charles Dickens

Washington is a very easy city for you to forget where you came from and why you got there in the first place.
— President Harry Truman

BEING THERE. 1979. Directed by Hal Ashby. Written by Jerzy Kosinski.
Chance, a gardener who has never left home, is evicted at age 50 when his
employer dies. After being injured in a car accident he moves in with Mr. and
Mrs. Rand, enormously wealthy philanthropists and political power-brokers,
who introduce him to important people and society life. His simplicity is mis-
taken (or seen truly) for wisdom, and the country is transfixed by a dream.
Peter Sellers gets all the plaudits for an almost supernatural performance, but
Melvyn Douglas and Shirley MacLaine are pitch-perfect too, along with Richard
Dysart and Jack Warden, who prove themselves among the coolest character
actors we've ever seen. The pace of the film is akin to a Buddhist meditation.

**THE EXORCIST. 1973. Directed by William Friedkin. Adapted by William
Peter Blatty, from his novel.** Beware imaginary friends, but invite Scandinavian
priests to pray for you. *The Exorcist* is a rare thing—a vastly popular film that is
also a magnificent work of art, containing within it one of the more profound
affirmations of life you can find in a movie.

WASHINGTON, DC—A WHOLE CITY CREATED TO SIT ON A HIGH HORSE, where the buildings are made to look like ancient Rome and American royalty have theaters named for themselves, where the whiteness of the National Mall contrasts with the most famous orator to preach there, where the marble and plaster dominate the discourse of a socially constructed city-state. Everyone has their headquarters in DC—the World Bank, the International Monetary Fund, the U.S. Holocaust Memorial Museum, the government that likes to think of itself as the leader of the free world.

In the movies it's a place where people wear cream-colored trench coats and meet by cold rivers to talk about whose career they're going to ruin next, or in dark underground parking lots to bring down governments and make journalistic careers, or on park benches eating lunches out of brown paper bags while the conversation turns to national security and the next military adventure overseas. It's a place where half a million people sleep at night, but where the population doubles during the day. In *The Exorcist*, of course, it's a place where there are demons in the attic whose evil can only be conquered by the practice of the good, which I guess shows that at least somewhere in Washington someone knows how the world really works.

It knows it's an important place, but its residents couldn't vote for President until 1961; even today its sole congressional representative has no vote and is considered "at large." Someone should tell her she should ask for her money back. Like London or Paris, Washington's got a heightened sense of its own importance. It's impossible not to feel tempted by that sense when you're there.

The statue of Lincoln is huge, impressing on anyone regarding it that to be president is to be wise and humble and BIGGER THAN YOU. He overlooks the reflecting pool where Dr. King dreamed aloud, where Abbie Hoffman reminded us that at least some property is theft, where Nixon took a night time stroll of sincerity to talk with students who hated him, where Clint Eastwood tried to seduce Rene Russo, where Forrest Gump was reunited with Jenny. It's also where the eighteen-year-old version of me sat one day, soaking in the city's humid sub-tropical climate with a girl who made me wonder but who stopped writing to me six months before inviting me to her wedding. Ah well.

Some days, the reflecting pool in front of Lincoln's memorial is so clear that it looks like glass—like you could walk on it. Which brings me to *Being There*—a film in which Peter Sellers "went into another dimension," according to the actor Ileana Douglas, grand-daughter of his co-star, to play Chance the gardener, a man who never got to leave the house he spent fifty years in, and whose knowledge of the outside world derives from a combination of television and horticulture. He knows something about reflecting pools and their power as visual aids. I first watched it with my mum on UK Channel Four on a Sunday night in the late 80s. I loved it then. I think I understand it now. Jerzy Kosinski drew inspiration for *Being There* from the themes in Heidegger's *Dasein*—presence, embodiment, standing still, allowing. Okay, so maybe I don't understand it, but I certainly want to go where it leads.

Chance is a totally free man, guileless, capable of love and loyalty because no one has yet told him that he is supposed to be or do anything limited to the absurdly narrow circle of self. When Alan Jackson in "Where Were You When the World Stopped Turning" helps some people feel better about themselves by singing, "I'm not sure I could tell you the difference between Iraq and Iran," you're in the ballpark of what Chance is like, except you don't imagine he'd want to drop bombs on anyone whether he could distinguish between them or not. Chance has no sense of his own self-importance, but television grants this to the culture, structuring our lies. TV in *Being There* is a singular paradox, containing both beauty and catastrophe—we hear about the weather somewhere else, Sesame Street teaches us how to speak to each other, uneducated and unelected men and women "anchor" our lives by telling us what to fear and what to buy, our unfulfilled sexual desires are turned into glossy commodities Bob Barker of *The Price is Right* declares, "IT'S A NEW CAR!!!!," and the relationship between age and wisdom is ignored, forgotten, or never seen for what it is in the first place.

When Chance is evicted by lawyers who have never been in the home he has known for half a century, he is told, "We will need some proof of your having resided here." His response, so obvious as to be both wiser than words can say and utterly lost on modern ears, is:

"You have *me. I'm* here."

In the simplest terms possible, Chance affirms what the cultural critic Lewis Hyde calls the "erotic life of property," and spends the rest of the film showing that it's the tricksters who make the world livable. The law throws him out of the house and he walks through streets beyond repair. Ten blocks from the White House is as far as you need to go to find one of the highest centers of urban poverty and crime rates in the country. Chance becomes a Mad Ranter, suffering the brokenness of the inner city, the grain and grey of 1970s films, and the Central East winter. Thankfully, a one-percenter crushes him between a limo and a sedan, and in, as they say, an unlikely turn of events he decides to help and bring him home. From then on, Chance is a king—in the world, but not of it. He meets the President, advises ambassadors, and has the ultimate validation of being on TV. Richard Dreyfuss, a man who knows, claims that everyone wants to be in the movies—I think what he means is that everyone wants to be seen. We feel invisible to the world until the world drops by to say hello.

When Martin Luther King, standing beneath but also beside that imposing white Lincoln, was nearing the end of his most-remembered speech on August 28, 1963, a speech originally titled "Normalcy, Never Again," his voice may have begun to exemplify an entirely reasonable fatigue. He had traveled through Scripture, Shakespeare, and the US Constitution. He had made his case and was about to alter the consciousness of a nation. A woman, who some say was the gospel singer Mahalia Jackson, shouted out,

"Tell them about the dream, Martin." And so he did. All men created equal. We cannot walk alone. *Their* freedom inextricably bound to *our* freedom. Hew out of the mountain of despair a stone of hope. Not by the color of their skin but by the content of their character. And then, this:

"I have a dream that one day on the red hills of Georgia the sons of former slaves and the sons of former slave owners will be able to sit down together at a table of brotherhood."

Chance doesn't belong in the Rand mansion any more than slaves in the massa's house. He's just a gardener—a man who has lived in something akin to indentured servitude for fifty years. He's a slave now setting others free. In that sense, he is a dream come true.

Chance ends up as a candidate for President, anointed in absentia by Illuminati-like power-brokers in the act of burying their dead king, while Chance retraces the original great leap for mankind, walking on water to remind us that innocence and magic are not unrelated. The spirit of Chance doesn't often show up in elected politics today—but it's there, if you know where to look. If a President were to dedicate him or herself to bringing more love into the world, everything would change. Woodward and Bernstein know it in *All the President's Men*—the pen is mightier than the tape recorder. The priest in *The Exorcist* knows it—evil can be absorbed and subverted by love. Chance knows it—innocence can be power.

FLORIDA

Development

MIDNIGHT COWBOY, 1969. Directed by John Schlesinger, written by Waldo Salt, from the novel by James Leo Herlihy. Two guys take a bus trip. It doesn't work out too well.

THE TRAJECTORY OF *MIDNIGHT COWBOY* IS FAMILIAR—BEGINNING WITH A MAN searching for his dream and ending with two guys going to die in Florida. I didn't know until recently that this is what *lots* of Americans do, but one of the most amazing things that happened to me while spending the better part of a year watching movies, most of which I'd seen before and liked, was the revelatory experience that comes when adult eyes take another look at things they saw as a child. We've all shared this—we see things that meant the world to us when we were younger and discover that the encroachment of cynicism, or a mature mind, or a re-shaped ego, no longer permit the same response. It works in the opposite direction too, of course.

And so it was when I sat down to explore Florida, a state that I knew for orange juice, swamps, and the day I visited Disney World, which was so busy that I got on only nine rides in twelve hours, an experience that is a contender for the Biggest Let Down of My Life.

I'd seen *Midnight Cowboy* before—the story of a man called Joe Buck and his friend Rizzo, debauched and broken in New York City, traveling to the Southern sun and a freedom that eludes them if it was ever there in the first place. I'd first watched it as part of my autodidactic education in cinema history, on a fuzzy VHS copy when I was about fifteen-years-old. I didn't understand it then, but this time round I was about the same age as Jon Voigt and Dustin Hoffman are in the movie. I'd been to New York and Florida, and my own vision of the American Dream was now tempered by cynicism.

Despite the cynicism, let me get this out of the road:there may be no more moving performance in American movies than that which portrays the collapse of Ratso Rizzo in *Midnight Cowboy*. Dustin Hoffman makes you agonize with this guy's brokenness and feel anger at how others reject him. But you also get this creeping sense of guilt that you might reject him too. This is the American nightmare—that in risking everything for your fortune, you might actually lose it all.

Here's how the Dream goes: You are born in some god-awful place, you go to a terrible high school where you have one inspirational teacher who tells you, along with everyone except your parents (although sometimes even them) that the first thing you should do, as soon as you can, is Get Out Of There. If you have a low cost of living and are safe where you are, like in a small town in Florida, then you should work even harder to leave, because a low cost of living and community safety cannot compete with the opportunity to get by on minimum wage working for a TGI Fridays on Staten Island.

The American Dream in *Midnight Cowboy* romanticizes the kind of future that likes to promise "You Can Have It All," and the reason it says You Should is that you can idealize your childhood and recreate it in the suburbs of the big romantic city, even though it might kill you before you can afford to escape. Neither Joe (whom we see implicitly as an impotent bystander to his girlfriend's rape back home in Texas) nor Rizzo (about whose past we know little, but can infer a lot) are surviving, and no one will help them. The aesthetes who think they own Greenwich Village offer hallucinogenic substances in place of compassion: They are the avatars of the broken parts of the 1970s: they know that if you want to get ahead in this version of the dream, you have to be ready to cash in on the primal desires of others and literally sell your body.

And so the depressing pilgrimage unfolds, with Joe and Rizzo blinded by superficiality and desperation into kidding themselves that the Dream is achievable without disregarding the needs of others. They walk over someone sleeping or dead outside Tiffany's, concerned only for how they look (among Rizzo's first words to Joe are "terrific shirt"), and are lulled into intellectual dormancy by commercial propaganda summed up in the slogan they see: "It makes even black whiter." They are reduced by the shame of looking for spare change in a vending machine—the foundations of a man's dignity stripped by the very process of trying to stay alive.

Their circumstances are desperate, but they are not empty of empathy. In fact, at the end of the day, there may be no greater love between two men in the movies—whether it's Rizzo cutting Joe's hair, or Joe cradling Rizzo in his arms, having zipped up his fly for him, the crumpled body Christlike, an epitaph for the era when America could get away with kidding itself that it cared for all of its own people.

The story of Florida—where it snowed badly in 1899, where the 2000 election proved the country's lack of mature democracy, where one of the country's oldest cities co-habits with its shiniest and most contrived new developments, where Hulk Hogan was born, where almost more than anywhere else in the US lives the story of removing people from their native land. The latter happened, of course, in every single state, but who knows what the displaced indigenous people of what is now Miami had left when they reached the end of their bus line? What will become of us when we find ourselves in Florida, in towns named after Spanish military heroes or Catholic saints, after realizing that a life cannot be built on, but only played at with, Warholian parties? *Midnight Cowboy* speaks for the demolition of the foundations of one man's dignity, and the emergence of "happenings" instead of neighborliness as a defining characteristic of American culture. Joe and Rizzo feel safe going to the warm south because they imagine they will be healthier there. But the bus won't even stop when one of them dies. The bus won't stop because capital must flow freely, even if people can't, because the terms and conditions of the ticket sale legally bind the company to treat you as a statistic and not a person. The bus won't stop because there isn't time to figure out the difference between need and desire; and Orlando theme parks must have their customers.

GEORGIA

SPACE INVADERS

There's no getting away from it if you're Irish.
— Mr. O'Hara in *Gone With the Wind*

DELIVERANCE, 1972. Directed by John Boorman, written by James Dickey, from his novel. Men interfere with nature. It wins.

GONE WITH THE WIND, 1939. Directed by Victor Fleming, written by Sidney Howard, from the novel by Margaret Mitchell. The American Civil War interferes with a woman's social calendar. She wins.

WISE BLOOD, 1979. Directed by John Huston, written by Benedict Fitzgerald and Michael Fitzgerald, from the novella by Flannery O'Connor. God interferes with an angry ex-soldier's atheism. God wins.

q WAS WALKING OUT OF AN ATLANTA BRAVES GAME IN THE BUSY SUMMER WHEN the Olympics had come to Georgia. The International Committee apparently had not registered the fact that average temperatures in July are, shall we say, somewhat higher than average *annual* heat in this glorious humid swamp, which was also one of the first legislatures to rebel against British rule, a former penal colony, and where the Trail of Tears began. I made my way out the main gates, jostled by the forward momentum of the crowd, swimming downstream to the multistory car park, embraced by a warm breeze, when a strange woman took my hand, and walked along with me for a few seconds before exclaiming (with a degree of conciseness that Georgians aren't known for), "You're not my husband!" Call it Southern hospitality, call it romance, call it what you will—whatever it was, it made me feel welcome. Which is how the South always makes me feel. The American South.

Before we get to *Gone with the Wind*, the most-seen film of all time, a film about trauma and epic violence, which at one point attracts the pyromania those of us who love, just love, to see a city burn, let's pause for some bluegrass. The dueling banjoes of *Deliverance* evoke the idea of a culture being destroyed, of people fighting against an invasion of their space. At the beginning of the movie the vanishing wilderness is about to be made invisible—they're "drowning the river" to make way for hydro-electric power. It is, as one character says, "just about the last untamed, unfucked up river in the South." It turns out, of course, to be just a little more fucked up than they imagined, but before they know this the city boys at least have the presence of mind to acknowledge that "this is where everything ends up. We may just be at the end of the line." The men in this story want to be thrilled by exploiting nature. They, the city-dwellers, the businessmen, the masters of the universe, think they know the edges of the unknown and are not afraid to lie to each other and steal from each other and take from the land. They believe nature is benign, but they delve into a state of nature that they don't understand. They happen upon primitivism of a kind that does not easily respond to post-industrial bargaining.

Because Georgia thinks that it's where it all began, *Deliverance* is an origin story, which means Georgia movie people think they can't do any-thing to stop violence other than using violence in return. When one of the mountain men gets shot, we're supposed to feel FANTASTIC. We identify with the men lost on the river, because we too want to find ourselves. And we derive comfort from pictures of our loved ones, as Jon Voigt does on the night he thinks he's going to die. He finds himself, alright—humiliation and attempted disempowerment leads to violence, he finds what he's capable of, and it will always haunt him.

When he is rescued at the film's end, he finds that the circle of indus-trialization is complete—touching his car makes him feel better and he eases into the hospitality that the South wants to be known for (and does pretty darn well, if you ask me). The town is going to die soon, he sees a church rescued from drowning on stilts and wheels and he knows it's later going to be towed away, a witness that may not have seen the facts, but a witness nonetheless. Its removal is both an accusation and a declaration that something beautiful is dying.

Deliverance in this sense echoes the quintessential Georgia film, perhaps the quintessential American movie, *Gone With the Wind*, for they are both about ways of life that are dying, and dying violently, and about what people will do to hold fast to what is dying. The absurd caricature of Scarlet O'Hara, a ridiculous reification of feminine wiliness meeting its shadow in the caricature of Rhett Butler, the man-as-beast in a dress coat, ready to abandon his children for a bit of a lark, raping his wife to teach her a lesson (and one that the film has her seeming to enjoy), and rather hoping that her next pregnancy might be ended prematurely with an accident.

Georgia has been poor for a very long time, which lends irony to the garish expense of the movie. *Gone With the Wind* is on a big canvas in every way, declaring its intent from the scroll that tells the audience how Mr. Selznick's organization "has the honor to present its Technicolor production of"......[wait for it]......PICTURES OF BLACK PEOPLE EKING OUT INDENTURED EXISTENCE IN THE FIELDS, followed hard by the most audacious title sequence EVER—four little words apparently too big to fit on a screen by themselves.

And we're plunged into burnt paint thrown on a screen, the technical skill of an army of art directors almost compensating for the embodiment of cliché that the characters are. Rhett and Scarlet, Ashley and Melanie (people who talk to each other as if they were royalty), Tara and the burning of Atlanta, those quaint slaves—we feel that these people exist in our heads, in our memories, in the space between spaces. Their story is the *ne plus ultra* of romantic movie origins: Men with "terrible" reputations and women who want only to stand on their own two feet, to love money, and learning to love place. Tara is filmed as a vision of heaven—the only thing wiser than this in the film is the slaves, who are both smarter and funnier than the other characters. People get married before the man goes to war, it seems, so that the woman will be able to personalize national grief when he doesn't return. Mourning in *Gone with the Wind* is a fashion statement—you get to wear black and look snazzy, and when a man wants to buy you at a charity auction, you can get even more attention than if your husband has been in his grave for only a few months. Not that sex with a non-widow is any less shameful: The lusts of the flesh—or power over other bodies—are the problem here. When one character says early on that "most of the miseries in the world are caused by wars, and when the wars are over, nobody knows what they were about," it's hard not to wonder why no one is listening, despite the fact that, in the movies. people *always* say things like this.

★

OF COURSE, THE MOVIE HAS A SUBTEXT AND A BACKDROP, ALTHOUGH IN THIS case the Civil War appears to have been fought over the autumn collection of the local haberdashery, so well turned out are the men engaged in battles that, as a caption tells us, occurred when "two nations came to death grips." The film was released in 1939, when the Depression was ending and memories of urban sorrow and unjust death were fresh, but close enough also to the end of Lincoln's war that surely some who saw it had also seen Atlanta actually burning down. Some also were about to lose their lives in a war that America did not yet want to join. The names of the dead are read and America is supposed to like this—calls it "closure"—which is what everyone's looking for in *Gone with the Wind*.

"You can tell your grandchildren how you watched the old South disappear one night," Rhett consoles Scarlet, yet again weeping over how her privileged upbringing as an oppressor of humans trafficked from halfway around the world is wafting away like so many strands of cotton. Ok, maybe she deserves a little sympathy—she is living in the traumatic aftermath of shooting in the face a straggly-bearded raping monster (rape by her husband being less unpleasant due to his more finely tuned whiskers, one presumes). Yet this is a woman who is obsessed with the survival of her house though not the slaves who live in it. You wonder if all those silhouettes of her against the sundown that make her look like a cardboard cutout are meant to indicate her shallowness—she doesn't know who she is apart from Tara and her daddy and the men she thinks she loves. The role that Tara plays is important because it raises the question of the place of place in shaping our identity. It raises it, but doesn't answer it other than to suggest that Georgia is a place where bricks and mortar mean more than family, which in my experience couldn't be further from the truth. Its values are not the same as the post-industrial revolution. Men are soldiers or fathers, women are nurses or wives, nothing happens that Scarlet can't reinterpret as a melodrama with herself at the center, and the movie ends with her declaring her intention to return to the womb of Tara to "think of some way to get him back." The best known Hollywood romance ends with the delusional revenge dream of a control freak. The past ain't past.

It's always there. Which is why, I suppose, the protagonist of *Wise Blood*, John Huston's film of Flannery O'Connor's novel, just wants to go home. Hazel has been turned by the army into a walking dead man. He visits graves where the departed are marked as having "gone to become an angle [*sic*]," and he hates churches whose preachers have "all got too damn good to believe in anything." He gets to the town of Macon and happens upon a crowd of grotesques hawking everything to everyone—a metaphor for the worst kind of religion. The real Macon is far more agreeable, miraculous even, though religion is, of course, the fundamental fact of American life, connecting people to God if not each other. He says that he has "come a long way since [he] believed in anything," but there is one thing he does believe: Religion cannot tell you that you are unclean, and this means you should not be afraid to show your shadow to the world.

★

Georgia warrants three films because they tell us something about three sides of Georgia—the natural world, political heritage, and religion, all of which are really about the same thing: survival. All three of these films present caricatures of an over-the-top personality that could be crazy, mingled with glorious Southern hospitality, and held in tension with the mild suspicion of outsiders that leaves a healthy proto-secessionist movement alive in Georgia today. But when the South is at its best, of course, it is the place that allows you to believe that *no one* can tell you that you are unclean.

Hawaii

Surfing

RIDING GIANTS, 2004. Directed by Stacy Peralta, written by Peralta and Sam George. Documentary about how surfing became a way of life, and how, by the end of the movie, there may be pretty much nothing else you'd rather do with your time on earth.

CAN'T STAND UP ON A SURFBOARD. AFTER AN UNFORTUNATE CONCUSSIVE incident at White Rock beach on the north coast of Ireland in 1984, I don't even like seeing the things up close. The real reason actually may be because I don't live in Hawaii. There are things that happen in Hawaii that can't happen anywhere else on earth (and as with Vegas, things that happen there can stay there). When surfers discovered the power of the North Shore in the 1950s, it must have been the shock of their lives. Surfing was already the drop-out activity du jour—it hadn't taken on the force of a religion yet (it had been only a century or so since missionaries banned it due to the state of undress and easy mixing of the sexes it encouraged). The North Shore was an invitation to something more than dropping out: It provided a reason for people to re-locate their lives and make a radical statement.

In *Riding Giants*, the survivgfors of post-war, pre-Sixties American life talk about how they enfleshed a dream in Hawaii, building a neo-subsistence culture from the waves up. Surfing was a way of life. They could play and fish and make love and ensure that no one went hungry as they shaped their lives, not around the making of cash, but the playing of breakers. They planned their lives around waiting. For waves, but presumably waves became something more than foamy water. They were like half-dressed (and warmer) variations on Vladimir and Estragon, though of course *Waiting for Godot* was written in cold, rainy Paris in 1956 and aimed to freeze hearts, while Hawaii was the epicenter of living free. Hawaii was the epicenter of living free. Of course, people sometimes die when they're surfing, which simply underlines the fact that the most incredible things are sometimes the riskiest (as when Susan asks whether or not Aslan in *The Lion, the Witch and the Wardrobe* is "quite safe," the answer is, "'Course he isn't safe. But he's *good*"). Out there in nature, as one surfing survivor says, "You're an insignificant rag doll," but if the karma is with you, you're a dragon slayer.

As with *Fight Club*, these guys inspire my envy. They don't just have a great war. They have a great life. Hawaii seems to be a place where you can still live near to nature without abusing it. Surf culture might be one of the few in which people actually depend on looking after each other. In fact, surfing may be the great leveler in American life—loved as much by leftist hippies as by warring minds of people like John Milius, whose screenwriting gifts gave us *Apocalypse Now* and *Conan the Barbarian*. There is, of course, a cloud in this silver lining—there's a hierarchy with fame; guys make their reputations by riding big waves, and sometimes you get the sense that these guys take themselves a little too seriously.

Better to live between two caveats, offered by two of the riding giants:

1: There are times when surfing [life] makes you call upon the deepest sense of who you are. (Which is not a bad way to live at the best of times.)

And . . .

2: If you're too deep, you won't make it. (Which is not a bad way to live at the worst.)

There is anxiety before exhilaration (as one says, "Your balls are in your stomach") and pitting yourself against the ferocity of the sea can make you into a better human. It can make you grateful for what you have, can "soften some hard corners," and grant the most supreme pleasure and contentment, which is being in relationship with nature and recognizing the immense comfort of knowing that one wave continues to roll through time, unending, unbending, and inviting.

There's something about Hawaii—its isolation from the main land mass of the US that grants it a kind of mystery. Its name might mean "homeland," and it might mean nothing—nobody is quite sure. Colonization has not necessarily been good for it—in the 1850s it lost twenty percent of its population to measles. But its ethnic diversity (sixteen percent have Japanese ancestry) makes its people perhaps a little more comfortable with difference. It has produced the coolest president of my lifetime so far, as well as being where

Dog the Bounty Hunter hunts his bounty, and where Paul Theroux chose to live after seeing pretty much everywhere else on earth. It's the place the makers of *Lost* chose to represent the center of the human universe, and its most well-known custom is that you should bring a gift and take off your shoes when visiting someone's home—partly as a mark of respect and partly to experience the earth with no barrier.

One giant relates how surfing ate his loneliness: "I surfed with this beautiful woman who allowed me to get away with shit as long as I didn't act too outrageously toward her." These days, of course, we all surf, and it doesn't take our loneliness away. We surf from home. Hawaiians would admonish us: "Malama ka'aina"—get out there and take care of the land. Take care of your soul. Life is art, not mathematics.

ꟼDAHO

SEX

If I had had a normal upbringing, I would have been well-adjusted.
—Mike (River Phoenix)

Follow the money.
— Deep Throat, the Idaho-born FBI agent Mark Felt, shortly before he brought down a President.

MY OWN PRIVATE IDAHO, 1992. Directed and written by Gus van Sant (with some input from an English Elizabethan playwright). A young man is lost in Seattle, having left Idaho for the big city years-months-days earlier. He sells his body because he needs money and love. Life doesn't work out too well for him, nor for an entire generation of American hipster guys. Have a nice day.

NAPOLEON DYNAMITE, 2004. Directed by Jared Hess. Written by Jared and Jerusha Hess. American heroism favors the little guy. And those who are willing to dance.

Т HE FIRST THING WE CAN BE SURE WE'RE SEEING IN *My Own Private Idaho* IS the word "narcolepsy" emblazoned in garish pastel colors on the screen. The second is River Phoenix, whom I can't look at in this film without remembering that he's months away from his own death, his own senseless death of a drug overdose in an LA nightclub owned by Johnny Depp. He's standing on an open road, like Tom Joad in *The Grapes of Wrath*, waiting for someone to pick him up. It's not long before just that happens, and he's being paid to get a blow job in a seedy hotel room from a fat man wearing a wife-beater. I suppose you could say that, as moments of snatched intimacy in the movies go, it's one of the more memorable.

When I was seventeen, I wanted to be River Phoenix—the perfect hair, the vulnerability-as-strength, the fact that he got to do things I could never imagine being able to do myself (have adventures in Stand by Me, be Indiana Jones' younger self, help Robert Redford steal unimaginable technology in Sneakers). In *My Own Private Idaho*, he plays a guy called Mike and he hates his life because he has lost his mother and he's wandering, like the rest of us, on the open Idaho road surrounded by tumbleweed and burnt light, moving to the music of a slide guitar. Oh, and he's in love with Keanu Reeves. That's to be expected, I suppose.

My Own Private Idaho has noble pretensions to Shakespearian tragedy, and while it serves as a good reminder of the indulgence of some American performance art (look at me! LOOK AT ME!) it works: Young guys wondering if it's possible to stay beautiful in a world that only wants to steal from them, in a country that will spit out its broken onto the streets rather than acknowledge a shared responsibility to care, scapegoating men whose only sin appears to be that they are honest about whom they want to love, while "civilized society" keeps its sense of sensuality under a net called "respectability." This is one of those movies that wants to portray America as a dumping ground for the vulnerable, leaving them only their exotic and impossible fantasies for comfort. In that sense, it mirrors the other great

Idaho film, in which the eponymous Napoleon Dynamite enacts himself into history through dancing like a prophetic fool. Napoleon and Mike are the same—whereas most American movie protagonists confuse desire with need, for these guys there is no difference. They want shelter and comfort, their parents have abandoned them, and sexuality has become a game in which their bodies are commodities.

As *My Own Private Idaho* moves from Idaho to Oregon to Washington to Italy and back again, it fills itself further with despair for a parentless generation. The primal fear, rage, and desire expressed when a person refers to himself as being "from a corrupt man" evokes the notion of the sins of America's fathers repeating on themselves. As bodies roll in and with and apart from each other, borne against some of the most astonishing landscape images ever photographed, we're all asking the same question as Mike: Is anyone ever going to love him?

Idaho wants to last forever (the state motto is *Esto perpetua*), and I guess if you base your corporate identity on how many gemstones can be mined under your soil, or what kind of potatoes can be grown in it, you might have a chance of getting what you want into eternity. But *My Own Private Idaho*'s vision is bleaker—it suggests that there will never be a resolution to the paradox of human yearning unless the conflicts of sexual desire and need for psychic stability can find a place to settle themselves. Mike says that he would love someone even if they didn't pay him, and there may be no more subtle definition of love than that. But he fears that no one will ever love him in return:

"I've been tasting roads my whole life; this road will never end. It probably goes all around the world."

In some sense, we're all looking for our own private Idaho—we want, as the Irving Berlin song, played on a squeaky Hammond organ at various points in the film, has it, "God to send his grace on us." We know that some people will steal from us, and some people will save us. But we're afraid to trust—we suspect that love might have more to do with commerce than we would like. It is claimed by many that "Idaho" means "sun coming down from the mountains," but apparently this is a made up story, a tradition invented to make the state feel more important. Mike's fear is that love itself is a hoax, and *My Own Private Idaho*'s declaration is that the American Dream—or at least the most popular version of it—is a lie.

ILLINOIS

VIOLENCE

An honest question is one to which you don't already know the answer.
—Parker Palmer

You get further in this town with a kind word and a gun than you do with just a kind word.
—Al Capone

THE UNTOUCHABLES, 1987. Directed by Brian De Palma, Written by David Mamet. The battle between Al Capone and the FBI is ratcheted up by the establishment of an incorruptible team of investigators led by Elliott Ness. Capone kills to stay in power; but Ness and company bring him down through exposing his tax evasion. One of the best-known mainstream thrillers of the 1980s, featuring an Oscar-winning performance by Sean Connery and some high camp from Robert De Niro as Capone. Kevin Costner anchors proceedings as an everyman in extraordinary circumstances. It's over the top violent, historically implausible, and at first glance there's not much to it other than extremely well-dressed sets and well-orchestrated set-pieces. So it's a hell of a lot of troubling fun.

TWO UTOPIAN CULTURES HAVE RISEN AND FALLEN IN ILLINOIS, AND THAT WAS before anyone from next door even knew it was there. We know that the Cahokia Indian civilization once existed, and we know it disappeared, but we don't know how or why. The Mormon city of Nauvoo fell apart for clearer reasons: human envy and the violence that goes hand in hand. You'd think that after losing one city of gold you might be more careful to keep a close eye on the other, but the people of Illinois are strangely unpredictable—for one thing, according to *The Untouchables*, they don't let you drink alcohol, and if they find that you do, they shoot you. The unfortunate guys who facilitate the drinking live in swanky hotel suites that they appear to share with about a dozen other men, while the cops who have to enforce this ridiculous law inhabit either tidy gingerbread houses or enormously long apartments, with perfect wives and love-notes in their lunch boxes. They are unfailing in politeness, but euphemize the murder of the wine class with neat phrases like "Take him"—which in the case of Elliot Ness actually means "shoot him in the face." Illinois (centrally located, freezing in winter, too hot in the summer) considers itself part of the Midwest even though it's not really in the middle, makes a lot of coal and corn, and more than anywhere besides Louisiana, is the home of jazz and blues. In *The Untouchables*, it is something close to a fascist state.

Crime is dealt with by criminal means. Despite Ness' statement that the law should be enforced by example, his Irish cop friend (played by Connery in his apparently immutable Scottish accent) tells him that the best way to respond to a bootlegger who "puts one of your men in the hospital" is to put him in "the morgue." There is violence in America, of course, but *The Untouchables* is an assertion that its spiral has so often not only been not ended by the state, but *sped up*. The word "Illinois" is apparently derived from a French adaptation of the Algonquian word for "s/he speaks normally," which could evoke an average state, or maybe just state the obvious: that in a world where the forces of law and order break their own rules to maintain them, everybody already believes the lie.

You're reminded that only eight decades ago, Prohibition was a key fact of American life; that after over half a century of lobbying, the country that considers itself the leader of the free world put an unreachably high shelf between people's hands and their mouths. It actually amended its constitution to ban the sale of alcohol, upon which it blamed all social ills. Perhaps this seemed fair enough, since a few decades of industrialization had given working class men-machines a reason to spend too much time in the pub. But, come on, it's not as if religion had been ill-served by the demon drink (I seem to recall Jesus getting things started with a fairly raucous party in which there was not only wine provided by the host, but magicked out of nothing but water by the new guy), nor would we have the writings of good Illinoisans like Ernest Hemingway or the music of other locals such as Miles Davis, without the presence of a decent bottle of whiskey. On the other hand, the same Puritanism that caused Prohibition has also been responsible for book-burning, which makes for uneasy bed-fellows with a national psyche that claims human freedom as its ultimate goal.

The US Constitution, a document outlining the notion of a nation, written by the descendants of Puritans, is held by some in the kind of awe otherwise reserved for sacred texts. The Constitution may be the most paradoxical list of rights and freedoms in the English language—it allows everyone to have a gun, but doesn't guarantee equal pay for women; it enshrines freedom of speech, but people go crazy when someone tries to pray in a public building or put the Stars and Stripes on a bonfire; it upholds freedom of assembly, but, for a period in the early 20th century, it allowed the law to tell people they couldn't have a drink. We've all known people laid low by alcohol, but Prohibition may be one of the few examples in history when an entire country was broken by enforced tee-totaling. Asceticism can be an addiction, too, and so can its nationalistic corollary. Even today constitutional amendments are proposed to make it a criminal offense to burn an American flag, which to my mind is the definition of diminishing something by denying its opposite. I suppose you could do worse than test the kind of nation the Constitution was supposed to produce by looking at Chicago, the third most populous city in the country, and part of a state that has been ranked "most average" on a range of social indicators such as employment, culture, and health care.

If you are to believe *The Untouchables*, the American Everyman lives in Illinois, his family never more content than when gathered round the radio to hear "The National Farm and Home Hour" after supper. It's a world where father knows best, men leave their problems at the office when they've had a bad day at work, and the job of a cop is to keep the community safe, or at least feel like it is. In this romanticized vision, even psychopathic gangsters can occupy a place of wonder—you're always dressed in a tux, on the way up or down opulent staircases, going to the opera, or getting a manicure and foot rub while your personal barber shaves you.

Despite its statistical averageness, Illinois has produced the universally accepted nominee for the country's greatest President, and in Lincoln's footsteps have followed Reagan (born there) and Obama (made there), so it knows how to leave its mark. But the social contract has broken down in Illinois, although if the frequency with which Chicago politicians find themselves on the business end of a subpoena is anything to go by, maybe it was never there in the first place. Illinois seems confused about which way is up. Do you get to be governor because you earned the votes or bought them? Do the police uphold the law or create their own? Is there a straight answer to an Illinois question?

Like I said, it's a confused state. "On a boat, it's bootlegging. But on Lakeshore Drive, it's hospitality," says De Nero's Capone, fictionally defining paradox before historically personifying it as a murderer who managed to get prosecuted only for tax evasion. Contradictions in terms seem to pursue Illinoisians everywhere—it was there that Ray Kroc started McDonalds, contributing to the health crisis and environmental degradation that our generation has to mop up; but he and his wife also gave over a billion dollars of the profits to charities working for peace and to end poverty.

In 1933, just as Prohibition was ending, the "Century of Progress" World's Fair was held in Chicago. I imagine well-known Illinoisans getting out of town when the rabble-crowds arrived, perhaps going to a dinner party held a few hundred miles away at the mansion Jay Gatsby bought with the profits from moonshine and guns. William Jennings Bryan is holding court with Walt Disney, trying to figure out how to make America more "American." Roger Ebert is talking with Michael Mann about the portrayal of cops in his *Heat* and *Miami Vice* movies, wondering if there is something innate in American tough guys that makes them want to shoot people while wearing dark glasses. Oprah is taking notes for another therapeutic show that teaches people to deal with their angst by talking about it in public—her next guests will be Ferris Bueller and John Candy's character from *Planes, Trains, and Automobiles*. Hugh Hefner's in his smoking jacket, showing off Cindy Crawford and her signature perfume collection, whose alcohol content means it has to be tunneled in from Canada. Frank Lloyd Wright is teaching Richard Pryor about architecture as a way of helping people to live well, and Pryor returns that satire is a way of showing people what's really wrong with their lives.

And in the corner of the room stands a sweating man, gently excitable eyes bulging from the effort of driving a tune from his horn. He's a man from Louisiana, but Illinois is where he found his mojo. He's a man who sees most of the century, is connected through blood to the recent history of slavery, is percolated in the violence and shadows of Prohibition, and he maybe wonders what kind of person wants to become a cop in a culture where "shoot first, ask questions later" appears not only to be a legal duty, but an acceptable way of becoming a man. He's fusing gospel and sharecropper work songs with the plaintive wooing of a mama's lullaby, injecting his repertoire from time to time with the whoops and hollers of a freedom song. He's casting a glance over this state and this nation and wonders why there is so much violence over so little to fight about, why a historic legal document is worshipped while people go hungry, why the rush to judge others when, as he later sings, we have all the time in the world.

He is Louis Armstrong. And he is today's reason that Illinois deserves better than to be reduced to the head for an eye, body for a tooth politics of *The Untouchables*. For Illinois did more than stop people drinking or shoot those who did. It is the crucible in which the only purely American art form was invented. And that should be a comfort to anyone who has figured out that there are no easy answers in life. For jazz doesn't present solutions either, because then, unlike Prohibition or gangsterism, it would be an ideology, and not a soundtrack to human freedom.

INDIANA

VISIONS

The magic of darkness breaking through into colour and light is such a promise of invitation and possibility. No wonder we always associate the hope and urgency of new beginning with the dawn. The beautiful danger is that no one can ever predict what the new day will bring.
— John O'Donohue, 'To Bless the Space Between Us'

CLOSE ENCOUNTERS of the THIRD KIND, 1977. Directed and Written by Steven Spielberg. Electrician Roy Neary wishes upon a star, and pursues a dream of aliens, because he believes that there is more to life than what we tell ourselves. And he's right. Relationships have broken up over one party not endorsing life for what it is—a mystical experience.

THE FIRST THING YOU SEE IN *CLOSE ENCOUNTERS OF THE THIRD KIND* IS THE DARK. The second is that it's beautiful. The third is that you don't belong there. Yet. Spielberg was obviously paying homage to Stanley Kubrick's *2001: A Space Odyssey* by opening with a completely black screen accompanied by a high-pitched sound, before an eruption of white light consumes the audience's field of vision. Opening titles proceed with the names (Dreyfuss, Truffaut, Zsigmond, Balaban, Spielberg himself) evoking an imaginary heist crew consisting of Polish rabbis and French chocolatiers. There's a sense that we are entering liminal space—a different place to any of those that we have previously known. When the screen brightens, we're peering through the dust into a wind-swept desert in Mexico, and people are babbling about things we don't understand. Almost the first words of the film are, "Are we the first to arrive here?" And this is why and how it represents America—the thrill of actual discovery mingled with the adolescent assertion that no one else did it before us. This is what America (and America's shadow) is about: invention (and colonizing), creation (and empire).

We meet a delirious man, old and poor, jabbering on about the vision he had the previous night, repeating his new mantra "the sun sings to me." We cut to an air traffic control room. The pilots squawking to the controllers don't want to report a UFO because there are times when no one wants to accept that there is anything that they can't explain.

Then, suddenly, we're in Muncie, Indiana—a house straight out of *The Wizard of Oz*, the house that Jack built, the house that those of us who have never been there believe is America: clapboard siding, huge yard, crickets sounding off everywhere, the medium-sized house on the prairie with the cymbal-crashing monkey, the house that we imagine to be standard in the country of our dreams. It intentionally evokes Dorothy's farm in Kansas, for Spielberg is reaching back into our childhood pre-history, nudging our inner innocent to come back to life.

A little boy is awakened by what turn out to be aliens from outer space.

His mother (Dad is so absent he might as well be on the moon) is terrified by the noises and lights and her inability to protect her child. Melinda
Dillon has made a career out of playing slightly unhinged mothers—in this
where aliens appear to destroy her security, in *A Christmas Story* where the
dogs destroy her oven-roasted turkey, and in *Magnolia* where her husband
almost destroys her daughter. Meanwhile, in the Muncie suburbs, Roy
Neary (Dreyfuss), ignorant of the fact that he is mere hours away from
being invited by aliens to go with them into the unknown, is enacting the
myth of American fatherhood, playing with his trains and failing to help his
son learn how to count. As a baby boomer, Roy may be fixated on the fear
of having no great task in life, no "great crisis," as *Fight Club* would have it.
The sons of this generation are looking to their fathers for guidance, but
their fathers are too deadened by suburbia to know or perhaps even to care:

"I don't have to do your problems for you. You do your problems for
you."

There is no organizing theme to Roy's life except sleeping and working
and eating and playing with his trains; indeed, he is so bored by the ordinary
and there is a part of him desperate enough for the prize of being alive that
he will eventually abandon his family to win it. He has more capacity for
dreaming than even his own children:

"You have a choice tomorrow night—you can either play Goofy golf
which is a lot of waiting and pushing and shoving and probably getting a
zero, or see *Pinocchio*, which is a lot of furry animals and magic and you'll
have a great time."

As I watch, I wonder if I ever become a father in America whether I
will have to struggle against forces that leave me able to be more playful
than my kids. I may be doomed to trying to persuade them that there is
more magic out there in the world than on an electronic device. Magic is,
of course, partly what this film is about: A man hears a voice that speaks
apparent absurdities, but he follows because, although he can't understand

it, there's nothing else he can do. It's the biblical story of Abraham, who left everything he knew for something apparently ridiculous only to become the father of a nation because he did so. It's the story of the Pilgrim Fathers who may well have felt they were traveling an Abrahamic route. It's the story of anyone whose inner monologue ever told them they were different.

So it's my story, too. I'm the mad guy in the Sonora Desert, jabbering away to myself about what the world is and is not, asking where the light came from and why it sings to me. I too say the light came from UP THERE, and I point—it comes from heaven and from the cinema screen, and other places too. I say the sun came out last night and it sang to me. The sun sings to me through the movies, and while this particular movie was made when I was three-years-old, I feel it understands me now. At one point, Roy's wife, played by Teri Garr, who, when given a chance, is one of the most perfect of pitch perfect comic actors, listens to him trying to explain something he can't articulate, just as in life the movies so often articulate for us what we can't speak, what we feel and not what we think we ought to say. Roy has seen something beyond profound, but his wife only worries about how to put dinner on the table. He's discovering the secret of the universe; she's telling him he should put fake tan on his face. The face that was burned by an alien spaceship.

One of the fascinating things about *Close Encounters* is that, for a quint-essential American story, it's relatively open to the rest of the world—we see traces of alien reconnaissance in India, Nepal, and Mexico, and we can assume that Indiana and Wyoming are not the only places they choose to land. In that sense, the film respects the audience more than many American mythic enterprises—it's an everyman story that really does have something for everyone. We can believe that something happening to a little guy in a house in Muncie is also happening to the whole world. This is perhaps the good side of American exceptionalism—at its best it is a country that sees itself as a gift to the rest of humanity. And what can be more human than a mother searching for her child? What can be more human than a man getting on a spaceship to find God?

And this may be the vision that America most believes about itself: There's something out there bigger than us, but it's not just *out there*— it's *here*. The American story, like all of Spielberg's stories, is a domestic drama with a metaphysical soundtrack, and there's only one authority that Spielberg respects—a man's vision of what might make him a *good* man. Every other rule is challenged, from employee responsibility to obeying military instructions, and eventually common sense. What stuns me is that Spielberg was younger than I am now when he made it. I'm getting older, faster than I want to, and I want my inner innocent to come back to life. *Close Encounters* suggests that I should just sit still and build something.

For much of the film's central section, Roy is compelled to mold a shape that he doesn't understand—from mashed potatoes, from plasticine, from the soil of plants he uproots in the garden, from clay. Tom Waits once wrote a song about such a man, his neighbor inquiring, half-amused and half-horrified, "What's he building in there?" There is a subset of America in which the suburban male is forever working on a project in the basement. In real life, the Unabomber constructed bombs in a shack, destroying the lives of others to make a political point. George Clooney's character in *Burn After Reading* enacted the Coen Brothers' coruscating satire of the flimsy reasons for the war in Iraq by using aluminum tubes to build a sex toy in his cellar, and Roy Neary sculpts Wyoming's Devil's Tower, the first declared national monument in the US, and the landing site for his particular ETs. Plasticine, of course, is for kids and Roy needs to, as St Paul and President Obama might say, put away childish things. The uprooting of the plants telegraphs his maturation—Roy needs a rupture. He gets it, but it comes at a price. The gifts that life brings us are sometimes accompanied by scars, and when Roy sees the light, it burns him, taking him away from what he has known maybe never to return—which is, I suppose, what the best movies are supposed to do.

Close Encounters is, like *Chinatown*, also a movie about cinema itself, with the magic of *Oz* and *Pinocchio* mixed with gentle jokes about *North by Northwest*. The climactic half hour takes place in an alien landing strip at the bottom of Devil's Tower, which is not only one of the most majestic images ever filmed, but a picture that evokes the feeling of being in the largest movie theatre ever built. It's not just aliens that are coming: it's the greatest film premiere on earth.

As the large plasticine alien emerges from the craft and does his peaceable wave-thing, we are moved, uplifted, possibly we are changed, and we know that there is something bigger than us in the world. As we look at the gracious face of Francois Truffaut, cast by Spielberg because of his association with Great Movies (and evidence against the charge that Americans never trust the French), we know that There Is Something Bigger, and that Something is not just America, nor is it cinema. It's being a Person. That's what Indiana, somewhere in its depths, knows.

Along the way, the religious figures do their thing, anointing the new astronauts on their way to forever; but ecclesiastical ritual pales alongside the vision of the alien mothership. The scientists congratulate themselves, but seem sufficiently under-awed by the majesty of the visitation that none of them try to board it. As Jesus or John Updike might say, "Only ordinary people can see the magic, and only the childlike can enter the kingdom of heaven."

(Note to Self—Things have changed since the Seventies: The striped cardigan of the guy who tries to escape from the army with Roy is terrifying. Second Note to Self: Things have not changed since the Seventies—the sign at a McDonalds featured in close-up says that they had served only "24 billion" then, but the buildings look exactly the same today. Third Note to Self: When people in America see things that inspire awe, they invariably say, "Oh my God!" whether they believe in God or not.)

Ultimately, *Close Encounters of the Third Kind* is America's cinematic prophecy of itself, reminding us that the new is often frightening, and that promise and danger can be the same thing. This is how America began. In promise and in danger. In *Close Encounters*, you have both: America is a place that worships its own myths of greatness, where the authorities make you wear gas masks when the air is clean, and pretends that there's no such thing as aliens; where salesmen try to scare people into buying protection they don't need; a place where the government militarizes human discovery and endeavor, is willing to harm its own citizens for the sake of what it determines to be national security, and tries to frighten a superior intelligence away by playing John Williams' music to spaceships. It's also a place where everyone is called by the same cosmological echoes—to be reunited with our parents, to get back to the source, to know that there is a God, to feel like we have done something significant. At the end of the film, Roy is no longer an outsider looking in, looking on, yearning to be part of things. He has melded with the core, which is where America says everyone can be—at the center of their own nation.

ꟼOWA

A DREAM YOU CAN DREAM
WHEN YOU'RE AWAKE

When primal forces of nature tell you to do something, the prudent thing is not to quibble.

— Ray Kinsella

FIELD OF DREAMS, 1989. Directed and written by Phil Alden Robinson, from WP Kinsella's novel. Thirty-five-year-old farmer, who regrets losing his father just a little more than having a dad in the first place, hears a Voice telling him what it means to be human: To plow under his corn and make a baseball diamond so that deceased cheating ball players can return to play ball and cleanse their guilt; to visit a reclusive writer and return him to society where he will feel inspired to write again, restoring his sanity; to allow an old man to be reborn in his youth and play the game he always wanted to, so that he might no longer live in regret; and to build a space where the whole world can come to sit quietly and be healed. It takes him a little while, however, to realize that his journey is not only for the sake of others, nor is it really about baseball. When he finally, angrily, demands to know, "What's in it for me?" the answer is simple: Saving his own life.

THERE ARE TWO KINDS OF RUNNING. THE FIRST I HAVEN'T DONE SINCE I WAS a kid. When I was a kid, the only sport that didn't reduce me to feeling infinitesimally tiny and existentially lost in the face of my peers was the one where you take a stick and a ball and you hit the ball in the air and around a diamond. In northern Ireland we called it softball, and it had no rules except those just noted. On Tuesday afternoons at 2:30, I'd pick up the stick, let some guy throw a ball at me, and I'd swing, imagining the sound of "eh batter-batter-batter-batter-sa-wing battah!" in *Ferris Bueller's Day Off*, or thinking about the noble-by-degrees cheats in *Eight Men Out*, or wondering why anyone thought forty-seven-year-old Robert Redford could play seventeen in *The Natural*. I'd swing for my dignity, swing for my life. Remarkably enough, sometimes I hit the ball. The bat actually connected and I got to run a base or two. I remember the feeling that biologists would understand, but I would not have known then, to be a rush of adrenaline swooshing up the front of my torso, cheeks flushed red, and the slo-mo advance when the cogs in my brain clicked my legs into gear. I dropped the bat, turned, and RAN.

The second kind of running is probably best described in Flannery O'Connor's "The Turkey," a story that ends with a boy running home in terror after being bullied and his turkey stolen by rough, abusive lads. It's gothic horror imagery—the boy is terrified, for the traumatic events have convinced him he can feel something that can only be interpreted as a death wind blowing behind him. He's chilled into submission as what seems to him the inevitability of his own future failure sinks its claws into his mind. The second kind of running is the running you do when you're afraid.

For most of my younger life, I was caught between these two kinds of running. In my mind's eye, the child version of me sometimes looks like a frightened, hobbled skeleton, clothed in fabric but no flesh—bones of anxiety. But sometimes the image that my memory reveals is different: The young me is smiling, laughing even, from deep within as I let go of the bat and start moving, alive in my own world, sure of something:

I know I hit the ball dozens of times. On a few occasions it flew far enough away that a few fielders had to leap into action to retrieve it. There was definitely even a home run or two. I have no idea whether or not any softball team of which I was a member won a single game. But my memory knows this:

I AM RUNNING.

★

"SEE IF YOU CAN HIT MY CURVE," SAYS THE GENTLY COCKY RAY KINSELLA TO Shoeless Joe Jackson early in *Field of Dreams*, the professional player's ghost having just arrived at Ray's farm. Joe can, of course, hit the curve. He's a paranormal being, so it's not unreasonable to imagine that he probably knows he's in a movie whose aim is nothing less than the birth of a new American myth: That the generational anxiety of post-war people can be resolved when they make peace with their parents, true community depends on love that can't be measured and can only exist in resistance to the driving-apart forces of privatized capitalism, and, as it turns out, baby boomers can be happy too. For a fourteen-year-old four thousand miles away from Iowa in Belfast, it meant that life might actually turn out okay in the end. But what could *Field of Dreams* teach me twenty years later and two thousand miles closer?

Now, I know what you're thinking.

"Another Kevin Costner baseball movie?" Sure. Because if it's alright for Kevin, it's probably alright for me. I've seen *Field of Dreams* more than almost any other movie. It is a comfort in trying times, and even in rich ones. We're watching a guy heal himself through giving to others. Along the way, he helps his wife end censorship in America, critiques the private ownership of the common good (he explains to the ghost that most ball games are played at night these days because the corporations that own baseball teams know they could make more money that way. The ghost cuts to the truth, saying that the lights "make it hard to see the ball"), prevents himself from getting killed by reminding the man threatening him that he's a pacifist, and does everything he can to avoid turning into his father before realizing the inevitability—and the hope—that you will eventually see two sides even to *that* story.

This film feels authentic amidst its own magic because its characters are actually doing something with their lives. They're farmers and librarians and doctors, but they are also people who believe in possibility—the possibility of magic, the possibility that people might actually learn to embody their greatest hopes.

Now, of course, for a quiet, self-effacing state, Iowa catches a good game. Without Iowa there'd be no Bix Beiderbecke or Glenn Miller to jazz us to sleep, no Buffalo Bill to keep the memory of the West alive, no Ann Landers to answer our problems in the papers. It's considered the safest place in America to live, where stewardship of the land is what it means to be American. And, in the 19th century, its very ground held miraculous powers, as when Ralph Montgomery fled his slave master in Missouri and became a free man as soon as he stood on Iowa soil. It might really be the place where dreams come true.

What kind of dream am I trying to make true when I'm awake? To become a free person? Definitely. Who is the father we are looking for? Myself? Maybe. *"What's in it for me?"* Well, says *Field of Dreams*, if you can learn to be at peace with your inner self and find true contentment in sharing the land and not charging people to use it, the answer to that question can ultimately be . . . everything.

KANSAS

THE MILITARY-INDUSTRIAL-HALLUCINAGENIC-PLANT-STRAW-SCARECROW COMPLEX

Teenage Loner Drops House on Witch
—*Kansas City Star* headline, September 1939

THE WIZARD OF OZ. 1939. Directed by Victor Fleming. Written by Noel Langley, Florence Ryerson, and Edgar Allen Woolf. A tornado flies teenage Dorothy into a fantasy land where she learns the meaning of everything. When children had longer attention spans, holiday TV schedules needed look no further. Now they think this movie is an antique. When I was a kid, I played the Lion in a school production. I don't know if my teacher, the magnificent Mrs. Smyth, she of the amazing rock-solid peroxide blonde hair, House of Windsor pronunciation, and overpowering perfume, had clairvoyant powers, but I turned out to be just like him—hairy and scared.

YOU WILL, I TRUST, FORGIVE ME IF I APPEAR UNSURE OF THE FACTS—FOR THE truth is, *The Wizard of Oz* features a Kansas that will not respond easily to reductionist analysis. I can ascertain that, as a result of the pandemic psychosis induced by whatever substances were airborne during the tornado, Dorothy Gale and the people of Kansas arranged for the brutal murder of poor angry Ms. Elvira Gulch by the (quite frankly, rude) means of dropping a house on her head.

Is this a Kansas characteristic? Well, what do I know about Kansas? It's flat, I suppose. Dusty. Tumble-wed. Has a city named after itself. Indigenous people lived there contentedly for thousands of years before Coronado arrived in 1541 to "civilize" the people. Lewis and Clark later explored it and national mail delivery there learned how to be Pony Express-quick. The open plains may have nurtured John Brown to see why human beings must be free from slavery. It's an expansive place where Amelia Earhart may have caught the itch to fly in order to explore the void; where Langston Hughes grew to became the man who sang with poetic vitality, ethnic fidelity, and sexual diversity; where Dennis Hopper erupted into an acting force of rare courage, confronting his audiences with their own fears of what lurks beneath the unintegrated ego; where, four hundred years after Coronado, the Supreme Court in Topeka ruled in Brown vs. Board of Education that racial segregation in schools was unconstitutional; where people today are abandoning their farms and moving to the cities in an epidemic of rural flight.

Kansas.

The only place in America where the ground reminds me of home.

★

THERE ARE LOW, GREEN, ROLLING HILLS, CATTLE IN THE FIELDS, PERHAPS EVEN some hand-built stone walls. There are farmers and traveling salesmen and people who enjoy "ordinary" life enough not to worry about money or fame, because that's the way it's always been. And, of course, there are teenage girls who believe that the fastest way to travel between two points is to don garish red shoes and summon imaginary friends.

But, in *The Wizard of Oz*, Kansas is boring, brown, ugly, and dry. The Kansas family unit seems to consist of a weak-willed father, a domineering mother, three male helpers (none of whom are too bright), and a little girl who seems incapable of making friends with human beings so committed is she to the belief that her dog understands the English language. The Kansas community revealed in Victor Fleming's self-evidently magical but strangely troubling film yields only two further members: a crackpot snake oil salesman, whose false marketing as a clairvoyant might lead to his prosecution, and a nice elderly lady on a bicycle who is attempting nothing less noble than to achieve a measure of justice after being viciously attacked by the girl's dog.

Once the scene changes, and we see Kansas turning into Oz, the movie version of the state seems to be a glimmering place in which small people are drugged into pretending that they're happy, when in reality they are slaves of an empire. Upon receiving the news of Ms. Gulch's death, the Ozians/ Kansans engage in what can only be described as a pseudo-satanic ritual— triumphantly singing and literally dancing on the grave of this vulnerable woman. Dorothy, unsurprisingly, is troubled, so Ms. Glinda, apparently a runner-up in the 1938 Miss Kansas regional finals and the mastermind behind the murder, manages to fool Dorothy into leaving the scene of the crime "for her protection."

Still affected by the airborne hallucinogen, Dorothy follows a path lined with flowers that look like pink-painted white chocolate and along a stream made from aluminum foil, passing through a poppy field, evidently for medicinal purposes.

Along the way, Dorothy meets three delusional men—a farmer, an industrialist, and an army deserter—and befriends them (Kansans are clearly not afraid to talk to strangers). After throwing acid on a Ms. Glinda lookalike already suffering with terrible jaundice, and engaging in animal cruelty by stapling wings to a large troupe of monkeys, Dorothy and her gang finally meet a man in a funny suit hiding behind a screen. Presumably he is the governor of Kansas. It turns out he is a weak leader, hiding in his office rather than dealing with the statewide emergency caused by the tornado. The governor gives each of the travelers the freedom of the state. Shortly thereafter, the hidden camera appears to have stopped working, and the film switches back to the farmhouse where Dorothy seems doomed to eke out an indentured existence with only her dog and her drug-induced flashbacks for company.

Ms. Gulch is still apparently dead.

Ding-dong.

One might say that this exceptionally disturbing film raises several questions for those who wish to understand the socio-psychological terrain of Kansas in particular and the Midwest in general. *The Wizard of Oz* is astonishing, given that it provides such an intimate, no-holds-barred look at the American family and political system. The cinema verité approach, revealing the day-to-day workings of a Kansas farm, the troubled psyche of an American teenager, and the sheer complexity of elected governance makes this film ripe for a new audience.

Let me count the ways:

The governor speaks of the poisoned chalice of state leadership: "I'm a good man, just a bad wizard." It's clear that the American people demand much from their political leaders, and this is entirely natural because sheep without a shepherd wander in dangerous territory. Another Kansan, Dwight D. Eisenhower, after he had served as what could be called national wizard, once said that "any man who wants to be president is either an egomaniac or crazy," and he yearned for the days when he would be called "ex-president." Yet he was not merely concerned with the state of his self-image or the freedom to take vacations, but rather, in terms that were once famous, and eventually became cliché, but more recently may have been forgotten, also said:

> We must guard against the acquisition of unwarranted influ-
> ence . . . by the military-industrial complex. The potential for
> the disastrous rise of misplaced power exists and will persist
> . . . Every gun that is made, every warship launched, every
> rocket fired, signifies in the final sense a theft from those who
> hunger and are not fed, those who are cold and are not clothed.

Midwestern stereotypes suggest a militaristic people, yet Wizard
Ike was the president who said "war settles nothing." In *The Wizard of Oz*,
Kansans danced when they killed their oppressors, yet the president from
Kansas said, "There is no glory in battle worth the blood it costs." The
people of Kansas may have projected their inner shadows onto the witch
and killed her, thinking it would make them free, but their best-known son
suggested a touching reason why political power so often turns into bully-
ing: "There are a number of things wrong with Washington. One of them
is that everyone is too far from home." The people want their leaders to
be perfect, but what they need is confidence that they will be looked after.
As for the wizard of Oz, he's terrified. In that sense, he represents the fears
we have about our leaders—that they are just old men, frail beings hiding
behind curtains using a loud voice to make us run away, and having only
the authority we give them.

The Kansas of *The Wizard of Oz* represents a high ideal: the notion that
home is where the heart is. When John Updike died, *The New Yorker* paid
tribute to a writer whose head would not have been out of place on the wizard's shoulders, whose magic, when applied, could even make Connecticut
Protestant intellectuals seem sexy. On his death, *The New Yorker* described
his skill of discernment thus: "He knew the difference between the point
and the purpose: The *purpose* of *King Lear* is to make you feel the tragedy

of life, and the point is to show that old men should not retire before their time." Well, the purpose of *The Wizard of Oz* is to make you feel like you're dreaming the dream of childhood; the point is that there's no place like home. Dorothy is lost on the road to the Emerald City and perhaps, in some sense, so are all Americans. The country as it currently sees itself is still just a little too young to know where—or what—it really is. Yet the dream of the magical land of Oz, with everyone dancing and nobody voting, just doesn't satisfy. Americans want leadership, but they also tend to exile the leaders who fail them.

The antidote? Well, *The Wizard of Oz* and the story of Kansas itself—a land that had been colonized by explorers and from which people later left to explore—is a parable for growing up. The farmer/scarecrow, the industrialist/tin man, and the soldier/lion represent the ages through which American society had to pass before it could discover the most profound truth—that what you think is happening always changes when you look back on it. As the governor/wizard says, it is a delusion to think that "simply because you run away from danger, you have no courage."

This is where America starts—in a dream that life could be different, and that the end of the rainbow will turn out to be closer than your own backyard. I want to leave my mark on the world, Dorothy wants to travel beyond the color spectrum because she feels it will bring her meaning. Fair enough. Maybe Kansas is as boring as she thinks. Though given the mark its people have left—unbridled human journeys, an end to school segregation, an actor unafraid of facing rather than exiling the shadow side of being human, a poet who sang beauty out of sorrow, and a president with enough battle experience to know the futility of war—it turns out that if you're looking for a heart, or a brain, or the right kind of courage, maybe there is no place like Kansas.

KENTUCKY

FAME

Madness is the only way of escaping in the face of a hostile environment.
—Sergi Sanchez

COAL MINER'S DAUGHTER, 1980. Directed by Michael Apted, written by Thomas Rickman, from the autobiography of Loretta Lynn. Loretta Lynn grows up as a sweet little girl with a knack for stringed instruments in the western coalfields of Kentucky. Life is hard. She marries her sweetheart. Life is hard. She works her way up the entertainment tree. Life is hard. She works some more. Life is hard. She has a breakdown on stage. Life is hard. She gets really famous and rich and builds a cute house that reminds her of the things that made her happy when she was younger. Life is hard.

ALL I KNEW ABOUT KENTUCKY BEFORE I GOT TO COAL MINER'S DAUGHTER COULD have fit into a bucket of fried chicken. There would be tales of bourbon distilling, tobacco growing, and hopefully some apocryphal stories about deep fried mice accidentally turning up in a certain Colonel's sandwich. From the evidence in Coal Miner's Daughter, however, it would appear that hot, greasy rodent phobia caused me to miss the opportunity to live in a modern utopia. According to this film, it would appear that poverty-stricken pre-war Kentucky is full of moss-covered tree forests from which big wooden houses are carved with gorgeous wrap-around porches. Within these houses live happy and enormous families who are lulled to sleep at night by the sound of contented crickets. The young Loretta Lynn thinks she's growing up in hell, but if that's hell, then give me Kentucky.

Young Loretta is played by Sissy Spacek, who at thirty is playing the oldest looking thirteen-year-old you ever did see. But the contrast between the Sissy we know and the Sissy we see's got nuthin' on Tommy Lee Jones with his hair dyed ginger. Tommy Lee plays Loretta's suitor, admirably waking up her father at two o'clock in the morning to ask for permission to marry her. These early days of motel-bound nuptials are a textbook example of why American sexual repression is bad for your health. Neither of them know what they're supposed to do in bed, nor even if they're supposed to want to. But human appetites is as human appetites does, so sex happens, whether they like it or not. So does hunger. For Loretta, it's music that feeds her soul, and when her husband gives her a ropey old guitar for their first anniversary, it's the most romantic gift imaginable.

And so, through the time-honored combination of determination, talent, and those funny little cowgirl tassels that women country singers sometimes have hanging off their two gallon hats, Loretta makes it. She is accused of trying to foment revolution, largely due to her advocacy of women's rights in songs with titles not too far from "Get Out of the Kitchen and Onto the Battlefield" and "I Ain't Making No Bed for No Man" and

"Take Yer Freaking Greasy Hands Off My Cowbells, Mister." She digs. And she finds her treasure, not in riches (although they help), but in a house that looks remarkably like the one she ran away from at the start of the movie. Granted, the décor is so chintzy it looks like the wallpaper was taken from Barbie's off-cuts, but it's got that same wraparound porch and a few rocking chairs, so it's home.

It's funny that it looks like home to me, too, even though I never had a porch or a rocking chair in Belfast. I know that I can never really go home, because what I mean by "home" in that sense is a return to how I saw the world when I was innocent enough to believe that I could find life without working for it.

I don't think Kentucky's going to be that home. For a start, it's subject to some of the strangest weather conditions in America. Look up "Kentucky weather" and you'll find voluminous articles on events as varied as the Mid-Mississippi Valley tornado outbreak of 1890, the Ohio River flood of 1937, the North American blizzard of 2003, and the Windstorm of 2008. So it's cold, and the wind blows harder than I'd like. And, while Abraham Lincoln was born there, its politics don't appeal to me. Things got so tense in the 1900 gubernatorial campaign that one of the candidates actually had the governor killed. The popular Kentucky brand of religion, too, might be a problem for me. Kentuckians like their God, and they like the Ten Commandments displayed on public property, but they like to exhibit them alongside other holy documents like the Declaration of Independence, the words of the "Star-Spangled Banner," and - we may presume - the recipe for hot wings. As you know, I'm all for the spiritual journey, but I'd hope to be more for salt and light than the imposition of cultural imperialism. And I think the Ten Commandments are probably secure enough to take care of themselves.

Coal Miner's Daughter does suggest something about Kentucky that might be what all of us need. Someone says early on that there are three choices in Kentucky: "coal mine, moonshine, or moving down the line." I guess he means to say that a good life isn't just going to happen to you. You have to work for it. And in Kentucky that means being open to change. In Kentucky, in order to have teachable moments, you have to stop thinking that you know everything (an appropriate thought, given that no one seems quite sure what the name of the state even means—folks vacillate between "dark and bloody ground," the Iroquois word for "prairie," and my personal and rather obvious favorite: "cane turkey"). The "unbridled spirit" of Kentucky, as the state tourism motto has it, is one that encourages people to live from their dreams, but not to get too excited about anything in particular.

We're only a generation or two removed from a time when people lived together in large households of moms and dads and uncles and aunts and grandmas and grandpas and kids and cousins and someone from back East and a wayfaring stranger and a couple of dogs. Sometimes the house on the hill with the huge porch and huge lot and huge family seems like the perfect way to live. If I had a house like that in Kentucky, I'd invite people from the neighborhood to come and join me. I'd ask Wendell Berry to talk to me about raising tobacco, writing poetry, and minding the earth; I'd wonder aloud with Larry Flynt about sexual repression in America and whether or not he's tending to people's souls or harming them; maybe we'd sit down with Private Lynndie England to explore the role of that same sexual repression in the Abu Ghraib images that made her famous and got her scapegoated for the sin of a whole war. And while we were talking about famous people, perhaps the Louisville son Muhammad Ali could get a bit a wistful, and eloquently reflect on the strangeness of a country that grants privilege to people who can punch well, or sing songs, or fry a piece of meat, while the work of digging for the fuel that keeps our houses warm goes unrewarded, unremarked upon, in the freezing and windy coalfields of western Kentucky.

LOUISIANA

RELIGION

THE APOSTLE, 1997. Directed and written by Robert Duvall. Preacher
makes a mistake and tries to atone.

I WENT TO LOUISIANA ONCE, TO NEW ORLEANS, EIGHT MONTHS AFTER THE Flood. There were still wrecked cars on the freeway, broken electrical poles on the main street, marsh grass on the road. Eight months after the Flood. It was sticky hot. But there was music and there were muffalettas, the biggest sandwiches I've ever seen, and people who seemed to thrive on the fact that where they lived was different. Now, if I've learned one thing on this journey it's that everywhere in America is different, and that everyone thinks they're more different than everyone else. But, please, take it from me, Louisiana is *different* different.

One of the things that makes it different is that it's French. Another is that people really know how to mosey. And another is that Robert Duvall made one of the most realistic films about American religion there. Religion may actually be the central fact of American life: The dream that we can always rise higher than we have before is the constant in American political speeches, and mystical sentiment isn't just present in the rocks beneath the Gulf Coast prairies, but also in those that chill a glass of Southern Comfort.

The spirituality of *The Apostle* is deeply alluring to me, because it makes space for every kind of motivation and confusion a human soul can permit. The temptation to charlatanry and the compassion to do miracles can co-exist in the same body at the same time. The film respects the audience enough to acknowledge that shadow and light appear together. Of course they do. The cracks are how the light gets through, right?

The Apostle knows that humans are a stew of emotions, gifts, talents, fears, mistakes, and blessings. It imagines that Louisiana might understand that life sometimes needs its bearers to be given a break. I've heard that Louisiana politics aren't necessarily the most transparent, and the humidity might get me down, but it's also the state that gave birth to one of the wisest, most fully alive, loving and human people I know, who remains indivisible from her Louisiana heritage (and would never want to be divided from it anyway). There's a million reasons to love it - not just drive-thru Daiquiri stands; or Dr John & muffulettas; or that it won't bow down after the flood; and it would be so easy to go back, because there it was so easy to feel love. And in their most honest searching, movies about love say it clearly: It is in the broken places that love arises. When we are not certain, when we are confused or vulnerable, when we cannot control our circumstances, we are free to be something more than robots. We might find our way to peace. We might sense the gentle breeze of a Louisiana port town, scooping up the smell of broiling fish and voodoo incense (the good kind), and feel within ourselves that we have arrived.

MAINE

MONSTERS

It appears we have a problem of some magnitude here.
—Stephen King, *The Mist*

THE MIST (2007), THE SHAWSHANK REDEMPTION (1994). Directed and written by Frank Darabont, from Stephen King's novellas. Monsters turn up in a New England town, and the people kill themselves trying to fight back. Meanwhile, an innocent man digs.

THE MOST HELPFUL THING I'VE EVER READ ABOUT WRITING IS BY A MAN WHOSE books scare me to death. Stephen King's memoir *On Writing* claims that his life is utterly ordinary—he has a daily rhythm of work that begins at 8:30 on a weekday and finishes when he has written 3000 words (he'd have written this book in five and a half weeks). Monday night's for football, Tuesday's movies, and he plays his guitar on weekends. He and his wife try to be about as regular as a couple in a 1950s sitcom. He says this is why he can write about such dark shadows as those that have chosen to visit his home state.

King's stories take place in a heightened version of Maine—small towns where people know each other, where the coast is agreeable, and where it gets really bloody cold in winter. They're also places where little girls can set things on fire by just thinking about it (which means she could be useful when it comes time to immolate the local vampire residence), nasty clowns and crazed fans want to kill you, solar eclipses seem to occur every two or three days, and the local curiosity shop is owned and staffed by the devil. These are small towns, but here, unlike in many other fictional American small towns, people aren't hiding from reality.

King presents his people as being just like you and me—suspicious of strangeness, needing to band together to help each other in times of crisis, but sometimes afraid to do so, subject to petty political jealousies and the tempting security of religious fundamentalism. King's monsters divide and conquer when people respond to them with violence. Much of the time you get the impression that the danger would pass if the Mainers would just get on with their lives and leave the monsters alone. But their projection of the need to be heroic (and the equation of heroism with killing) gets in the way.

That's certainly the case in *The Mist*, in which people end up sacrificing their own children to combat an enemy that was going to disappear and leave them alone in a few hours anyway. This has been a present reality in Maine ever since Americans and Brits started fighting each other over it.

People in King's Maine are all looking for the same thing—family stability and economic security. They all think that they'll find this through destroying an external enemy, but they're wrong. The people who survive in King's stories of Maine are the ones who fight the inner battle, who conquer the demons inside. This is why Andy Dufresne is already free long before he escapes from Shawshank prison: He has confronted his fears, and meditated his way into believing that, while his body is where he happens to be, his soul isn't bound by the physical cage he finds himself in.

I can imagine standing on a stretch of Maine coastline and feeling the same thing. I can imagine standing there in the coldest Maine winter and experiencing the adrenaline rush of endless possibility that is always present when I look at the sea. I know with Stephen King that enormous pain and struggle can erupt into the most mundane life. I know that we can have parts of our own personalities hidden from us, and that if we don't learn the discipline of self-awareness, we might become our own worst enemy. But I also know that the most powerful demons I need to confront are the ones that remind me of myself. If I lived in Maine, I'd want to avoid the vampires and the Mephistophelean antique seller. I'd rather sit in a small town coffee shop, or browse an independent bookstore, or go to the local prison where I might meet King's humanity in the form of a vulnerable prisoner with miraculous powers, or develop a friendship with another like-minded person that lasts forever, or be inspired to find myself freer already than I ever thought possible. Sounds great. But it's bloody cold in the winter.

MARYLAND

DEATH

THE ACCIDENTAL TOURIST, 1988. Directed by Lawrence Kasdan; written by Kasdan and Frank Galati, from Anne Tyler's novel. Travel writer Macon Leary (William Hurt) deals with the trauma of his son's murder and his own consequent divorce by hiding in overseas trips. He is saved by a happy woman whose brokenness is close to the surface too. This is one of the most honest emotional films about grief and the burdens we carry. Maryland resembles a quiet hell until Leary looks up from his life. When he chooses to put his suitcase down and take with him the only artifact of real life he needs—a photograph of someone he loves—you'll remember times when you've done the same yourself.

Question: How many Marylanders does it take to change a light bulb?

Answer: Thirteen—

Frederick Douglass to liberate the light bulb from exploitation at the hands of the electricity slave-drivers.

Thurgood Marshall to issue the court ruling on the legality of such liberation.

James M Cain and Dashiell Hammett to fight over who gets to write the perfect noir thriller entitled *Awake in the Dark* (Tagline: *How He Turned Her On and Exposed the World*).

Philip Glass to write a gorgeously repetitive minimalist score to the thriller.

Edgar Allen Poe to turn it into a ghost story.

Tom Clancy to decide that there's a Soviet bugging device inside the light bulb and that someone needs to nuke the house.

Tori Amos to write a song about the most creative way to self-harm while waiting for the power to come back on.

John Wilkes Booth to shoot the man watching the screwing.

David Byrne to let it illuminate his over-sized white suit.

Cab Calloway to scat it to glorious illumination.

Billie Holiday to sit under it, in her solitude, and compose.

Jim Henson to turn it into a reason to feel happy about life.

Maryland has the highest median household income in the U.S., and it likes to think of itself as America in miniature. It's the same size as Belgium— not too big to be ostentatious, not too small to be ignored. Average income, average size. I suppose everyone's averagely happy. The state was created as a refuge for fleeing Puritans and Catholics when Virginia made the practice of Anglicanism mandatory. Named for a Queen—Henrietta Maria, Charles the First's girlfriend—its best-known political export was Spiro Agnew who was also, of course, the second best-known tax evader to be convicted in

the U.S.. The state absorbs the residue of DC, becoming therefore a kind of
fantasy world in which the capital's political dreams are born, producing
in Agnew a vice-president, in Carl Bernstein a journalist who helped bring
down his Commander-in-Chief, in Matt Drudge the progenitor of the gossipy
morass that passes for political discourse today. Drudge's fellow Marylander,
H.L. Mencken, might be turning in his grave, but no one from Maryland's
too worried about that. Or anything else.

All I knew about Maryland before I came to America, other than that
it was where Tom Cruise puts Dustin Hoffman on the train at the end of
Rain Man, was that it was the name for a way to cook chicken in pubs whose
speciality was really Irish Stew. But I haven't met anyone outside the UK and
Ireland who knows what I'm talking about. The outside world's vision of
Maryland has been more recently circumscribed by Baltimore in *The Wire*,
so you'd be forgiven for thinking that the whole state is merely the stomping
ground for two gangs—those that sell drugs and those elected to make a
living out of not being able to stop them. But if you visited Baltimore before
HBO got its hands on it, you'd more likely have seen a city where the camp
master John Waters rooted his vision of America as a small town absurdist
circus in films such as Pink Flamingos and the more mainstream-palatable
Hairspray. The Wire says it's a war zone, Waters says it's *Queer Nation*, but
in *The Accidental Tourist*, Maryland is neither and nothing particularly interesting has ever happened there. No one wants to talk about anything
except what's not happening: who doesn't love who, why they can't get on
with their lives, how not to travel. The film's protagonist, Macon Leary,
presumably the quintessential Maryland man, is a writer devoted to helping
reluctant business pilgrims feel as if they never left the monotony of their
grey domestic lives, taking with them only the "few necessities in this world
which do not come in travel-sized packets."

The suburban landscape is as grey as the suits Leary advises his readers to pack in case of unexpected funerals; traveling with the accidental

tourist is advertised as being "like going in a cocoon." It's no wonder that when you look at William Hurt's face all you see is brokenness and loss. At one point, he actually says that he believes "people are basically bad." The mottled green of the tree leaves, the dark brown autumn, and the quiet roads: Maryland is where people withdraw. This is a realistic proposition, I suppose, given that it has to be the state whose existence most people forget (though why you would want to—with towns that have names like Silver Spring, Greenbelt, Port Tobacco, and Accident—is beyond me.)

But what Leary wants to forget is the grief he suffers over the loss of his son. This death has given birth to clarity of vision regarding a dormant marriage that feels a few lifetimes too long. He's married to someone who needs him to be "the kind of person [he's] never been, and that isn't fair to either of us." These Marylanders are people who think they're not going to recover from the past, and they depend on regimen and routine to pretend that they aren't really there. But they're only getting worse. And so into Leary's life erupts a woman who represents both a threat to his routine and a magnet for his hopes—Muriel the dog-walker, who undresses him and lets him lie down, to sleep and be comforted. In the rush of US political life, in the fear and anger expressed in its recent foreign policy, this might be just what the country needs: to go to sleep and be allowed to. To not have to keep one eye open, because the broken shell of a traumatized nation knows that it is being watched over by friends.

Until this point, Leary has been waiting, but without knowing it. Waiting. Waiting for . . . what? He doesn't want new experiences. But there are some things you can't ignore, like the voice of Muriel and people who call each other by name. He eventually finds a path away from where he's been dying and gets another chance to decide who he is. Maryland. America in miniature. Another chance to decide who it is.

MASSACHUSETTS

SCAPEGOATS

I was stretched between contemplation of a motionless point and the command to participate actively in history.
—Czeslaw Milosz

JAWS, 1975. Directed by Steven Spielberg; Written by Peter Benchley and Carl Gottleib. Great White shark terrorizes small town holiday resort; thudding music accompanies three archetypal men who chase it until one of them finds an innovative use for an oxygen tank. Maybe the best film of its kind.

HI. My name's Bruce. I'm a man-eating shark, but don't let that scare you—I'm dead, so can't do much harm, I guess. Though they haven't told me all the rules yet. Just woke up. Never imagined heaven would let my sort in. But, after that bloke rammed a gas canister in my jaws, fired a harpoon, blew me up, and recreated the world, I found myself waking up in a hospital ward with "Special Cases" etched on the door. Nice lady in a white suit told me that every so often, they get folk up here they don't know what to do with. Apparently sentient beings without a conscience usually just get turned into clouds, but in cases like mine, where they think there might have been a miscarriage of justice, you get an interview to determine whether or not you warrant a free pass to Nirvana.

Not that I know what fish utopia looks like. I guess for me, it's pretty much what my life was like until those guys started fishing deeper than they should have. Lady at the window gave me a disappointed nod and sighed something about agricultural and marine processing methods in the post-industrial age being monstrosities that will be the death of the food chain as we know it. Tell me about it. One day I'm happily chomping my way through the ocean, enjoying a little plankton here, a big tuna there, and next thing I know it's like closing time at KFC—there's nothing on the grill except grease and human fingers. Gotta swim toward shore. It's not that I wanted to eat that naked woman. I mean, I like a hot blond chick as much as the next predator, but I'd rather have some New England clam chowder. It's just that the good people of—what was it called again? Oh yeah, Massachusetts—keep stealing my dinner.

Lady says it's a common story, says that Massachusetts folk are refined and intelligent. They've got lots of colleges in the state, lots of smart people. Some guy called Chomsky who knows a lot about why we talk the way we talk, and how injustice is sewn into the current democratic process. Some other guy called Mr. Poe who writes scary stories about ravens and people who seal their uncles into cement. And a woman writer—Edith

Wharton—whose focus seems to be the destruction of the human soul at the hands of social convention, whatever that means. Like I said, smart people, but scary. And scared.

Everyone that I ever met in Massachusetts seems like they're afraid of something—that naked woman seemed afraid when I was pulling her under, the deputy was afraid of the body parts he found, the mayor of losing money and reputation, the chief of losing his job. Fear drives these people, the residents of what they call Amity Island—only I know this is a pseudonym for Martha's Vineyard, presumably because the real mayor wasn't any more interested in stirring up panic than his fictional counterpart in the movie they made about me. The good thing about fear is that being in touch with your flaws might just make you a more humble person.

But Amity's the kind of place where getting drunk gets you killed; where city politics prefer the advancement of neckties and pastel suits over the protection of people's bodies; where if you weren't born there, you'll always be an outsider. Massachusetts in *Jaws*—my biopic, I suppose, though I can't for the life of me figure out why they didn't call it " Bruce"—is a place where only the belongers belong, where small town Americana meets aristocratic and dynastic lineage. It's a state where money gets you anywhere. As Quint the shark killer says, "I'll catch him for you, but it ain't gonna be easy. For ten thousand dollars you get the head, the tail, the whole damn thing." Imagine, the democratically-elected government of nice people by the nice people for the nice people paying off some foreign goon so he could end my beautiful life? It's hard to know what to say to that.

So they showed me the movie and, I gotta admit, other than the ending, I *liked* it. The sheriff, Chief Brody, seemed decent—the guy's just trying to make a life for himself and be a good police officer, which in Amity means he's kinda like a family therapist to the whole town. There's a nice bit of domestic utopia with him and his kid at the dinner table, making faces at each other because he looks sad. I know the feeling. Some of the camera work's a bit wobbly—I guess they filmed a lot of it at sea for authenticity. And there's what I think they call a "crash zoom," where everything moves really fast toward and away from the cop at the same time. Cool. Made me excited. Plus, I'm in the movie.

When they get on the boat, now that's when the story really goes somewhere. Seems to me, they wanted to make a movie about two species, fish and people, but they ended up going smaller. It's a film about what men from Massachusetts are supposed to be like. There's three of them on the boat—a college boy (he's smart), a salty sea dog (he's strong), and that nice sheriff (he's decent). They've all got their flaws, but between 'em they might make one whole human. Anyway, they're out on the boat, looking for little old me, but really figuring out who has the biggest you-know-what. Man, those are some tense guys. You'd think they didn't know that Massachusetts has one of the most liberal marijuana policies in the country. Chill, Chief Brody. I ain't gonna hurt ya unless you insist on destroying my natural habitat. I mean, let's face it, there's an average of one fatal shark attack per year in the whole United States. You'd think I was a serial killer or something.

Anyway, as you might know—cuz they tell me that the movie's pretty popular—it ends with bad news for me. I've still got a headache from that explosion. When I woke up in the hospital, the doctor told me I'd been in for a few hundred years—took 'em that long to piece me back together. He broke the news that I'd been forced to eat a gas canister, been harpooned, and blew up. Said that the good news was that the people of Massachusetts didn't fish in the deep sea anymore. They were too scared of my family to go on the water at all. Gave me a book, an old one from Persia called *The Epic of Gilgamesh*. I like books. Dad used to scare us kids by reading horror stories like *Moby Dick* and *A River Runs Through It* to us when I was just a tiny shark.

Anyway, *Gilgamesh* is about how these ancient people believed everything came about. Apparently it's the oldest book humans have found, so it must have some insights into what they think about themselves. A long

long time ago, a couple of gods had already been bouncing around for a few millennia. They got lonely and decided to make new gods, little kid gods, to keep them company. It was fun at first, but after a while the cosmic games of catch (in which they threw planets at each other) got wearing, and Mom God and Pop God figured on a change. They decided, as gods are wont to do, to kill their kids. Not very fair, but I suppose you could also say that the kids weren't playing by the rules, making too much noise at night and all. At first, Mom and Pop ran into a problem. Basically Pop got killed by the kids before he could get them, but Mom was too strong. So the kids re-grouped and made a plan. The strongest kid would kill Mom, and the other kids would make him ruler of the universe.

Now this is where it gets weird. The strong kid snuck up on his mother, kissed her, blowing a poisonous gas into her mouth. Then, from a distance, he fired an arrow into her stomach, whereupon she exploded, and from her entrails the kid built the world. The doc told me that this is called a "myth of redemptive violence," the idea that you can bring order out of chaos. I says to the doc, "Sure doc, but it's the exploding gas in the stomach that chaosifies me." Doc tells me he understands, he's seen cases like mine before—guys who think people need to get over their obsession with violence and can't understand why everyone hates them so much—but never so similar to the myth.

I guess people from Massachusetts are big believers in the myth of redemptive violence. Doc says it maybe started with the pilgrims who came from Plymouth. They were abandoning everything they knew for the promised land. That's a kind of violence itself, I suppose. Their descendants eventually used pretty hefty force to bring what they called "freedom" in the revolution to kick Britain out. Two of their favorite sons, Jack and Bobby, were shot down by people who obviously thought their deaths could bring some kind of renewal. Lotta blood. No one seems to learn from the past.

There's more to you, Massachusetts, than the fact that you once blew up a shark to feel better about yourselves. You've produced amazing word-smiths: the nature-men poems of Thoreau and Emerson, the crazy-falutin' comedy of Steven Wright, and artists and musicians like Whistler, Rockwell, Jack Lemmon, James Taylor, Sam Waterston—folk who reflect the landscape of the American soul pretty well. For Neptune's sake, I know you gave us Eli Whitney without whom slavery might have ended sooner, but you also produced JK Galbraith and Mr. Spock. Where would progressive politics be without them? Sure, it seems limited to a lot of elegant white men with sculpted craggy faces, but you've done your part. You're where the philosophy of the nation was fostered, where Benjamin Franklin and Thomas Paine gave birth to modern political radicalism, and where the beauty, grace, materialism, nightmares, and wish-fulfillment of the Kennedys gave rise to one of the most stunning political rhetorical turns of phrase: "Ask not what your country can do for you, but what you can do for your country." You've got it all going for you, Massachusetts. So why, then, do you root your foundational philosophy—your real religion—on a story that involves children killing their parents? Why do you insist on giving credibility, a whitewash of respectability, to war? Why don't you want to go the extra mile and figure out what it might mean to live in peace? Why can't we all just get along?

"We're gonna need a bigger boat," someone out to get me said; the doc says this is what war-mongers always want. A bigger boat. Here I am, a harmless fish, going about my daily business, and the good people of Massachusetts want to turn me into their bitch. It's as if all American violence is scapegoated onto me. They never look inward. They don't ask themselves what a non-violent response to a man-eating shark would be. Stop eating my breakfast, for a start. Don't run away from your grief. Face it. And then keep going.

MICHIGAN

LOVE AND DEATH

ROGER AND ME, 1989. Directed and written by Michael Moore. A documentary film-maker makes his mark on the world by trying to get an interview with a late capitalist people-eater.

SOMEWHERE IN TIME, 1980. Directed by Jeannot Szwarc, adapted by Richard Matheson from his own novel. Christophers Reeve and Plummer vie for the same woman, Jane Seymour. This is understandable, because she's Jane Seymour, but also somewhat confusing because she lives on Mackinac Island in 1912 and Mr. Reeve is a Chicago playwright in 1980.

THE MAJOR PLOT HOOK IN *SOMEWHERE IN TIME*—A FILM SO POMPOUS THAT IT treats Rachmaninoff like hot candle wax, but so strangely resonant at possibly subliminal levels that I cry every time I see it—avoids getting in the way of physical logic: All it takes to send Chris back to the past is some dextrous self-hypnosis and snazzy dressing. He and the lovely Ms Seymour meet as if they'd always known each other and acknowledge the love they've always had, but because the movie needs a crisis and we can't be permitted to just enjoy two beautiful people getting what they want, Captain von Trapp shows up to spoil things. He wants to turn Jane into a famous actress, which of course means that he has to drug the other Christopher, put him in a wardrobe, and eventually propel him seventy years into the future when he will die of a broken heart.

But before that happens, we learn that people in Michigan dress for dinner, live at an astonishing island hotel, can't get an interview with the head of General Motors, and will do anything for love, including abandoning the present. There's something about *Somewhere in Time*—maybe it's the costumes, maybe it's the fact that John Barry's music is one of those pieces that walks the delicate line between cheese and glory, beckoning you back to yourself, or maybe it's the fact that it speaks a language that doesn't require complicated words, saying things like, "The human journey is made of goodbyes. Goodbye to childhood, goodbye to youth, goodbye to life."

Norman Mailer once remarked that

> the resemblance of cinema to death has been ignored for too long. An emotion produced from the churn of the flesh is delivered to a machine, and that machine and its connections manage to produce a flow of images which will arouse some related sentiment in those who watch. The living emotion has passed through a burial ground—and has been resurrected. The living emotion survives as a psychological reality; it continues

to exist as a set of images in one's memory which are not too different, as the years go by, from the images we keep of a relative who is dead.[4]

I don't imagine Mailer would have devoted much of his time to something so slight as *Somewhere in Time*, but if he had, he might have been surprised. *Somewhere in Time* is about a man who sees an old photograph that makes him feel the way nostalgic movies do, and who dies in order to love, which, when you think about it, is what we're all doing. It's not pessimistic. In fact, it's pretty clear it's on the side of the angels—the protagonists end up literally becoming celestial beings, forever united in finally resolved desire. On this evidence, Michigan looks pretty transcendent.

Of course, Michigan's most famous cinematic son is Michael Moore, whose films are like *Somewhere in Time*—dreams about personal loves, nightmares about sociological deaths. Both Moore and Richard Matheson know that our deepest desire may be to return to where our dreams began. They romanticize the past because the present seems too difficult (or real) to deal with. They may be right. People gather every year at the hotel on Mackinac Island to re-enact *Somewhere in Time*, and Moore makes variations on the same story over and over to warn us how far we may be slipping from what we used to hope for.

In Michigan, aside from all the lakes and all the coastal lighthouses, and Stevie Wonder, and one of the nation's largest Arab-American communities, there is of course the Ford Motor Company whose story might be seen as the story of twentieth century Michigan. Now this axis of radical economic change has become an industrial wasteland. It's no wonder people might want to live in the dreamy past: It's too easy to believe the lie that when the economy doesn't work anymore, neither can you.

It's funny, watching these, because I look at Michael Moore and

---

4   From *The Spooky Art.*

Christopher Reeve and their apparently doomed plans, the sentimental-
ization and melodrama, the yearning for something more, anything more,
something to make the dream of life worth dreaming. Both *Somewhere in
Time* and Michael Moore's films convey what love can be—that is, the ex-
tension of oneself for the sake of another; and they both present a love that
transcends death. We know the tragedy of what happened to Christopher
Reeve, and we know that Michael Moore never got to meet Roger; we know
that things don't always work out perfectly; we know that everyone we love
will one day die. But still we're left with the feeling, watching *Somewhere in
Time* and *Roger and Me*, that if you wouldn't drop everything to travel back in
time for love, or if you wouldn't do everything you could to save something
you care about from destruction, then what *would* you do?

MINNESOTA

WORKING FOR THE DREAM

A SIMPLE PLAN, 1998. Directed by Sam Raimi, written by Scott B Smith, based on his novel. Family man steals money; nearly kills him.

PURPLE RAIN, 1984. Directed by Albert Magnoli, written by Magnoli and William Blinn. Poor talented kid wears sequins; conquers the world.

THIS IS WHAT HAPPENS WHEN YOU LISTEN TO YOUR INNER GIVE-THE-BENEFIT-of-the-doubt whisper: Yesterday morning, feeling a little sluggish, I decided to begin the working week by watching *Purple Rain*, Albert Magnoli's extended music video showcase of a certain Prince Rogers Nelson's talents, and a film that I had not been permitted to see on its original release given my official status then as a nine-year-old child. I thought it might wake me up, get me in the mood to do some writing. It turns out to be a film of such unique character that I think I can only respond with something like stream of consciousness narrative. Let's call it "word association film criticism." Here goes:

Prince has a hairy chest.

He lives with his parents in Minneapolis.

He has no friends.

His enemy is another musician who can't play too well. Clearly Prince thinks this film is an analogy for the relationship between Salieri and Mozart.

His enemy throws women into dumpsters.

There's a beautiful enchanted evergreen forest on the immediate outskirts of town.

He's tiny.

His girl is the reason I wasn't allowed to see this movie when it was first released. Finally I'm vindicated.

If this is what the 1980s were really like, why do I miss my childhood?

The music is everything you'd expect.

Morris Day as the bad guy is terrible.

Everyone is terrible.

The poster's more dramatic than anything else in the movie.

Prince's hairstyle makes him look like Marie Antoinette.

It's still Prince, for goodness' sake.

It's a movie built around a soundtrack.

Does that make it all bad?

Mostly.

But the title song's pretty great.

In *Purple Rain*, Minnesota appears to be the most thrilling place in America, or at least Minneapolis nightclubs do. It is where the most epic and long-lasting rock song of my childhood was born, where men love women and drive them around on motorbikes without helmets, only stopping to stare at each other in existentially meaningful ways (and to play with hand puppets). Prince (in the film he's called "the Kid") eventually conquers his enemy, performing a rather excellent song in a nightclub, and getting the girl to kiss him and take her top off. He is, as another Kid would later announce, the king of the world.

O Minnesota, how do I love thee?

★

SOME YEARS AFTER *PURPLE RAIN*, SAM RAIMI, THE DIRECTOR OF THE *EVIL DEAD* movies, brought us *A Simple Plan*. This film is set in the Minnesota country-side, a place of real beauty despoiled by the curse of the love of money when a couple of small town guys find a satchel stuffed full of cash in a crashed plane. It's the shadow side of *Lovesexy*—Prince in *Purple Rain* wants money too, but somehow you feel that the mega-wealth he achieves isn't going to lead him to kill three people, ruin his marriage, and fritter away his soul. I guess you could call this one a morality tale, whose politics are best summed up by one character responding to the fact that they have found the American Dream in a "fuckin' gym bag":

"You *work* for the American Dream. You don't steal it."

A reasonable point, I suppose. More reasonable, actually, when you notice that the protagonists' lives are already going along just fine. They have a nice house, stable employment, live in a good community, baby's on the way. They don't realize that their American reality already is the American

Dream. These two movies seem to indicate something about the Minnesotan ethic—if you work for your dream, you deserve it; but if you steal someone else's dream, it'll kill ya. Lust for riches makes people do things they wouldn't otherwise do, like kill people or wear velvet ruffles or write epic slam poetry about Batman. They'll do anything to pick apart the shackles that hold them to their economic limitations. In this cinematic Minnesota, as in the rest of the country, everyone's worried about money. It rips marriages apart, it sets brother against brother, it starts wars. Makes Minnesota look like a frightening place to live, but that's at least partly to do with the fact that the crime story has become the dominant narrative in American fiction.

Minnesota movies are ambivalent about whether or not the residents actually want to live there. It's a state that exists in a strange reality. "Minnesota" means "somewhat cloudy water." Of course it does. It's got this reputation for being boring, but it has one of the healthiest populations in the nation, its diversity reaches to both Norwegian and German, it's got some of the oldest rocks that our race has yet found on earth. It's where *Little House on the Prairie* came from, and where Bob Dylan's stone started rolling. It has produced Keith Ellison, the first Muslim member of Congress, and gave breath to F. Scott Fitzgerald. I have a feeling that Robert Bly, its poet laureate, would caution me against running too quickly to the far borders of his state. He'd remind me that the spiritual journey, the path to maturity, takes *work*—that dreams come with a price, and that if life is a struggle you might as well continue with the struggle (or the state) that you are already in.

We may be born free but are destined to live our way into a kind of trap from which only we can free ourselves. The trap, the one that tells you you're only as good as your income or your abs, is waiting for us all. And there's only one way out. You have to take your talent and force it to do what it's supposed to do. There are no shortcuts. That's why *A Simple Plan* ends with desolation and *Purple Rain* with triumph. When you steal your dream, you can't enjoy it. When you work for it, then you're really living. So sayeth Minnesota.

MISSISSIPPI

Soul Music

CROSSROADS, 1986. Directed by Walter Hill, written by John Fusco. Old African American musician teams up with young Karate Kid to get his soul back, having sold it, in the traditional style, to the devil down in Mississippi. After many adventures, the Kid defeats evil by fusing classical music with Delta guitar. We see that the world can never be the same again, and nothing is better than playing the blues.

ABOUT 12,000 YEARS AGO, SOME FOLK TURNED UP IN WHAT WE KNOW TODAY as Mississippi. They hunted and gathered hard and well for a few thousand years, and they built a few mounds here and there. Everything was rosy in the garden of the Chickasaw. The Spanish arrived in 1540, followed by the French in 1699 who imaginatively baptized the area "New Louisiana" before setting to work. The typical story of displacing indigenous people followed in their wake, and even the French were eventually assimilated by demographic shifts. Finally, in the early years of the twentieth century, a Turning Point: A young musician, guitar in hand, participated in what was to become a noble and long-lasting tradition of meeting Lucifer at a four-way dirt road intersection, signing his soul away in exchange for fame, fortune, and the right to sing the blues. We know this, because in 1986, Walter Hill made a film about it, and we care because the Mississippi revealed in *Crossroads* might just be the most exciting state in the Union.

I think I have been searching for this film my whole life. I'm troubled by how difficult the task has become of finding a place that the movies could make me call home. So here I stand, at the crossroads. And here it is—your typical young Julliard-trained-classical-guitarist-meets-soul-selling-Blind-Willie-and-falls-for-the-beautiful-Jami-Gertz-but-has-to-abandon-her-so-that-he-can-beat-the-devil-and-get-Willie's-soul-back comedy adventure story. We stand at the crossroads, the musician and I, and I may have found my way forward.

Because *Crossroads* and Mississippi have got everything you could want.

You've got your religious names for towns.

You've got your old mentor and your young kid learning from each other.

You've got amazing rain and thunderstorms.

You've got lines like "A blues man never travels the lonely road without a pistol," "There are no goodbyes on the road, it doesn't work that way," "I can put you in the county home for criminal women," and my personal favorite, "The blues ain't nothing but a good man feelin' bad thinkin' about the woman he was once with."

You've got folk who find cars just lying there on the street with the keys inside, folk who stay in old barns when they're hiding from the police and the robber barons and who knows what else, folk who believe their dreams depend on finding songs lost by guitarists who sold their soul to the devil.

You've got a film whose duration is mostly taken up by the two protagonists cussing each other out instead of just talking.

You've got two guys wearing amazing hats.

You've got a bar owner who ends a riot by shooting the ceiling of his own joint.

You've got some of the strangest racial politics you could think of.

On top of all this, you've got some lovely photography, sepia-toned images of the South, and a story that just rollicks along and makes you believe that a life lived lolling on a porch swing, picking at a guitar, and moaning about how she left you broken-hearted but you're not gonna let it get you down might not be so bad after all.

Crossroads presents Mississippi as one hell of a rich and exciting state. For a start, the name means "Great River," but there's more than one flowing through the state. And they sure know how to name a river. There's the Big Black, the Pearl, the Yazoo, the Pascagoula, and the Tombigbee. It's the poorest state in the country, but it's so open-minded that it repealed its ban on inter-racial marriage as long ago as 1987. It bottled the first Coca-Cola, named the first teddy bear, and gave birth to Elvis.

Crossroads is one of those movies whose *deus ex machina* out-*machinas* the *deus*. The final guitar duel between good and evil is marvelously alive with humor, even though the future of the whole world is at stake. The climax seems to underline the fact that the state is unthinkable without music. So is life. But I don't know how to play the guitar, I don't know if I could put up with the humidity, and if I have to sell my soul to Satan, I'd need something other than the ability to sing like BB King in return. For the world only needs one BB King.

MISSOURI

AMATEURS

In no other state but Missouri would the James brothers be tolerated for 12 years.
—The Chicago Papers

THE ASSASSINATION OF JESSE JAMES BY THE COWARD ROBERT FORD, 2007. Directed and written by Andrew Dominik, from Ron Hansen's novel. The homoerotic adventures of a gang that steals and kills and then self-destructs. The amoral killer at the center becomes really famous.

WAITING FOR GUFFMAN, 1996. Directed by Christopher Guest, written by Guest and Eugene Levy. The homoerotic adventures of a gang that puts on a play and then self-destructs. The theater director at the center disappears into obscurity.

KANSAS CITY, 1996. Directed by Robert Altman, written by Altman and Frank Barhydt. The erotic adventures of a petty thief, his wife, and a gang of jazz fans who self-destruct. The thief gets tortured to death, the wife gets strung out, and the jazz keeps playing.

GOT STUCK IN KANSAS CITY, MISSOURI ONCE WITH NO CAR, NOT MUCH CASH, and a host whose job took him away from hosting for fourteen hours a day. So I spent an entire week watching the same movies over and over again. The fact that the city I was in apparently had only two movie theaters, and that it was the summer of 1996, somewhat limited the potential for me to do anything like enjoying my sojourn. The slate of available releases was limited to Kurt Russell saving the world by ending it in John Carpenter's *Escape From LA*, Samuel L Jackson shooting a rapist in Joel Schumacher's film of John Grisham's novel *A Time to Kill*, and Robin Williams rapidly aging in Francis Ford Coppola's *Jack*. Each of these happens to be among the weakest of their respective director's output. None of them needs to be seen twice.

That particular week left me somewhat reticent about returning to the cinema of Missouri, but it's not nicknamed the "Show-Me state" for nothing. After a little research, I discovered that Missouri's probably the best place in America for an amateur like me to live, if by "amateur" we mean those who do what they love and love what they do without much care for how other people perceive them.

Waiting for Guffman and *Kansas City* are films that represent the notion of an American artistry that doesn't depend on an understanding of the art by outsiders. They are delirious evocations of that desire within us all to perform, to be seen, to make the kind of music to which others can dance. If you've been around non-professional theatre companies, you'll know how tense things can get when the butcher and the baker decide to put on a production of *The Crucible* with tinsel wigs and fake trees; if you've met a middle-aged actor whose conversational tone indicates a sense of failure and missed opportunities, you'll know how easy it is to become detached from a sense of the common good; if you know any musicians, you might recognize how the power of performance can tempt an artist away from family. Each of these films has the same ending—change the way you think about ambition and then your work will take care of itself. Show me, but let me show you too. This is not a solo endeavor.

Of course, Missouri has had its share of lone rangers—chief among them, it seems, was the outlaw Jesse James who, despite working in a team, carried the same sense of existential isolation we would recognize in the shark from *Jaws*. In *The Assassination of Jesse James by the Coward Robert Ford*, a film about a man who does evil, but whose death may still make you cry, James is portrayed as a southern guerrilla who still wants to fight the Civil War after it's long over. He's what some would call a man's man, so of course he's played by Brad Pitt, partly because Pitt's a far more nuanced actor than his populist reputation suggests, but mostly because most movies can embrace only a limited imagination of masculinity. So does the coward Robert Ford, a young man so lacking in an independent sense of self that he worships Jesse, wants to become him, and eventually kills him, because, he might guess, it's the next best thing.

I want to be famous. Or at least part of me does. In my less mature times, I want recognition for all the hassle and struggle and talent I think I have. And, this being the funny part about being human, I'm really scared to be seen. I'm terrified that if I get on a platform, I will either misuse it and mess everybody up who reads or listens to me, or I will appear as naked as the emperor in the old story—that you will see me for who I really am and mock me or despise me or just ignore me. *The Assassination of Jesse James by the Coward Robert Ford* understands me because it knows that all of us want to be seen, and it knows the power of the temptation to leave everything that matters for the sake of celebrity, which is, of course, a concept about as unreal and impermanent as they come. If the best things in life are free, then celebrity may be one of the most expensive things you can imagine.

There is a magic part of my brain that turned on when I first went to the kind of movies that made me fantasize about how my life could somehow be as exciting as the characters I watched. That my *self* could be as large and full as Eddie Murphy in *Beverly Hills Cop* or Steve Guttenberg in *Cocoon*. I'm different now, but there is a through-line from the childish things of Eddie and Steve to Jesse James and Robert Ford. I still want to be seen, but the films I'm watching these days don't often portray the kind of life I'd like to have myself. All the guys in the Jesse James film are bad guys—it is cast of actors whose faces are made to look so craggy and lived in they look like a geological periodic table of the Midwest. Just listen to the names and you'll see them: Sam Rockwell, Sam Shepard, Paul Schneider, Jeremy Renner, Casey Affleck, Mr. Pitt. They are not happy. They are trudging the American nightmare.

This is a film that tries to tell the truth about the violence of selfishness, how greed dehumanizes the greedy and oppresses those from whom the greedy steal. It is also about what it means to be a fully actualized self. In *Jesse James*, as in *Guffman* and *Kansas City*, men identify themselves in the light of how they think others see them. They have no independent selves. Their egos are as massive as the Missouri sky and as delicate as the snow that falls gently on the farm when Jesse comes to kill a man in return for a perceived slight.

These Show-Me State movies are all about perception. How we hide our identities like contraband comic books under the bed, how certain kinds of behavior attract the interest of the public, how some of us would give anything for the chance to be on TV for fifteen minutes. There's a compelling, disturbing scene in *Jesse James* when Robert helps Jesse take a bath—the fake intimacy evoking the mutually parasitic eroticism of the celebrity/paparazzism cycle and its shadow of violence. Celebrities are scapegoats—we project our desires onto them, we want to be them, but we love it when they fail. When the real Jesse James was killed, the body was photographed and the images sold. More people made a pilgrimage to see James' body than President Garfield's. Death was vindicated as the American obsession. Missouri's misery ruled.

Now, of course Missouri isn't all bad—there are some nice bridges, amazing caves, and a restaurant near Cape Girardeau called Lambert's where they throw bread rolls at you from across the room. If you ask nicely. Wander round the state for long enough and you're bound to bump into signs left by one of its many poets—Eminem, Burt Bacharach, TS Eliot, Charlie Parker, Wilco, Mark Twain, Rush Limbaugh. You could spend days ruminating on the fact that the state derives its name from a Native word meaning "those who have dug out canoes," and how, when Missourian Harry Truman inaugurated the CIA, he dubbed its first director "snooper-in-chief." It's true. You think about Missouri and it occurs to you that the complications of being a person might be better represented here than anywhere else in America. It's the Show-Me State, so you want to be seen. It's got six thousand caves, so you want to hide. Its President ratified the government spying on its own citizens, so hiding in a Missouri cave might be wise. Saying "I'm from Missouri" means "I'm skeptical." I want to be famous. I don't want to be famous. I want to be seen. I want to hide. You're showing yourself to me. I don't believe you. I want to give Brad Pitt a bath. I want to run away. I want to do the show right here.

MONTANA

RECONCILIATION

Montana has the richest grass on the face of this earth. That's why the cattle are quiet.
—*Cattle Queen of Montana*

BARBARA STANWYCK · RONALD REAGAN

CATTLE QUEEN OF MONTANA, 1954. Directed by Allan Dwan, written by Robert Blees and Howard Estabrook. Barbara Stanwyck stakes her claim to land in the West; nasty Indians and Ronald Reagan try to stop her. She recruits nice Indians to work with her, and manages to get Ronnie to reveal his soft side. Remarkably enough, they all actually do live happily ever after.

A RIVER RUNS THROUGH IT, 1992. Directed by Robert Redford, written by Richard Friedenberg, based on the story by Norman Maclean. A pastoral film which happens to be, coincidentally, about a pastor living in 1920s Montana. He sees astonishing natural landscapes: rivers, mountains, Brad Pitt. He's a puritanical type, so of course he has two diametrically opposed sons. One is a good worker bee, never in trouble, always does what his dad says, and gets to survive. The other possesses an independent conscience and a thirst to actually enjoy life. He gets killed, of course.

THE FIRST TIME I BEHELD THE WORD "MONTANA" WAS WHEN I WATCHED Marty McFly see on the Hill Valley cinema billboard that his President (in 1985) was appearing in a western (in 1955) entitled *Cattle Queen of Montana*, which might suggest a cross-dressing farmer beauty contest. The state, and this mysterious film, became permanently imprinted in the generous plasticity of my then ten-year-old brain. A quarter century passed—nearly as long as Marty traveled back to the future—before fate sat me down to watch the movie to help me decide if I could stay in this country for the rest of my life. The irony was not lost.

So I did a little research into Montana before watching *Cattle Queen*. And aside from the fact that it carries the burden of being the only state in the Union that failed to get a Navy battleship named after itself in the Second World War, it's also the place where the first contact between aliens and humans occurs in *Star Trek*. Perhaps the extra-terrestrials were attracted by the names of Montana's towns. They already sound as if they were made for other planets: Butte, Missoula, Kalispell, Anaconda, Cut Bank, Sidney. Or perhaps, given the connection between spirituality and aliens in science fiction, they were drawn by the words spoken in *A River Runs Through It* that "under the rock of Montana is the word of God."

That said, everything feels schematic in that movie—too well planned. Man may be "a damn mess," as the pastor says, but the film is too perfect for its own good. It's trying to tell a story about the universal notion that you can't help your family, because they blame you for why they need the help in the first place. But it tries too hard, spelling everything out, issuing platitudes like a seeping wound (when Redford—who has often done much better than this—narrates that "grace comes by art," my regretful reflex was to say, "Not in this movie"). Tom Skerritt, playing the father figure, has one of those faces that belongs on Mount Rushmore, and his words are just a little too chiseled as well. Perhaps this is the point—it's so formal that when you're watching people sitting together having a repressive meal in a floral-printed dining room, the movie feels like you're actually never going to get out of that room. Gorgeous image inexorably follows gorgeous image—there's always a train going off into some beautiful, unknown distance, and the light always has a pretty brown hue. It's like overdosing on salted chocolate. Nothing surprises, except perhaps the movie's politics. It wants to celebrate the vast open spaces of the American West, but the liberated son gets killed because of this very freedom. And so the benefit of *A River Runs Through It* is not so much what it does, but what it reminds you of: The towering figure of Mark Twain writing about the rural nation and the potential for safety in smallness. It reminds you of community, of resisting the death-dealing of privatized capitalism, of the notion that what you see shapes how you behave. You are reminded that if you see life as a competition then one of you is bound to lose, and that the inevitability of family dysfunction is carved into the narrative of American existence.

★

A River Runs Through It also, naturally, drives home the fact that Montana is huge. Big enough to contain both David Lynch and Evel Knievel, for a start. Beyond that, what you see in Montana is just how easily America could rule the world of human recreation: You can't open your eyes in Montana without seeing somewhere to swim, to shoot, to sail. It's a pilgrim's state—it's a place people moved to because they wanted to get away from something, which of course also means that they wanted to get *to* something. What they wanted to get to was home. They carved out a swathe of land, bled their way into domesticity, and made the most natural decision of all—where it's beautiful, that's where we'll stay.[5]

On the other hand, *Cattle Queen* is sadly not about cross-dressing cowboys, but the trials of homesteading. We meet Barbara Stanwyck, a butch girl

---

5   Or, these days, "That's where we'll pay someone to build us a summer home where we can spend two weeks a year."

laboring under the magnificent name of Sierra Nevada Jones, horse-riding with Daddy to take possession of her parcel of land. Wherever they are coming from, they do not feel secure; so they want to move to a place where they can eat "thick steaks and count their money." Alas, Daddy is soon killed by the folk whose land they've stolen and Barbara is reduced to skinny dipping while a peeping Tom observes her. The fact that this particular Tom is in real life named Ron gives the movie a kind of sacred imprimatur: If it's good enough for Reagan, it should be good enough for the audience. (We later see Ronnie shoot a match flame out from Jack Elam's fingers, and you can imagine that this would have been the perfect image for a critical retrospective of his Presidency. But perhaps snuffing out light and warmth from the hands of the indigenous poor is a little too nuanced for prime time.)

"This is my land," exclaims Barbara when she recognizes the threat to take it away that emanates from the people who owned it first. This, and other constants of the western genre, finds its way into the map of the *Cattle Queen's* cinematic terrain:

Stampeding buffalo, check.

Talking about the country as if it's a new car, check.

Statements of American exceptionalism sounding like teenagers trying to outdo each other, check.

Ruthless Indians, check. (In perhaps the most egregious denunciation of Native Americans, the script has the future President say, "White women's scalps are especially valuable," adding sexism to bigotry based on skin color.)

Primitive Indians, check. ("I see you have learned the soft ways of the whites.")

Wise Indians, check. ("The greatest challenge is not how to deal with the white, but how to keep your own tribe together.")

Indians with pathos, check. ("Is it too much to believe that I am a human being too?")

People who manage to get over their grief resulting from horrific violence by the time the sun comes up the next day, check.

Partly because it's trying to do so much, *Cattle Queen of Montana* ends up as one of the most politically fascinating films of its time. It was made in 1954, but even then it was attempting American historical revisionism. It doesn't state unequivocally that one truth about modern America is that white people stole land, indigenous people fought them, and they never learned. But it comes close. Sure, some of the Indians talk like Yoda; sure, the hard-jawed white hero never shows fear; sure, it repeats and endorses the notion that you can bring order out of chaos by killing people. But it's in the climax that *Cattle Queen* stuns. After the killing and the stealing and the loving has been done, after Barbara has been emasculated (and I use that term advisedly, because her character arc begins with her being in charge, but must of course lead to the removal of any obstacle that might prevent Ronnie from being the man of the house, and by the end of the movie her traditional femininity has asserted itself out of nowhere), the sunset is waiting. Waiting to be walked off into, as if the sun knows that that's what the sun's job is. Ronnie has turned into a good guy, Barbara has turned into a well-behaved girl; they join hands and march off to their promised land.

But there is something new. They are not alone. Ronnie is on one side of Barbara, and on the other is the Good Indian. The new green and wild Montana thus becomes one in which a white woman will set up home with a white man and a red one. For that to be suggested in the context of the time of the film's release is fascinating. Fear of miscegenation and legalized segregation ordered the day for so many, and the civil rights movement was only just being born. And yet, despite the problem of heroism being defined as killing people, despite the cliché and trying-to-have-it-both-ways, *Cattle Queen of Montana* ends with perhaps the most hopeful image in American cinema: The oppressed native and the next president are united by a loving (albeit tamed) woman. So many American stories claim to resolve themselves with things being blown up. But by someone offering one hand each to former sworn enemies, this film reconciles race in America.

NEBRASKA

GROWING PAINS

*"Look, Dad. I have a bad outside hook shot, I'm allergic to eggs and have a six
dollar haircut . . . I mean I have problems . . . I don't need this one."*
*"Son, I was hoping I wasn't going to have to tell you about it. Sometimes it skips
a generation. The werewolf is a part of you, but that doesn't change what you are
inside."*
—Scott (Michael J Fox) talks to Dad (James Hampton) in *Teen Wolf*

TEEN WOLF, 1985. Directed by Rod Daniel, written by Joseph Loeb III and Matthew Weisman. In 1985, reflecting the wonderfully humane me-first society, not so much ushered in as refined and enshrined as a religious idol by a Hollywood actor previously most famous for co-starring in a film with a chimpanzee, then occupying the White House, Michael J Fox wants to win a game for his high school basketball team. Becoming a werewolf teaches him valuable life lessons. He gets the girl, and the hoop, and the incredibly hairy armpits. Ronald Reagan is still president.

SIXTEEN-YEAR-OLD SCOTT HOWARD HAS A PROBLEM, BUT IT'S NOT THE FACT that he is possessed by the spirit of the twenty-four-year-old Michael J Fox, the most vibrant and engaging of 80s teen idols. He lives alone with his kindly father, they both feel the loss of his mother, he's short and easily put upon by bigger boys at school; he's in love with his best female friend, although in typical best female friend style, she only thinks of him as a brother; he's on the basketball team but can't jump high enough for it to matter; he's got tests and all the stress of being an American teen to contend with. He's also living in the 1980s, so he's stuck with the horror of leather ties, pink cardigans, mullets, and homophobic jokes as an unquestioned fact of comedy (he does have an eccentric-but-cool best male friend, as the protagonists of all such '80s movies do, with said eccentricity-but-coolness manifested of course by roof-surfing on top of a speeding car).

On top of all this, Scott Howard lives in Nebraska which, despite the fact that Bruce Springsteen thinks it's worthy of an eponymous album, is also boringly right dead in the middle of the country—cold and landlocked, literally surrounded by America. He lives in one of many tiny towns (nearly 90% of Nebraskan towns have populations of less than 3000 people), where there's nothing to do on weekends except drink. And he's a werewolf.

To which the only possible response can be, now we're talking. Nebraska might seem average in every way, with the possible exception of the people it produced. L Ron Hubbard did reasonably well for himself, I suppose, as has Warren Buffett. The state also managed to produce not only Malcolm X, but also Fred Astaire and Marlon Brando. Without the producer Daryl Zanuck, there'd be no *Gone With the Wind*, and without *CliffsNotes*, a Nebraskan original, where might any of us be? Without Congressman Leo Ryan, murdered by People's Temple members as a precursor to the Jonestown mass suicide, we wouldn't know much about the CIA's activities in the 1970s. And in a very weird coincidence, the Kool-Aid that would eventually be mixed with the poison that killed the 900 members of the People's Temple was invented in the state where Congressman Ryan was born, and remains the official soft drink of the state to this day. Yet Nebraska seems to want to think of itself as average—even its name means *flat*. Maybe that's what makes it accessible.

Teen Wolf is a perfect snapshot of Reaganite social history—it starts by investing the bouncing of a basketball with a kind of tension better suited to Cold War nuclear brinksmanship. Its characters are poor and therefore fertile ground for the seeds of rugged individualism to grow. The magnificently named Coach Bobby Finstock underlines their economic disenfranchisement by explaining the losing streak of the team to the principal thus: "If our guys had sneakers like that, there's no telling what they could do." He also provides the kind of sage advice that could help us all in times of trouble:

> Never get less than twelve hours sleep, never play cards with a guy who's got the same name as a city, and never go anywhere near a lady who's got a tattoo of a dagger on her body. Now you stick with that, everything else is cream cheese.

"I'm sick of being so average," our hero says early on, and we may presume that his blue collar fellow Nebraskans would have identified. They wanted to get up and get out, and their president was telling them that not only could they do that, but that selfish ambition mingled with commitment to the team—for the sake of winning, always winning—was the American way. It was the very *meaning* of the nation.

Now, if that is the meaning of the nation, what is the meaning of Michael J Fox? Every generation has a surrogate who gets to live our dreams for us; and *my* generation's teenage surrogate was Michael J Fox. Unlike many people who become famous when they're too young to know what it means, he appears to have responded to life with a degree of maturity gained, according to his own account, via the challenges of illness. But in the 80s, in *Teen Wolf* and *Back to the Future*, he embodied an idealized vision of what being a teenager could mean. Because he was short and weak and didn't look like a jock, you felt like you could be him someday. You didn't need to suspend disbelief when he got into a time-travelling DeLorean (made in Belfast!) or grew hair all over his face because you were willing to let him do anything as long as he won. You identified with him, you rejoiced with him, you felt the pathos when his high school principals bullied him, or when it looked like he wasn't going to get the girl. You didn't see the contradictions inherent in stories that claimed to be about "what you are on the inside" while ending with an economic victory that caused suffering to others. The American hero has an alarming tendency to bully the bully. Biff in *Back to the Future* is reduced to a kind of indentured servitude in Marty McFly's garage, and the jock in *Teen Wolf* is likely destroyed by the post-werewolf victory tailgate party. Like I said, you don't see these things—you just want to be Michael J Fox.

In most American movies, the hero doesn't seem able to bring conflict to a conclusion without a violent conflagration. Yet *Teen Wolf* imagines something a little more nuanced. At the end, Scott is confronted with a critical, life-defining choice—he knows he can win as the wolf, or he can risk failure as himself. He chooses the latter because it is the deeper victory. His battle is with himself. He doesn't actualize himself by putting a ball in a hoop, he wins by doing something that only pretending to be someone else has enabled him to do. But the victory wouldn't be real if he did it in disguise. There is a lesson here, from Nebraska, about fear and ambition. One part of it is that growing up may consist of imagining what somebody smarter would do and then doing it. The other is that people who take life too seriously may be doomed to unhappiness. Because imagining, like America sometimes seems to do, that contentment derives from always being number one, well, that's the road to Iran-Contra, to Baghdad, to being sneered at by the rest of the world. These are temporary mistakes, with temporary rewards. But trying to be yourself, and laughing about your mistakes? If this is the spirit of Nebraska, where railroads may outnumber people, it'd take a silver bullet to stop that train.

NEVADA

Five Haiku About Las Vegas

CASINO, 1995. Directed by Martin Scorsese, written by Nicolas Pileggi. Wise guys run a few hotels, make a lot of cash, hurt a lot of people, wear a lot of clothes, stab a few people in the neck with fountain pens, snort a lot of coke, blow up a few cars, bury some people alive. Who says you can't have fun at work?

THE GODFATHER PART II, 1974. Directed by Francis Ford Coppola, written by Coppola with Mario Puzo. Patriarch tries to keep control of his family by killing most of the people he knows.

SULLIVAN'S TRAVELS, 1941. Directed and written by Preston Sturges. Rich director pretends to be poor and discovers that the movies really do make a difference.

OCEANS 11, 12 and 13, 2001, 2004, 2007, Directed by Steven Soderbergh, written by Ted Griffin, George Nolfi, Brian Koppelman and David Levien. Rich guys steal from other rich guys so they can get richer. The rest of us are supposed to think this is funny.

Casino

Casino killers.
Money laundering. Vegas:
Big. Like US Steel.

Sullivan's Travels

Sullivan's road trip.
What do people really need?
Tell stories. Save lives.

The Godfather, Part II

Olive oil buys stuff.
Family's most important.
Don't kill your brother.

Ocean's 11

George Clooney, Brad Pitt.
Stylish casino thieving.
Smug. Like the city?

★

A BONUS HAIKU
Vegas. What happens
There should stay there. Heat. Gambling.
Guns. Elvis pastors.

NEW HAMPSHIRE

FREEDOM

It's a story they tell in the border country; but it could happen to anyone, any-time, anywhere.
—The Devil and Daniel Webster

ON GOLDEN POND, 1981. Directed by Mark Rydell, written by Ernest Thompson. Henry Fonda and Katharine Hepburn try to figure out how to die in beautiful lakeside light.

THE DEVIL AND DANIEL WEBSTER, 1941. Directed by William Dieterle, written by Dan Totheroh and Stephen Vincent Benet from Benet's story. Jabez Stone sells his soul to a mysterious man called Mr. Scratch. He gets rich and unhappy, but a US Senator rides to his rescue by invoking the freedom of conscience clauses played at in the US Constitution.

WHAT ABOUT BOB?, 1991. Directed by Frank Oz, written by Tom Schulman from a story by Alvin Sargent and Laura Ziskin. Obsessive-compulsive home-worker Bill Murray teaches anal-retentive psychotherapist Richard Dreyfuss to relax.

THREE THINGS ARE CERTAIN ABOUT THE UNFOLDING AMERICAN STORY—DEATH, taxes, and Presidential candidates spending an inordinate amount of time in New Hampshire (a place which, in *The Devil and Daniel Webster* is referred to as having been made out of "hard luck and cod fish"). No one is quite sure why the New Hampshire primaries are so important. Perhaps it's the fact that the state was the first to define itself as a sovereign nation after the Declaration of Independence, or that the peak of US politics can be mirrored there by the possibility of actually *driving* to the top of a mountain (one of whose ranges is called "the Presidentials"), or maybe it's one of those old realities that will maintain itself simply because it's always been done that way and no one sees any good reason to change.

The protagonists of our New Hampshire films don't see any good reason to change either. Henry Fonda's Norman Thayer in *On Golden Pond* feels that he's going to die soon, that he's given enough of his life to other people, and what has worked before (being rude and grumpy) should work again. Mr. Scratch's purposes in *The Devil and Daniel Webster* have been well served by the unfortunate tendency of human beings to pretend to ourselves that we enjoy money more than happiness. Dr. Leo Marvin (Richard Dreyfuss) in *What About Bob?* is the kind of psychiatrist so dedicated to the repetition of what he learned twenty years ago that he has failed to grow in any discernible fashion. Of course, given that these are male archetypes in Hollywood movies, they're about to discover that stay is here to change.

New Hampshire films attract a certain kind of cinematographer—the light is always golden, the landscape always appears to be the kind in which you would enjoy sitting on a porch reading books by old men with beards. It's the perfect state for libertarians who like rocking chairs, who want a little bit of conservative Americana without the politics, who want to remember who they were when life was simpler. All three of our protagonists feel this way—Jabez yearns for past innocence when he recognizes what might be considered the unintended consequences of selling his soul to the devil, Norman wishes life was as easy as sitting by the fire and not having to talk to anyone, Leo has been merely holding it together for so long that he has forgotten why he wanted to help people in the first place.

These films are also asking us to remember an era, or at least a romanticized vision of an era, when being American meant hardwood floors and open fireplaces and a pioneer spirit and families living together and music and good food in the open air. It also meant, for many, to quietly ignore genocide against the indigenous people and an economy dependent on the trade of Africans in chains. As for us, well, we can't ignore it anymore. and so, if the movies are right, change awaits.

On Golden Pond, *What About Bob?*, and *The Devil and Daniel Webster* are uncommonly wise films, for they understand that there is only one way to be happy, only one thing we must face in order to avoid causing havoc in the lives of others. That one thing is how to let go of the illusory power of material objects, to accept that a good life depends on making peace with the prospect of death. In these films, death may not be so frightening after all. In fact, it might almost be comforting because the people to whom it comes have discerned that describing our destiny as dust might not be as bad as it seems. It certainly might not be the end of us—we cannot be sure if there is or is not an afterlife. But of *this* we can be certain: The fear of death produces violence. New Hampshire's movies take this fact seriously enough to ask the question we all might benefit from asking ourselves:

Will the country so addicted to an invented history, on which it builds a spectacular but imaginary future, figure out what we all must ultimately face? Will it learn how to *die* to old, self-centered dreams, so that something new can be born?

NEW MEXICO

THE PRICE OF A PERSON

In the battle between commerce and pride, commerce will always win.
—Paul Schrader

ACE IN THE HOLE. 1951. Directed by Billy Wilder. Written by Walter Newman, Lesser Samuels, and Wilder. A venal journalist turns up in Albuquerque to manipulate a small town newspaper for his supper; in the process, he allows a man trapped underground to die just so he can get the scoop. The world above ground is not much less malevolent than the indifferent earth, turning the tragedy into a reason for as many people as possible to make money, while families have a good day out. Not for nothing was the film's original title *The Big Carnival*.

I F I WERE A HIGHER INTELLIGENCE, OR MORE LIKELY A FRIEND OF A HIGHER intelligence—or even more likely, working in a higher intelligence's travel agency—and my higher intelligence client came to me wanting me to organize a tour to the kind of place a higher intelligence would like to visit, and he/she/it didn't want to go to Machu Picchu, I'd probably choose New Mexico. It's the most alien landscape in America—tumbleweed central, parts of it look more like a *Star Trek* location than a *Star Trek* location, and it's easy to imagine ET feeling at home there. Now, of course, those statements contain a lot of assumptions—chief among them, I suppose, that anyone is actually reading this book, followed closely by the notion that we could ever know anything about a higher intelligence. The "Is anybody out there?" question can therefore apply equally to life on other planets and to my prospects as a writer. New Mexico's a good place to think about both. The science fiction genius Arthur C Clarke once wrote at the end of *Rendezvous with Rama*, the most magnificently meandering novel I've ever read, that "everything happens in threes" as far as our extra-terrestrial friends are concerned. I'll take him at his word.

So.

Three fascinating facts about New Mexico:

1. Why New?

Calling a place "new" anything raises at least one obvious question— what was wrong with the old one? Or what was so good about it that you'd want it to happen twice? I suppose the new's of this world exist in part because the people who named them wanted to leave something behind, without entirely abandoning a sense of home. The one time I visited Santa Fe it was pretty clear that they got more than they bargained for—it seems to be a mingling of Old World adobe theme park with New Age self-help ghetto, where everything's made out of corn and deep fried at least once. They should have called it New Maizeco.

2. Contrasts.

If a place can contain the world's most PhDs per square inch, the largest stockpile of nuclear weapons on earth, and the official landing site for our alien brothers and sisters, it's no wonder that they named one of the local towns Truth or Consequences. I guess the choice between Roswell and Los Alamos adds up to that—one might set us free (or terrify us), the other could kill us all (or save us).

New Mexico is one of the most poverty-stricken states in the Union, where the desert poor collide with Hollywood stars (whose lives are so elevated they might as well already be in outer space) and writers in their Santa Fe and Taos second homes. Pockets of wealth, beauty, and art offer themselves for sale to alien visitors from out of town and the next world. If other-worldly creatures are indeed drawn to New Mexico, it has to be at least partly because of the physical terrain—flat enough for a high speed spacecraft landing, red enough to feel like a Mars away from home, and sparsely populated enough for little green men to hide. There are parts of the state so isolated that you might as well be on another planet. Of course, the very *name* of the state implies alienation—many of the people who used to live south of the border are made into strangers by policies that prevent them traveling back to see their families. People from Mexico are aliens in New Mexico. It's a funny old Other-world.

3. Outsiders.

In *Ace in the Hole*, Kirk Douglas plays a failed journalist exiled to Albuquerque who digs deeper than most for the big story—he literally goes underground to find a man trapped in a cave due to a landslide. Kirk hides the fact that there's a way to rescue the guy so he can maintain exclusive rights to the story. On the outside, the circus of local government and law enforcement, clergy and candy-floss sellers, fearful family members and hangers-on form a community devoted to the ultimate question: How can we monetize this man's pain? Which, of course, is a way of pretending he's not one of us. Alien.

Eventually, the guy trapped in the cave dies due to exposure. So does Kirk, but he goes out with a bang, the most embedded journalist in history. It's one of the most chilling performances of human venality you'll find outside the *Meet the Press* studio. And it feels like reality, because it's pretty obvious from a sampling of US prime time television that turning human suffering into dollars is a national sport. Game shows bribing marriages into oblivion through public confessions, close-ups of the aftermath of murder, the publication of psychiatric records that destroy people's careers—all in the public interest.

Most of us would like to believe that we have come a long way since the Roman circus where animals and human beings *killed* other people for our entertainment; or even the Victorian circus, where we merely *abused* the disabled and disadvantaged. Today's circus may look like it only mocks the *powerful*—the fabulously wealthy humiliated as they emerge drunk and bloodied from a nightclub, or photographed while getting an embarrassing haircut. We like to tell ourselves that people are not harmed by the pornography of other people's social humiliation. It's easy to suspect, however, that the visible bruises and alleged substance abuse problems of a celebrity here or the obvious mental illness of one over there are neither healthy fodder for our entertainment nor does the public status of their subjects warrant our gloating, no matter how economically powerful they may be.

Wilder's film about this potential corruption of making the flow of information subject to commercial dictates has Douglas' character saying, "Bad news sells because good news is no news." I guess this is believed to be true only because the public appears to like it that way. Inasmuch as all violent political conflict may have something to do with economics or economic power, so all commercial broadcasting may have something to do with violence. The economics reside in the willingness of an audience— us—to consistently consume crap.

Ace in the Hole wants those with public platforms to recognize that they have immense power, which could be used to inspire compassion and mutual respect. This stands in obvious contrast to the current addiction to imagining that acts of horrific violence (rare in reality) are just waiting to pounce on every one of us, to seeing sex only as something tawdry and available for the laughter or prurience of others, or to the impeding of absolutely vital conversation about the future of the nation and the world in exchange for something that is itself socially violent and intellectually dishonest.

The science fiction author Philip K Dick predicted that the future would consist of every human being selling to each other the same hamburger back and forth. E-bay may have proven him more correct than even he would have feared, but the nutritional quality of what is served up by much of our entertainment and news media is not unworthy of the comparison to junk food. Yet I'm cautioned by the fact that it isn't just Kirk Douglas who wants to make money from a mingling of his words and someone else's tragedy. All writers feed upon the lives of others. We may, more or less, be seeking to alleviate suffering, but there's a desert place between manipulation and selflessness that most of us inhabit. We want to see creativity as a gift, but are inhibited by the need to make money. We may not be hiding trapped men underground, but we know we may be feasting upon the carrion of history.

So, New Mexico, what have you got? Nuclear physicists and radical anti-nuke activist priests alike. Watercolor artists who hated living in New York City or Portland. People who make Milagros for a living to fend off the evil spirits that would prevent them being able to enjoin day tourists to part with their surplus cash. Monetizing. What is it that draws poets and artists and junkies and priests? Does the desert offer the kind of water that thirsty souls seek? When you look into the invisible distance are you aware that the possibilities of life on earth are endless? Is there a sense that New Mexico could be the place you leave to go ANYWHERE? Or that the horizon is so far away that, when you're there, no one really knows you exist?

NEW YORK

WORK

KING KONG, 1933, Merian C Cooper. Monkey pants and dies.

LENNY, 1970, Bob Fosse. Comedian rants and dies.

DO THE RIGHT THING, 1989. Directed and written by Spike Lee. Radio Raheem dies, the people wonder why, Mother Sister and the Mayor sigh.

SMOKE, 1995, Wane Wang & Paul Auster. Storytellers smoke. They'll eventually die.

CHOP SHOP, 2007, Ramin Bahrani. Car mechanic kid tries. To be continued.

AVID THOMSON WROTE ONCE THAT WHEN HE LOOKS AT PICTURES OF HIS father as a younger man than he is now, he can see himself "imprisoned in the past." It's a bittersweet memory, for his father was one of those fathers whose whole life appears to be one big regret. We can probably all identify with the central idea that we can find ourselves in the images of our own past, sometimes in a way that leads to grieving, sometimes liberation. These images don't have to be family photographs, of course. We often see ourselves in the movies we watched as children.

For a long time, as far as I was concerned, America was New York. While the first film I have a clear memory of seeing is *The Black Hole*, a fair proportion of my childhood was taken up with observing King Kong hanging on for dear life to the side of the Empire State Building. Later, I saw Woody Allen and Diane Keaton sit on a park bench by the Brooklyn Bridge at dawn, making Manhattan mythical in *Manhattan*. I followed the murky sepia tracking shot that showed young Vito Corleone asserting his dominion. I stood out of the way when Scorsese's yellow cab emerged from the street steam that always suggests a supernatural underworld concealed by New York's surfaces.

Of course, in a sense, America is New York. There's probably nothing in America that you can't find in New York, unless you're looking for prairies and marmots, I suppose. It was impossible to decide on only one film from the Empire State, so I made a random selection of five. They each taught me one thing:

LENNY SAYS THAT AMERICA IS STILL SCARED OF THE FREEDOM OF SPEECH, BUT THAT the veil will always be pulled back and there's really not that much to be afraid of behind it. We might need an angry jester like Lenny Bruce to threaten us into taking our own freedom seriously.

King Kong reminds us that America always loves a spectacle, but circus's come at a price.

Smoke is my favorite New York film for the same reason as all my favorite films in this book: It says that, amidst the haze and the violence of the city, human community is possible. A New York film that says you will never experience life unless you slow down.

Chop Shop pulls back Lenny's veil to reveal a hidden world of poverty behind the façade of the most romantic cityscape in the world. These are the hands that built America.

Do the Right Thing, which begins with the Universal logo making you feel like you really are entering another world, pivots to Rosie Perez dancing you and raging you and seducing you into Brooklyn, as Public Enemy invites us to "Fight the Power," is really *West Side Story* with more sociological depth. Or it's at least that; in focusing on the hottest day of the year on one New York City block, Spike Lee manages to tell the truth about how easy it is for humans to negate ourselves by asserting dominance over others.

But it's also wildly entertaining. Lee risks so many different styles, making a magnificent genre stew—it's a musical and a drama and a horror film and a worship service and a political tract and a whole world in two hours. It's about the joy and complexity of the human mind, and the pain of working that out. It ends, famously, with two contradictory quotations from Martin Luther King and Malcolm X, one dreaming of a nonviolent world, the other engaging with what he saw as the nightmare he was living in. Like everything else about America, its very paradox is the point. Maybe they're both right?

Or maybe—and I like to think this—the characters in *Do the Right Thing* (who themselves embody another brilliant paradox—as with Shakespearian characters, they feel like archetypes and real people at the same time) are holding out for realistic hope. At one point, Ossie Davis, the self-styled mayor of the street tells his hoped-for (and possibly historic) romantic partner, Ruby Dee (his real-life spouse) something that may eventually stand as an elegy for the era we're all still living through:

"One day you're going to be nice to me—we may both be dead and buried, but you're going to be nice. At least civil."

At least civil.

★

Manhattan's favorite son, Woody Allen, has said that the reason he lives in the Big Apple is that "It's the only place in the world where I can get Won-Ton soup at 4 o'clock in the morning." The fact that he can't think of any reason why he would want to eat Won-Ton soup at 4 o'clock in the morning is moot. He's just comforted by the fact that his city never sleeps. It's probably the most diverse city on earth, and in that sense maybe New York tells the truth about the world. These four movies certainly tell some truth: that sex is everywhere, that the New York attitude is not to be afraid, that violence not eroticism is obscenity, that sometimes you have to take risks in order to be free. It's a grid in which the taxi drivers move too fast, and where the transit lines criss and cross, and cross again the map of Manhattan, proceeding like the viral modeling programs in epidemic disaster movies like *Outbreak* or *Contagion*, while also representing one of the most extensive and useful public transport systems in the world.

New York wants to have a happy ending culture—what should be rather than what is. In *Chop Shop*, where a corridor of car repair units ends up looking like an Old West town, horse-shoeing options dotting the main drag, you'll see attempts to make us care about otherwise marginalized people. You'll be reminded of the role that work plays in how a person is formed and of how the city can be a tough place for a kid. This quintessential New York cop movie implies that crime is waiting behind every door, and the soundtrack of the city is a discordant contrast of sirens and fast heartbeats, the alert always just around the corner.

While the typical New York love story wants us to think that true romance is only possible on the island, *Chop Shop* understands New York to be the industrial engine of America, a country best defined as one big hustle. People come here to make it but end up disconnected from their families and on their toes because everyone has bought the propaganda that says people are always going to steal from each other. But amidst their suspicion and economic challenges, they get by. They grill hot dogs and feed pigeons; they cook, they eat, they sleep, and they work. They get by, cogs in Uncle Sam's machine. Between the Highline Park, reclaimed railroad land on the lower West Side turned by a fashion designer into a redeemed green space, and the broken blocks of the South Bronx, New York lives in the tension between creative madness and fear, between sleepwalking in a dream of making more cash and waking up to smell the roses in Central Park. New York: if I can make it there, I'll make it anywhere.

★

I GOT TO GO TO LINCOLN CENTER FOR A YO-YO MA CONCERT A WHILE BACK. NOW, I realize that that is a loaded statement. Lincoln Center. New York. Yo-Yo Ma. A trio not to be sniffed at. So before this chapter inspires judgment about the cosseted lives that writers lead, let me add that a) it was a free concert; b) it was in the open air and we were under a muggy sky that threatened rain (although thankfully it failed to deliver); and c) now that I live in North Carolina, New York is about as far away as Cork is from Belfast, so the romance of the Big Apple is somewhat diminished when you can perceive it as a kind of neighbor. Not that I'm ungrateful—New York City is unique, a place that appears to represent the culture of the whole world. Eight million people trying to get by, living amidst the greatest playground on earth. It was good to wander up and down Broadway—which is far more than a theatre district—eating Middle Eastern food, watching Argentinian films, listening to Senegalese musicians, all of whom seem to feel at home here as much as I do. Which is to say, kind of.

New York is a city of (and maybe *in*) exile. For a start, it's on an island. When you want to travel through it, the easiest way is to go underground—you leave one part of the city and emerge in another without knowing where you've been. On the subway cars are French couples animatedly discussing their dinner plans, African American guys listening to their iPods, white Wall Street executives trying to hide what they do for a living, and a multiplicity of tourists identifiable by the fact that they are attempting not to look as nervous as they feel, for this city is both daunting and thrilling.

That's the paradox at the heart of New York City—it's both/and all the time. It may be the noisiest place you'd ever want to visit, but you can also hear astonishing live cello music in the middle of a traffic intersection. Its concrete megaliths rise up to chisel out the most recognizable skyline on earth, but its city center is dominated by the most astonishing urban park. It's the heart—or at least *a* heart—of America, which has come to mean it is one of the most ethnically diverse places you could imagine. And, despite the reputation it earned in the 1970s for urban decay and violence, New York *works*. You could get lonely and bored here; or you could be so overstimulated that there simply isn't time to do anything properly. New York is like some of my local politicians—so sure of itself that it doesn't care whether or not you like it. And that's what makes me think of home.

New York is only a few hours away from Belfast and Dublin and Galway and Armagh and Lisburn and Portrush. It's full of people who left the island of Ireland because they saw better opportunities over here. When you talk to the Irish and northern Irish in New York, this most extravagantly interesting of cities, you hear the same themes being repeated. The Manhattan Celtic exiles love where they live now, but it's not home. They still miss the *craic* and the landscape and the people they left. But they disdain Irish politics. They are confounded as to why, if a city like New York can function the way it does, Belfast and Dublin seem to struggle to do the same. Perhaps I'm too wistful, exaggerating the community cohesion of New York while downplaying the parts of Irish society that really do work. If so, blame it on the distance and the fact that I'm living in a kind of limbo, between my old home and the new one that hasn't fully formed itself yet. Whatever the flaws in my perceptions, being here leaves me with a firm sense of one thing: I think we might all agree that we're tired of public discourse being dominated by people telling us what's wrong with the world. It's possible to make a city in which people who are different get along with each other, celebrate the wonders of the space around them, have their stake, and maybe even eat it too.

ꟼORTH ꟼAKOTA

RESISTANCE

Whenever sufficient numbers of people withdraw their consent, the Powers inevitably fall.
—Walter Wink

If every man were to regard the pain of others as his own person, who would inflict pain and injury on others?
—Mozi, 5th Century BCE Chinese philosopher

FARGO, 1996. Directed and written by Joel and Ethan Coen. Desire destroys a man and kills his wife. He's lost in a sea of the kind of greed that makes the most sense: He's swimming in debt, accrued, it appears, from failed attempts to finance an escape from his father-in-law. People die because of his greed, while police officer Marge Gunderson shakes her head in sadness and seeds the world with hope.

THE MOST DISTURBING THING ABOUT *FARGO* IS THE FACT THAT THE COEN Brothers don't feel the need to explain why the protagonist is in financial difficulty. They just take it for granted that this is the way of the world, that everyone in the audience will identify with the notion of not being satisfied with what they have and how quickly a sense of lack can turn itself into fear. And it doesn't take very long for this fear to transform itself into violence. With this film, the Coens helped take away our sense of safety in small towns, for *Fargo* suggests that there may be someone who wants to kill you no matter where you are. Marge wants to intervene—she's seen the world and knows that people often want to abuse each other. But in her world, no one would be hurt because they lack cash. People would experience each other's pain as their own. Kindness would not be a rarity.

One of the strangest things about *Fargo* is that most of it doesn't take place in Fargo, but one state over in the town of Brainerd. The Coens have said that they titled their movie after the South Dakota town of Fargo "because it sounds more interesting than 'Brainerd.'" But I think they're kidding us. They want us to remember that we usually imagine absurdism and terror existing only in some other place, when really the line between good and evil runs through the center of every person, wherever we are.

The main theme of the extraordinary, lyrical score by Carter Burwell is based on a Norwegian folk song called "The Lost Sheep," rightly so, for *Fargo* is ultimately a film about the epidemic of existential lostness that elides with our era of late privatized capitalism. The love of money is killing us. To really think of it, the cruelty on display in this movie is astonishing: a wealthy man who will not help his son-in-law tormented by financial panic; another man who will take money to torture a vulnerable woman; another man who seems to enjoy the experience of feeding a human body into a wood chipper.

And yet, the accelerant for the narrative in *Fargo* is something so simple and so easily mocked that you might think the Coens were disparaging the liberal intelligentsia in their audience. Marge Gunderson is a conservative Midwestern woman police officer of the kind who might have voted for George W Bush, who enacts the drama of life without being melodramatic. She doesn't overdo it. She sees a murder, she solves it, she laments the terrible event, she goes to a diner. She has not forgotten her despair at the horror of which some people are capable, but she knows that at the end of the day, the most important thing she has done is to praise her husband for winning a competition that will land his painting of a duck on the three-cent stamp. On the surface, an insignificant stamp, but one that everyone eventually needs. The heart of *Fargo* is not the fact that there are people out there who want to kill—there are far more people in this movie who are trying to help each other cope with the pain of living. There are people who are willing to give up their lives for the sake of their children. They're not particularly bothered by the agenda that the larger media culture wishes to impose. There are conservatives who want to forge an identity for themselves rooted in a vision of life prescribed by a tradition of hospitality, not *Fox News*.

In the "real" world there's another deceptively simple person from North Dakota, called Marcus Borg. He's one of the leading voices in intellectually-grounded, practically-embodied, humanity-affirming theology and philosophy, which means that his words might be just what the parts of America where ideas of Christendom still prevail need to hear. "Ideas matter," Borg says, "much more than we commonly think they do—especially our world-views and values, namely our ideas about what is real and how we are to live. We receive such ideas from our culture as we grow up, and unless we examine them, we will not be free persons, but will to a large extent live out the agenda of our socialization."

As I was writing this, I checked out a news website that collates the "most-read" stories for a given day, the agenda, one might say, of that day's socialization. A list of ideas that matter, I suppose. According to this site, the most important things happening in the world at 3:38 pm on this particular Tuesday afternoon were, in ascending order:

A ninty-eight-year-old woman was being evicted from her government-assisted housing for allegedly being abusive to other tenants.

An oil-trading company that scarred 30,000 Africans through toxic waste dumping was being fined.

A doctor who faked a wound on a sports player to help the team cheat was being suspended.

The way that the internet connects us was being celebrated.

Scientists were suggesting that they may have found a genetic cure for color blindness.

Belgian farmers were spilling three million liters of milk to protest their inability to make a profit.

Maryland was setting the date to execute a man convicted of killing eleven people with a sniper rifle.

Denmark was deleting a YouTube video that suggested easy promiscuity as a fun reason to visit Copenhagen.

Jimmy Carter was saying that much of the criticism of President Obama was racist.

The President was calling Kanye West a "jackass."

Ideas matter. Our ideas about what is real and of how to live matter. The ideas of Marge Gunderson matter. On the day that Kanye was being insulted by Barack, in North Dakota, in the midst of some of the most extreme climate changes on the planet, the Midwesterners evoked in *Fargo* were living in a place with a small enough population that they not only knew each other, but when something awful happened, they were awake enough to notice.

OHIO

Safety

RAIN MAN, 1988. Directed by Barry Levinson, written by Ronald Bass.
Tom Cruise turns into a real actor; Dustin Hoffman does his thing. Autism gets
a spotlight.

OHIO MIGHT BE THE SAFEST PLACE IN AMERICA. AT LEAST THE OHIO YOU see in *Rain Man*. This is the state most likely to succeed. It occupies the perfect geographic location for commerce—the river to which it gives its name belongs mostly to Kentucky and West Virginia, so it's not stuck with the maintenance bills. Even the more than thirty earthquakes it had in the first decade of the 21st century apparently weren't felt by anyone. And if they *had* felt them, they could hide in one of the best public libraries in America. Like I said, it's a safe place.

Is *Rain Man* an accurate portrayal of autism? The answers have always been ambivalent. Maybe Dustin Hoffman's performance is magnificent, or maybe it's a one note guess. Maybe it shows how to count cards properly and make a lot of money, or maybe it's a lie about gambling. Perhaps the film is entirely unrealistic—as in the scene when the brothers need to blend in to a casino crowd of Hawaiian shirt-comported obese gamblers and they choose to wear exactly the same shiny, ostentatious suits. Hard to be sure.

What I do know is that every time I watch it, I am spellbound by the story of two brothers finding their way to each other. It's an uncomplicated narrative—cynical younger brother Charlie wants to steal inherited money from the brother he never knew about, so he kidnaps him from the care home in Ohio and they drive across America, presumably on tires made by Ohio-based Goodyear. (Turns out that cars have quite an interesting history in Ohio—the first police vehicle showed up there too, in Akron.)

The journey goes in circles because Charlie doesn't get his money and his older sibling Raymond doesn't get "cured"—for a film whose reputation suggests sentimentality, it's actually more honest than most. Turns out they struggle with emotional engagement, and eventually Tom realizes that his brother will only thrive where he feels safe, back in Ohio. But not before the siblings dance together in an image evocative of the thesis at the heart of *Forrest Gump*—that two halves of the national culture need each other. They can't hug, because it oversteps Raymond's boundaries, but they can start to heal.

It may not be factually realistic, but it's psychologically truthful, so I'm moved by this Ohio story as these brothers' drive through the empty spaces of the Midwest, on the there-and-back-again exploration of what a full life could be, taking in a glass-half-full, half-empty vision of American culture (an obsession with trivia on television mingling with the grace notes that sound when strangers are willing to take you into their home to prevent your suffering).

The movie begins to wind down when Charlie provides pancakes for Raymond with maple syrup on the table, "just the way you like it." I like the look of Ohio. I wonder how it would treat me if I moved there. I wonder if there's a care home willing to take me in to heal my unease, some nice roads to drive on, and an older brother who can let me know that everything's going to be alright.

OKLAHOMA

DANCING

FOOTLOOSE, 1984. Directed by Herbert Ross, written by Dean Pitchford.
Kids in a small town resist the religious fundamentalism of their parents by dancing against the rules. Two-stepping is banned because a kid died a few years back due to over-exposure to fun. It takes an outsider—Kevin Bacon—to pierce the defenses and teach people how to get groovy. *Footloose* is set in Oklahoma, where Elmore City banned dancing until a school prom was allowed to facilitate some human movement in 1980. The music from this film was a huge part of my childhood: without it, I never would have heard the mighty name of Kenny Loggins. Nor would I know what it's like to play chicken with over-sized farm equipment. Nor would the astonishing montage of scenes have been possible in which Kevin Bacon teaches Sean Penn's late brother Chris to dance in order to attract the womenfolk of Oklahoma, but is so delicate with his pirouettes and so intimate with his tango that it ends up looking like early inspiration for *Brokeback Mountain*.

N 1977 THE TULSA EVANGELIST ORAL ROBERTS HAD A VISION. IN THIS VISION, Jesus appeared to Oral. He was 900 feet tall. Jesus, that is, not Oral. Ten years later, Oral pleaded with his followers for donations to prevent God 'calling him home'. Oral was able to manage another two decades without succumbing to death by Messiah. On an ordinary day I would usually pronounce myself ambivalent as to whether this story says more about Jesus, Oral, or Tulsa, but when I watched *Footloose*, which was filmed in Utah (another state known for its religious seers) but clearly set in Oklahoma, I had a kind of epiphany too. I think I finally figured out America's greatest hope.

It's still makeable.

★

I'M A SIMPLE GUY, YOU KNOW. SOMETIMES I WANT NOTHING MORE THAN TO BE allowed to play chicken with a couple of tractors in order to win the right to have sex with Lori Singer. It's not too much to ask, is it? So I identify with the itchy-toed, good folks in *Footloose* living in Elmore City, Oklahoma, where there's not a whole lot else to do except hang out at the burger shack and listen to Pastor Moore rant like a televangelist caricature on Sundays. They're only allowed to listen to "uplifting" music that doesn't confuse people's minds—those tunes generically mislabeled classical—because, as Pastor Moore says, "Every day, the Lord is testing us."

Every day the Lord is testing us. Oklahoma people have been tested a lot. A landing place for the Indians who survived the Trail of Tears. The site of a massacre in 1921 when the Ku Klux Klan murdered three hundred people. The site of the Dust Bowl, where the crops failed and nearly everyone died. The bombing of the Alfred P Murrah Building. For an Oklahoman looking back, it would not seem unreasonable to assert that the locals are quite simply terrified of doing anything that might unbalance the scales of the universe. Stay within the boundaries. Don't step out of line. Dancing kills.

Oklahoma—what can you say about Oklahoma?

OK—well, I suppose it had a film named after itself . . .

"O what a beautiful mornin'". . .

Even though they're the buckle of the Bible Belt, they've got more registered Democrats than Republicans . . .

The state drink may be milk, the state fruit strawberry, but according to USA Today they've got one of the best Oktoberfests in the world . . .

And, oh yeah, everyone is repressed, but at the same time just one step away from being totally liberated, ready to be themselves at the drop of a hat or a record needle. In *Footloose*, they didn't allow dancing because the pastor's eldest son got killed on his way home from a dance once, or a disco, or eating a hamburger, or something. No one really remembers why, but the main thing is, they're happy to say, everyone does everything for the same reason:

Because they are afraid.

The whole town is poisoned by the death of the older brother, which gives them a kind of biblical history to draw on as well as a well-worn psychological archetype. The new guy is someone to be suspicious of. Outsiders have a way of degrading all the standards a community holds dear. You can imagine the town elders saying to themselves, "We gotta be careful. Once we start tapping our toes to music, it's only moments before we slide down the slippery slope of jumping onto the roofs of cars, running tractors toward each other at high velocities, or standing in front of a fast-approaching train. These are, I suppose, the things that bad religion can make you do. But none of them is worth trading in our rage and terror. Because if we didn't have rage and terror, where then would we be?"

Oklahoma means "red people," and while this derives from its Native American name, it could also refer to the look on the kids' faces when the preacher catches them having fun. People dance for many reasons—in prayer and worship, to ask the gods to send rain or sunshine or bring a good harvest, to stay physically fit and show community spirit. To celebrate life. People are represented by their feet. So of course Elmore City Oklahomans ban themselves from using them.

Everyone in this place is full of anger and fear. It's as if a self-destructive melancholic teenager drank some potion that turned her into a town. They're frightened of intimacy with each other, of sex (which is, in their case, the fear of letting go), of allowing the unexpected to happen. Concurrently, it doesn't bother them, or at least they don't notice when their daughters are being beaten up or standing in front of trains in order to be able to know they are alive. They are numbed by fundamentalism, scared of nothing so much as facing reality.

This makes perfect sense in Oklahoma, because it was to this state where modern America banished the sight of its original sin. The Romans and the British Empire already knew it, and the authorities of the 19th century merely imported it: Manifest Destiny has to hide its genocide somewhere. The Trail of Tears leads to Elmore, a receptacle created to hold the leftovers of the people the pioneers didn't manage to kill. In that sense, Oklahoma and *Footloose* represent what America used to be: ancient pagan peoples colliding with red-faced Christians living in the same open coffin. In *Footloose*, the whole state is a reservation, a fundamentalist ghetto, a prison of the mind, a forgotten frontier in the war of ideas. But they're not so far encased in the jails of their own creation that they can't get out and dance.

Other Oklahomans might react to the psychological entrapment. Will Rogers would make a pithy joke about it. Gene Autry would say "aw shucks" and amble away on his horse. Senator Daniel Patrick Moynihan would bomb East Timor. James Garner would be Maverick laconic. Ron Howard would make a feel-good movie about it. Chuck Norris would kill someone with his bare hands or by hitting them in the face with his chin. Gary Busey would open his eyes and mouth wide and make us believe that surprises are still possible by going on *Celebrity Wife Swap* and appear to have the

wisdom of a Zen priest. Brad Pitt wouldn't care, because he doesn't have
to. The Flaming Lips would inflate an oversized panda and bounce it off
the heads of the religiously repressed. T Boone Pickens would find a way
to turn dancing into an alternative energy source for windmills. Timothy
McVeigh might blow up the church, the dance hall, and the local corn silo
for good measure. Oral Roberts would raise money to build a bigger church.
Dr Phil would analyze.

And the state's sons Bill Moyers and Cornel West would help us understand it all. It wouldn't take much to figure it out:

Dr. West might say that justice is what love looks like in public.

Mr. Moyers would respond with a smile and a question that lets Dr
West say more, because Moyers always behaves as if the other person is
more interesting than he is himself.

Dr. West could answer: "Oklahoma tells us who America is. The fact
that it can both ban dancing and have the biggest beer festival in the country adds up to one thing, and one thing only: America is ungraspable. It is
never merely one thing. It is still makeable. It can still be the embodiment
of our best hopes. You shouldn't give up. You probably shouldn't play tractor
chicken either. But let the music play."

OREGON

CHILDHOOD

Happiness. It comes on/unexpectedly. And goes beyond, really,/any early morning talk about it.

— Raymond Carver

THE GOONIES, 1985. Directed by Richard Donner, written by Chris Columbus from a story by Steven Spielberg. A group of kids find a treasure map and search for its object in order to prevent their homes being foreclosed on. It is an extraordinary adventure, featuring pirates, danger, romance, and excitement. Along the way, they grow up.

As the centerpiece of my eleventh birthday party, at an age I was supposed to be innocent enough to live unafraid, on or about the 23rd of January 1986, I went to see *The Goonies*, which at first blush seems to be nothing more than a kids' adventure story, though for me, it was an earthquake. While it may be fair to say that childhood can grant fearlessness to those lucky enough to be unaware that they have it, it is also a time when we perceive everything as equal—children can look at the movies and think that they are as real as anything else. The film-makers may only hope to entertain, but if they produce magic in the mind of a child, they can be responsible for a myriad of unintended consequences.

So, on my little piece of northern Irish soil, the experience of watching *The Goonies* was akin to being in the presence of a miracle worker who claims to heal your blindness and surprises even herself by being right. Afterward, I began to apprehend clearly things that had previously been invisible. I felt as if the ground of my being had been shaken, my psychological foundations loosened, my heart made more vulnerable to the morose ethnograph of 1980s Belfast. For the first time, I feared that there was a gap between my dreams and the realistic possibilities of my life. Of any life. I suddenly knew that nothing was ever going to be the same again.

There was something so magically exciting, so adventurous, so beyond my experience about the way the characters in this movie—seven kids living on the windswept coast and among evergreen forests in Oregon—related to each other: the nerdy computer guy, the fat kid, the frat boy, the brother in the frat boy's shadow, the "fixer" played by Corey Feldman as a kid who you just knew would one day turn out to be Corey Feldman as an adult, and the two hot chicks who inspired some of my earliest experiences of at least one of the seven deadly sins. They all seemed to live round the corner from each other, in a town built on hills by water, where the fact that it seemed to be always raining didn't really matter because they had BMX bikes with little flags sticking out of the back and they owned a treasure map.

They were an integrated community—Chunk, the fat kid, who at the time reminded me of myself, was as much part of the deal as the brilliantly named Brand, the frat boy who wore a red sweat band, hung upside down from a metal pole, and had the kind of muscles I could never imagine having myself. And the bad guys were great bad guys—the Frattellis—perhaps the second Italian family name I had ever heard (after Corleone). The Frattellis were the very definition of larger than life and they scared me half to death. Their caliber is evidenced by the fact that one of them went on to be a Bond villain, and the other became the turncoat in *The Matrix* who likes to eat fake steak. But most of all there was Ma—the late, the angry, the magnificent Anne Ramsey, a woman blessed with the nastiest looking face in all of cinema. Danny De Vito's character—her son in *Throw Momma From the Train*—hated her so much that he wanted to put that film's title into practice, and it wasn't hard to see why. Ma Frattelli was like the kind of grandmother we've all met—the one with the craggy, evil visage and steely demeanor that masks a heart of warmth and generosity, only, in Ma's case, without the warm and generous part.

Anyway, here I am at my eleventh birthday party, sitting at the Curzon cinema on the Ormeau Road, where I used to watch stuff with Dad and my brother Brian (and where, during the 1980s, a translucent overhead projector slide would often appear over the film to inform drivers that they should move their cars because the army was about to carry out a controlled explosion and it might be best for us if we were actually able to get home that night instead of finding that the vehicle we arrived in was now smoldering on the nine o'clock news. Dad also always removed the spark plug from the car when he parked on Ormeau Road. I guess it never occurred to him that a well-seasoned Belfast car thief might actually bring spares. But then again, I didn't spend most of my adult life in fear that someone might shoot me dead because of their perception of my politics or religion. By that measure, I think Dad had a right to be paranoid.). I had my friends with me:

Paul, who turned out to be a doctor and who often tells me that he wishes he had an interesting life like me, to which I usually respond by saying that I wish I had a boring life like him, if that's what it takes to be financially secure and in a stable relationship; Rob, who is also a doctor and never got into trouble at school because his dad was on the board of governors, and was the only kid I knew who appeared to care about what he might think of himself in the future, which has something to do with integrity, but maybe also something to do with growing up too fast; and the Other Rob with his inseparably best friend Tim, who both lived in the more exclusive part of an already exclusive town, but one of whose fathers once hosted a birthday party that involved giving us kids a leg up over a wall so that he wouldn't have to pay the 40 pence admission fee to the Ulster Transport Museum. Who else was there is lost in the haze of both being too young to remember and having done too many things since then that the space for not forgetting has been squeezed out.

So we're at the Curzon, we're watching the *The Goonies*, and the kids are going to have to move out of their town because unscrupulous developers are—wait for it—BUYING ALL THEIR HOUSES TO BUILD A BIG (and therefore EVIL) . . . GOLF COURSE.

Such economic conflict is a tradition in Oregon, beginning with the Kalapuya's entirely reasonable disdain for British fur trappers, traveling on through the threat felt by poor rural areas when Portland and Salem started their sprawl, over the hurdle of how environmentalists feel about industrial logging, and ending up with the uneasy truce today where people on one side of the mountains are known for communitarian spending policies while those on the other side might prefer there to be no taxes at all. So the Goonies are good Oregonians, but for some reason none of the parents can afford to buy replacement houses for the already huge ones they already live in, and nobody has heard of residents' associations. So the only way they can stop the malevolent developers (whose corporate interests are no

doubt wildly divergent from Warner Brothers' surely benign, perhaps even
Gandhi-like, ambitions) is to use the secret treasure map found, naturally,
in the attic to search for the pirated goods hidden a few miles away in a secret cave by a swashbuckler laboring under the marvelously unthreatening
name of One-Eyed Willie.

They have to, as you might expect, negotiate the rather tricky obstacles
placed in their path by the Frattellis, a gang dedicated mostly to counterfeit-
ing money and hurting people, but only hurting them in the way you can
get away with in kids' movies. Nobody actually dies, or if they do, it's a clean
death, in a hospital, surrounded by breathing pumps and white uniforms,
later on, after a decent interval has passed and the film is over. The Frattellis,
for their part, restrict their evil deeds to faking a suicide in the film's first
scene, making the kids drink very unpleasant looking water, tying the fat
kid to the ugly one, and chasing the others while shouting various epithets
such as, "Come here kids, I'm gonna get ya'."

The kids' parents are strangely non-plussed by the disappearance of
seven children on the same day that the Frattellis are known to be in town,
but this is the United States of America in 1985, in the peaceful enclave of
the Pacific Northwest, where Nike was created, where you can still find
perhaps the best bookstore in the English-speaking world, and when David
Lynch has not yet informed us that sometimes slightly dodgy things can
indeed happen behind white picket fences.[6] The police in Astoria, for that
is the name of the town, appear not to have been informed of the potential
kidnapping of seven children by a violent gang, or if they have, they seem
more interested in refereeing a 4x4 truck drag race on the beach.

Eventually the kids find a cave, find the treasure, and find themselves.

---

6   Lynch, one of the most intriguing and elegant film-makers, now concentrates on trying
to raise $7 billion to fund global transcendental meditation teams as a path to world peace.
If this is his penance for making *Dune*, then it's understandable; however, I sometimes think
it might be cheaper just to give every household on planet Earth a copy of *The Muppet Movie*
to make us feel better about ourselves.

The Frattellis get caught. The fat kid gets to keep the younger, gentler Frattelli brother. The unscrupulous developers get bought out. The families get to keep their not-as-huge-as-they-should-be houses. The pirate ship floats into the distance, its skeletal commander still pulling the strings. Roll credits. And I try to keep it together, don't want to cry in front of my friends. Don't want to show them what I'm feeling. Don't want to feel what I'm feeling. These guys aren't as much fun as the Goonies, and I'm not as cool as any of them. We won't find a treasure map. The closest we'll get to adventure is playing on the building site behind my house, pretending that it's the desertscape from *Star Wars*.

This moment occurred over twenty-five years ago. I have to pause as I write this, because the memory is so thick that the air feels heavy. I'm writing in a cold room. The grass in the garden outside is dead. I am, literally and in other ways too, chilled by remembering the vast hope that my life could be as cool as theirs, and the immense drop between that and the reality of what was to come. And yet I still smile when I think of *The Goonies* because while I may not have lived the adventure, at least I still have the thirst. *The Goonies*, like *Back to the Future* and *ET*,[7] made me cry because they offered a vision of childhood that was unreachable to me.

Real-life northern Irish teenagers of my generation weren't like American movie ones who get to be jocks, or drive at sixteen, or have a school prom to be king at. Most of us didn't get to go to college away from home, we wouldn't know what a tailgating party was even if we were sober enough to appreciate it, we didn't find treasure maps and defeat bad guys. I was so afraid as a child that I don't remember often taking time to simply enjoy myself.

---

7   Whose common denominator—as story writer, executive producer, or director—is, of course, Steven Spielberg, a director who happens to be that rare thing—both popular and talented. Any artist capable of creating both the transcendent journey, both self-centered and universal, of *Close Encounters of the Third Kind* and the comprehensive demolition of received wisdom about violence in *Munich* cannot be anything other than a master of both the form and content of narrative film-making, but also something altogether deeper than that.

At this point, if you could hear my inner monologue, you would hear something like, "Hold it. So, what you're saying, Gareth, is that you were lonely and fearful as a child, and that because of what was going on in your world then, you're stuck there?"

Well, maybe. But if I were in Portland, the radical author and Oregon transplant Chuck Pahlaniuk might look up from a Powell's bookstore reading where he's signing copies of *Fight Club*, and quote himself to me, saying:

"People are all over the world telling their one dramatic story and how their life has turned into getting over this one event. Now their lives are more about the past than their future."

I'm admonished. Let's move on.

PENNSYLVANIA

DIGNITY

ROCKY, 1976. Directed by John G Avildsen, written by Sylvester Stallone.
Poor brute finds that the gift second place lasts longer than first.

ONE OF MY UNIVERSITY TEACHERS HAD A SIMPLE ANSWER TO THE FREQUENT request of students to outline what topics they needed to cover in a paper to get a decent grade. She used to encourage people to read widely, or to avoid certain pitfalls, or just be sure that they didn't plagiarize. But she grew tired of the assumption that she had predetermined the contours of a meaningful essay, as if the meaning of life could be distilled into a flowchart. So she started giving the same answer to everyone who asked what they should do to pass her course, and perhaps unwittingly explained the task of being human:

"I don't care what you write. Just hand in something you can respect."

★

IN THE SUMMER OF 1993, I LANDED IN AMERICA FOR THE FIRST TIME. IT HAD BEEN calling me, in my overdeveloped dramatic imagination, as if I were the young Vito Andolini, or Eddie Murphy, or the Irish family led by Samantha Morton and Paddy Considine in Jim Sheridan's gorgeous film *In America*. My blood was Irish, which means that it was American too, since the flood of emigration to the holy land of stars and stripes and donuts has not stopped since the Potato Famine. Young men would get on the boat or the plane as soon as they could, and they wouldn't come back. They used to have Famine wakes—weeklong tragi-comic parties where families would say goodbye to their ship-bound kin for the last time because they knew they'd never see them again. Some would die on the boats, and most of the survivors would simply never return.

I landed in Philadelphia and went straight across the Ben Franklin bridge to Camden, New Jersey, then the fifth poorest city in the country, where I spent the rest of the summer volunteering with a program aimed at addressing the educational needs of disenfranchised children. Most of the time I just wanted to see Philadelphia again—a city with a Greek name, classical architecture, a heightened sense of itself, and an optimistic motto. The City of Brotherly Love. Big cities in America are like that—the country's so young that it needed to invent a history of elegance. So Philly has the Franklin stuff and the Liberty Bell, and the largest collection of Rodin sculptures outside Paris, and the Art Museum where Rocky invented the Stairmaster (is there a more exhilarating moment in popular American cinema than when he gets to the top of the museum steps?).

Rocky comes from the meatpacking district, and when you grew up in a city that didn't have a meatpacking district, such an origin sounds mysterious, romantic even. Until you go to the Philadelphia meatpacking district, which of course is now where hedge fund managers hibernate in lofts, and see that spending your day cutting into flesh is probably good training grounds for feeling like an animal yourself. Rocky's journey from meat to man does something unusual in the history of popular American hero narrative. He doesn't win the fight. But it doesn't matter. The question is whether or not he can make himself feel like a person again. And maybe the most beautiful thing about it is the fact that this movie actually did have an effect on real life.

If you watch the footage available on the internet of Sylvester Stallone accepting his Oscars for *Rocky*, you might catch a glimpse of what he was like before he couldn't go anywhere without people shouting, "Adrian!" in his general direction. He's just excited to be there. He's humble. He is—as the story that would otherwise be a cliché goes—life imitating art. He was down to his last three hundred bucks when Irwin Winkler and Robert Chartoff gave him one final shot at the title. They made the film together. It opens with a picture of Jesus and ends with a guy losing a fight but regaining his dignity. Out of the presumption that it was sentimental nonsense, I never watched it until a Philadelphia friend gently threatened to end our relationship over my ignorance. He spoke so seriously of it that I capitulated, assuming that I was about to be served up some of the most pungent cheese I'd ever consumed.

I was wrong.

I often am. *Rocky* is my favorite American hero story for many reasons, chief of which is that he doesn't need to defeat someone else in order to win. He's like the boys-becoming-men in *Fight Club* because he knows that growing up is violent; he's like Roy Neary in *Close Encounters* because he has a dream that he can't ignore; he's like the Goonies because he has a map and he knows that reading the map is not the same thing as walking the path; he's like Scott Howard in *Teen Wolf* because his battle is with himself and the acclaim of the crowd doesn't matter. He just wants to be able to look in the mirror and not feel ashamed. He seizes the day.

Now, I've known the phrase *carpe diem* for over twenty years now, first hearing it when Robin Williams tried to teach his privileged but wounded students in *Dead Poets Society*, shot just across the Delaware river from Philly, but as anyone who has tried to carve a life that subverts averageness will tell you, it's easier said than done. The *diems* always seem to be just out of my *carpe*. But when I think through the lens provided by *Rocky* about the kind of day I'm trying to seize, things become clearer.

Of course the Declaration of Independence was signed in Philadelphia, and sometimes you have to start again or go back to the source. There's a set of rules for the American hero that goes something like this:

PROBLEM

"We only have fourteen hours to save the earth!" —the beautiful Dale Arden to Flash Gordon

PLAN OF ACTION

"We're going to Minnesota to find Moonlight Graham." —Terrence Mann in *Field of Dreams*

SETBACK

"Of all the gin joints in all the world she had to walk into mine."
—Bogart in *Casablanca*

REGRET

"I coulda' been a contender" —Brando in *On the Waterfront*

NEW PLAN OF ACTION

"I don't know, but I'll think of something" —Indiana Jones in
Raiders of the Lost Ark

NEW SETBACK

"Luke, I am your father" —Darth Vader in *The Empire Strikes
Back*

TEMPTATION

Sing "Hakuna Matata" so often that you forget your responsibilities and loll in the jungle. - Simba in *The Lion King*

NEW PLAN OF ACTION

"He puts one of yours in the hospital, you put one of his in the
morgue." —Sean Connery to Kevin Costner's Elliot Ness in
The Untouchables

VICTORY

Get the Nazis and their wicked French advisor played by an
English actor to open the Ark and be killed by the Angel of
Death/push the German terrorist played by an English actor
out of the skyscraper window/Stand up on your desk and shout
"O Captain, my Captain"/Tell the investigating panel to go
fuck itself/Raise a glass to Eddie Murphy on the beach or Dan
Aykroyd on the boat while their butler played by an English ac-
tor suns himself/Get to the top of the steps at the art museum.

★

IN ROCKY, WHEN THE MAN ASCENDS THE STAIRS, HE'S TRAINING, OF COURSE. BUT
what is he training for? Pennsylvania may have given birth to America as
we know it, but now it seems content merely to outdo the other states in
producing pretzels and has become the snack capital of the United States.
Richard Gere and Gene Kelly were born there, but they were quick enough
to dance their way out. Jim Cramer wants you to make enough money to be
able to afford to live somewhere else, the films of Philadelphia transplant M
Night Shyamalan suggest there's something creepy under the surface and
the most people can hope for is to not get killed by a ghost (although his
The Village, which asks serious questions about how to live with fear and
shadows, may be the most thoughtful film about the post-9/11 retributive
over-reaction—an over-reaction that included the critical mauling of his
movie). What can Pennsylvania offer our hero when everyone seems to
want to leave? Maybe Pennsylvania's a bit more realistic about life. Maybe
Rocky personifies this state: He knows mammon doesn't make you happy,
he knows winning isn't everything, he knows what it's like to lose it all. It's
pretty clear that the boundaries of his ambition have been reduced to just

trying to get by. He's a working man, like the rest of us. He wants to prove to himself that he can do something better with the typical time-limited circle of ego. By the time the big fight comes around with its cash trappings and ridiculous pomp, Circus Americus, he doesn't give a damn what anyone else thinks. He just wants to do something. And, despite his chosen means, this fighter has been so wounded that he wouldn't want to hurt a fly.

So, when *Rocky* climaxes, we are with him in the ring. We're not concerned about the racial politics of him fighting a black guy, nor the philosophical contours of using physical violence as a metaphor for life in an already violent world. We're enraptured by the memory of our own struggles to get through the day—our failings, the ambitions that burned out, the loves we betrayed, the regret that sometimes makes life feel far too long. Rocky's not fighting Apollo Creed—he's purging himself. He's becoming stigmata for his, and our, sins. He's prefiguring Morgan Freeman's Red in *The Shawshank Redemption*. Having devoted the first thirty years of his life to slowly dying in urban desolation, he's allowing his outer shell to be pulped into the kind of pupa from which he can emerge re-born, and get busy living.

Pennsylvania doesn't care who you are or where you're from, and certainly not whether you win. It just wants you to hand in something you can respect.

RHODE ISLAND

GETTING WHAT YOU WANT

THERE'S SOMETHING ABOUT MARY, 1998. Directed by Peter and Bobby Farrelly, written by the Farrelly brothers, Ed Decter & John J Strauss. Ted loves Mary, but Mary doesn't know it. Everyone else in boring Rhode Island loves her too. But a prom night humiliation kills his hope, and fifteen years later he still hasn't moved on. There's just something about her. He decides to get her back and travels across what Gary Oldman's Dracula might call "oceans of time" to find her, along the way being accused of murder and theft, being hooked in the mouth with a fishing line, and, in one of the most ridiculous, amusing, and humane scenes in all moviedom, discovering a new organic hair gel. There are dodgy private investigators, serial killing hitch-hikers, unethical therapists, pleasant restaurants, a Greek chorus, a beautiful woman, and a gun. It's not stretching a point to suggest that this might be the result if *It's a Mad Mad Mad Mad World* had been remade starring Jean-Luc Godard, the Marx Brothers, Alfred Hitchcock, Gene Wilder, Elizabeth Kubler-Ross and the Dalai Lama. Ted's embarrassment transforms itself from what he thought was defeat into finally facing his reality: Only when you've lost everything can you truly experience anything.

WE KNOW FROM PENNSYLVANIA THAT EVERY AMERICAN MOVIE HERO FACES pre-requisite setbacks. Indiana Jones wouldn't be of much interest to any of us if he knew that boulder was made out of paper mâché. If John Wayne found his niece by just going round the corner to pick her up from the nice Comanche family next door, *The Searchers* would never have been made. Should the Scorpio Killer have decided to make Dirty Harry's day by shrugging, "It's a fair cop" and confessing straight off the bat, we would imagine that early Clint Eastwood might have made somewhat less of an impact on the canvas of cultural fascism (or late Clint on that of reflection and lament). The American hero must face setbacks, otherwise none of us will care about his journey. More than that, without observing how heroes face challenges, the audience has no point of identification or learning. The hero in *There's Something About Mary* teaches, and teaches well, because his struggles take place in the most ordinary of places—ordinary enough that it could be anywhere. Rhode Island looks so bland — it's full of rained-out car parks occupied by chunky vehicles, grey-green-grassed playgrounds, and men singing in trees. If cinema is about desire—getting what you want, and then dying—and if you can measure desire in terms of what you *don't* want as what you do, then *There's Something About Mary* is as good a place as any to explore what kind of person I want to be in America.

Ben Stiller plays Ted, a guy living in the past, believing that he is forever doomed to repeat the day when he was macro-humiliated by catching himself in his zipper, accused of voyeuristically sneaking a peek at his prom date, and bleeding in a hospital ward instead of dancing in his ruffled tuxedo. Like America, he's trying to grow up, but holding on a little too tightly to the dreams of history. And dreams he needs, because he lives in Rhode Island, which despite its quaint full name ("Rhode Island and Providence Plantations") is neither an island (mostly) nor all that quaint, at least not in this film where everyone is reduced to living in characterless suburbs. And so it's possible that Ted's emasculation may have been the only exciting thing to ever occur on that street. The worst thing in the world happening in the worst place in the world, the ritualistic humiliation of a young man by an older man, the exposing of the most natural and typical activity reduced to the most horrifying thing a guy can do, a life reduced to three little words, writ large and across eternity:

"He was masturbating!"

These words have pursued Ted to the point where we find him, shoulders hung down, almost as if he's hiding within, or from, himself. His therapist is so bored with this client's ruined life that he regularly disappears from the treatment room to grab a snack while Ted recounts to the wall. He's such a failure he can't even get the therapist to care.

The Greek chorus of two musicians who follow Ted's adventure evoke the fact that every American life has a soundtrack—for me, it's usually NPR. But a couple of days ago I rented a car with an XM satellite radio and was enlightened to discover that, amidst the couple hundred play-by-play sports channels, I was at the mercy of something called Playboy Radio, which is exactly what you might imagine it to be. Aural porn. A guy called in to talk to Candy and Cindy, saying that he was a truck driver on the interstate, with one hand on his phone and the other on something else. I got onto a side road quickly in case I was in the path of Mr. Trucker and changed channels to the uncharacteristically moderately named America Right, which appeared to be a clearing house for Bill O'Reilly wannabes. So as to develop a special place in the hearts of American fairness, the next channel along was America Left. I did. I'd rather have a couple of guys with guitars following me.

Before the action moves to Miami, the film-makers apparently lacking faith in their home state to provide an answer to ageless questions, we learn some ancient truths:

1: That beautiful women will sometimes date absolutely the wrong guy.

2: That we will lie to protect our ego from perceived threat (Ted tells Mary that "I haven't thought about that in years" when she asks him if he has recovered from his prom night injury.)

3: That until we learn to accept what Jung called the 'shadow' it will always have more power over us than our gold. Living under the shadow of your shadow will make you believe that things that hurt you when you were five-years-old will still hurt you today, and that "true love is not nice."

4: Sexuality is at the heart of how men understand themselves. Or at least men from Rhode Island. Or at least the part of sexuality that can be embarrassing. Or at least the consequences of tearing part of your ball sack in a zipper with only your girlfriend's dad to help you free yourself.

5: Some desires will never go away. True heroism never stops trying to satisfy the best of them.

6: The world is crazy, messy, and beautiful. The only way to experience it is through an epic journey that could be compared to the battles of Achilles, the quests of Hercules, the romance of Shakespearean protagonists, and the wanderings of St. Francis. Life is big. There will be crises and pitfalls, and the only way out is through.

Rhode Island is the smallest state in the Union, but it's also a state of firsts (I imagine it feels like it let itself down by being only the second state to abolish capital punishment, and it wasn't the first to legalize medical marijuana either). It likes to try to shake off the stigma of organized crime by championing its achievements:

1: The first state to abolish slavery.

2: The first Baptist church in America.

3: The first female newspaper editor.

4: The first synagogue in America.

5: The first colony to declare independence from Britain.

6: The first state to decriminalize prostitution.

7: The first film featuring a main character whose girlfriend unwittingly uses his semen to style her hair.

It's also the state that produced Cormac MacCarthy, one of the finest contemporary American writers, on whose book the Coen Brothers' film *No Country for Old Men* was based. *No Country for Old Men* and *There's Something About Mary* have more in common than the provenance of their authors: They're both about transcendent desire, and how it can lead to violence or transfiguration, and that, at the end of it all, the fact that we can experience desire and interpret its nuances is what makes us human. Ted will, of course, eventually be dead Ted. But, like Sheriff Ed Tom Bell, the audience's identification figure in *No Country for Old Men*, he will have died with his desire, and maybe some hope, that there is a future, even after death. This will have happened because he has discovered the meaning of life: to love another and be loved, and then to die. And so it is only right to end our thoughts on the woman about whom there is quite a deal more than just "something" with a prayer to her generosity:

Hail Mary, indeed so full of grace, so blessed amongst women are thee. Pray for us sinners, now and at the hour of our death.

SOUTH CAROLINA

HEALING

THE PRINCE OF TIDES, 1992. Directed by Barbra Streisand, written by Becky Johnston and Pat Conroy, from Conroy's novel. South Carolina football coach Tom Wingo goes to New York and gets more than Won-Ton soup from his therapist, Dr Lowenstein, who, mysteriously enough, bears more than a passing resemblance to a 19th century Polish cross-dressing Talmudic scholar.

I T USED TO BE THE LAW IN SOUTH CAROLINA THAT COCKTAILS COULD ONLY be poured from mini bottles. The presumption was that there would then be less anti-social behavior motivated by alcohol. Problem was, there's 30% more booze in each mini bottle than a standard pour measure. South Carolina's on to something, if you ask me.

In *The Prince of Tides*, it's a place where magical things can happen— like holding your breath underwater or Nick Nolte speaking in an accent that makes him sound like Rue McClanahan from *The Golden Girls*. The simple, beautiful landscape images bluntly composed by director Barbara Streisand reveal the South Carolina coast to border one of the most physically elegant of states. The fact that Streisand sees this tale of tragedy and healing as the cinematic equivalent of one of her barnstorming musical anthems—hit a beat here, raise a key there, pull on the heart strings in the other place—means that the images are somewhat crowded out by one of the most over-egged hybrids in Hollywood history. Traumatic drama meets almost comic romance as recovery from horrific childhood abuse somehow mingles with having an affair with Streisand's bouffant therapist, whose arts are so devilish they have the power to activate Nolte's healing mechanisms just by reciting her name.

So, at one level, it's a terrible movie—everything moves at stretch-neck speed toward a resolution that you saw coming before the film even started. Manhattan has never looked more like the tasteless movie version of Manhattan, the gay characters are so archetypal they even adore the director's music, ominous father figures act like Dracula, pompous Southern mothers behave in the 1950s as if they're still doing antebellum time, wives can tell things about their husbands by that clairvoyant sense only spoken of as "I know," people do a lot of staring off decks into the ocean with their hair blowing in the wind, and they all live happily ever after. The script sounds like it was put together by Doug the dog with the robot voice from *Up*. It's shot like an ad for a bra. Its score is so obvious you half expect Barbara to show up at the end to announce with glee that *"The Prince of Tides* is filmed in front of a live studio audience." It's like a bad *Saturday Night Live* skit, which these days is not much different from saying it's like a *Saturday Night Live* skit.

The Prince of Tides is not, therefore, what you'd call cinematically rich; but, and I didn't expect this, it turns out to be full of emotional truth. Truth that—damn it, it's true, so I'll say it—actually helped me construct some understanding of the place in which I find myself.

It was the last film I watched in researching this book, so there was a lot riding on it. It ended up saying something so clear and so obvious about America that I'm disappointed in myself that I hadn't seen it before. The central character in the movie says that he envies the kind of family for whom one day brings no more excitement or trauma than the previous one, or the next—the kind of families "who live out their entire lives without a single thing of interest happening to them." He wishes he was boring like them. He once idolized his mother, but hates her now that he sees her failure to protect him from her husband. He remembers his dad and could love him if he hadn't caused him so much pain. And in that sense, he is like how the rest of us view America. We want to love it; in fact we *could* love it—it represents something we hope for—if only it did not do so much violence to us by its arrogance and failure to distinguish between need and desire. We'll find a place in it when it's ready to be at peace with itself. Until that day, we're responsible for our own journeys, which have sometimes felt like dragging bare feet over glass or stones. But they may eventually become ones in which we are buffered from unnecessary sorrow.

It's fair enough to ask for this—to ask that we might find some way out of our sorrow. We suspect that the way to escape the prison of merciless angst is to find a home for our homeless souls, but who knows how to find the way home when you think you've never been there in the first place? Nolte's character has only ever felt safe in his fantasies, underwater, where he "found a silent soothing world, where there was no pain, a world without mothers and fathers." But avoiding reality has left him unable to feel anything. He has to run away from South Carolina to New York in order to be healed. For the first half of its running time, you may assume he's looking for a psychiatrist because he's enraged at his agent for putting him in the movie, but eventually a tale of the most ordinary horror unfolds. He's lost because his dad treated him like a thing and strangers violated him. He's still a frightened little boy, unsure of his place in the world. It's the oldest story—in which the boy must become a man through trials and suffering—so I can't deny that it speaks to me. Granted, I've been in therapy, but none of my counselors ever burst into "Evergreen," nor prescribed repeated viewings of Yentl for my depression. Having said that, walking along the South Carolina coast has helped.

Nolte has the luxury of living in a beach house, but before he can get to it he needs to hear Dr. Barbara respond to his pain. She's expositing all over the carpet while his behavior varies between sputtering to hold in his rage and uttering finely-honed dry witticisms about childhood suffering in a Charleston drawl. He's the Blanche Dubois of male repressed memory syndrome; she's such a bad therapist she's like the member of the heist crew who screws up the plans beforehand but knows how to use duct tape when a bank robbery goes wrong. You could see the story as redolent of the history of relationships between the former battling parties of the Civil War—Nolte is suspicious of Northerners because he has seen what happens when you let outsiders in, and the country can't relate to itself because it hasn't healed its own memory. This could easily be a metaphor for all human journeys—a cocktail of regret and hope and seeking to avoid repeating the sins of our fathers.

I think Barbara Streisand wants to see *The Prince of Tides* as the inspiration for peace on earth (she and Nolte look like gods on the poster).

It may have more clichés per square inch than any other film I can think of.

But it speaks to me.

It says that America may tell you that you're her favorite, but you're not.

Sure I want to live by the sea, and bring home a plush alligator to my kids when I return from a trip to heal my inner child.

Sure I want to emulate that most cinematic image of a man standing by a window, smoldering cigarette in hand, contemplating his regrets.

Sure I want to go to New York to catch my healing and then go back to the beach where I can make all the South Carolina journeys I can think of.

There I could go to the center of the recent history of the nation, where the first shots were fired in the first state to secede from the Union. We could reflect on how South Carolina immediately disenfranchised black voters after the abolition of slavery—even thirty years later, only 5000 made it onto the electoral rolls from a total black population of 800,000 in 1896. I could go to Hyman's Seafood Restaurant in Charleston where they serve the most amazing hush puppies and have little plaques screwed to the tables to tell you where Oprah or the guy who played Smokey in *Smokey and the Bandit* once sat. But most of all, what I think I'd like to do in South Carolina is stand on my deck overlooking the ocean and recognize what Tom Wingo recognizes at the end of *The Prince of Tides*—that there are no crimes beyond forgiveness, that mystery is a better sustainer of life than concrete answers, and that one of those very mysteries is the fact that it is in choosing to love other people that you learn to love yourself.

SOUTH DAKOTA

BOUNDARIES

There ain't no word in Sioux for goodbye.
—Graham Greene, *Thunderheart*

THUNDERHEART, 1992. Directed by Michael Apted, written by John Fusco. Val Kilmer investigates mysterious goings on at an Indian reservation, and finds his inner indigenous. Turns out he's a boy named Sioux.

NORTH BY NORTHWEST, 1959. Directed by Alfred Hitchcock, written by Ernest Lehman. Cary Grant tries to escape from meta-level bad guys in the form of James Mason and his unrequited lover Martin Landau. After facing death by crop-duster, broken car brakes, and nit-picking mother, he confronts his deepest fear: Will Eva Marie Saint prefer the concrete visages of four former Presidents to Cary's wooden charisma?

SUPERMAN II, 1980. Directed by Richard Donner and Richard Lester, written by Mario Puzo, David Newman, and Leslie Newman. Strong guy defeats bad guys; lies to his girlfriend.

WHEN CLINT EASTWOOD LEAVES HIS KIDS AT THE BEGINNING OF *UNFORGIVEN*, he tells them, "If you have any problems, go see Sally Two Trees," for he knows that he can trust his children to a culture that will treat them as human. Clint's films have always been empathetic to the American Indian peoples, and his protagonists often found ways to wrong-foot their oppressors, as if the man with no name were not actually one of them. Moving up and to the right from Wyoming we find Val Kilmer trying to convince himself of the same thing. He was sent to a South Dakota Indian reservation by the future presidential candidate Fred Dalton Thompson, back when he only *pretended* to be a politician. *Thunderheart* attempts to bring the plight of American Indians to an audience of the powerful. Kilmer (these days a possible future New Mexico gubernatorial candidate) and the audience are invited to go back to the scene of the crime. They will see that *everyone* is implicated.

Now, of course, I am a European and therefore also part of this *everyone*, an inheritor of a tradition that includes both life-enhancing, humanizing political dissent (Mennonites and Amish, the Reformation, the anti-slavery movement) and racist, destructive control (conquests both political and economic, slavery, genocide). I am a European, and so, even though I was not born when it happened, the siege at Wounded Knee, when locals from Pine Ridge cooperated with the American Indian Movement and others and occupied a town to make their case for justice, feels like it has something to do with me. As an immigrant to the United States, I benefit from a system that disenfranchises people who were here before me. (I suppose I could also say that as an immigrant I may also identify with the notion of being marginalized, but I wouldn't want to stretch the point. Right now my privilage permits me to be in a nice basement office in a rural cottage, eating a nectarine, and writing about movies for goodness' sake.)

There are two kinds of South Dakotan landscape in movies (if we exclude Kansas in *The Wizard of Oz*, whose imagery may owe more to L. Frank Baum's time as a failed businessman in Aberdeen, South Dakota. He never lived in the dustbowl state): flat dust bowl or statuesque mountain. At the end of *Thunderheart* we hear the mantra "This land is not for sale" because the land is sacred, and should not be touched—a necessary boundary given what has happened to those who have tried to live on it. However, the landscape in *North by Northwest* couldn't be more different—the magnificently named Gutzon Borglum has helpfully sculpted Abe, Teddy, George, and Tom onto the face of Mount Rushmore as an invitation for Eva Marie Saint to choose her favorite President before being abducted by Cary Grant and held prisoner on the top bunk of a train sleeper carriage. In modern America, the sacredness of the land has to be searched for since the gobbling of space by business is so often the country's default definition of progress. (South Dakota was ahead of this game: In 1981, it became the first state to remove caps on interest rates, opening the floodgates for oppressive credit to have its way with the poor.) But behind the land grab is beauty, the indigenous vision of shared space, communitarian tradition witnessing against the absurd notion that a human being could "own" land (and clearly General Zod, one of Clark Kent's arch-enemies, agreed, given how his eye-laser blasts the Rushmore sculpture in *Superman II*, making an alien monster perhaps the strongest defender of Native rights in cinema history. He's the only character who respects them enough to try to return the land to its natural state).

Native Americans have, of course, been forced to live under a way of thinking about land that runs entirely contrary to their beliefs. They've been given some of it back, in small parcels, with the garnish of gambling rights and a free healthcare system to deflect attention from genocide. The people exist as a witness to a tradition that includes pacifism, but in these films they are allowed to defend themselves the only way the American caricature knows how: with guns, only with guns. No conversation necessary, invited, or welcome.

South Dakota films weave together the distant and recent past in their narratives. *Thunderheart* exposes a potted history of the American Indian. It tells us about forced boarding education, the original Wounded Knee massacre, and the breaking of treaties alongside found footage of the 71-day-long siege. (For the fact that South Dakota has the lowest state income tax, among the lowest unemployment, is suffering from an epidemic of rural flight and produced George McGovern, *Little House on the Prairie*, Sitting Bull, Calamity Jane and Wild Bill Hickock, we shall have to look elsewhere.)

The sorrow of this people's mistreatment by the nation that often seems to claim for itself a monopoly on freedom is palpable. In that sense, *Thunderheart* is an important document; it might seem churlish to raise questions like the ones I'm about to pose, but they were those that occurred to me while watching.

Is the lionization of warrior traditions a necessary part of the process whereby an oppressed people's dignity is reasserted? In other words, do you have to endorse the use of violence just because it is employed by people who are suffering at the vulnerable end of a power dynamic? Let me be clear: The film's sympathies lie where they should—with the people who are oppressed. And its failure to ask whether the violence is justified does not equal an endorsement. The clearest surprise in watching these movies is the place of indigenous people in the United States—and how when we are powerful we might feel shame for how we got what they used to have. The fact that *Thunderheart* doesn't ask whether or not violent tactics in resisting injustice are justified is par for the course in American cinema. But when the death toll at Wounded Knee has been counted (two Indians dead during the siege; sixty in its aftermath, leaving the Pine Ridge reservation with the highest per capita murder rate in the country), and the elder statesmen and women of the movement have said their piece, one thing is clear: in South Dakota lies the nation's unfinished business.

TENNESSEE

IT'S PART OF THE DESIGN

NASHVILLE, 1975. Directed by Robert Altman, written by Joan Tewkesbury.
All of America comes to the Big Sleepy for a bit of pre-Bicentennial politick-
ing—musicians, soldiers, parents, lovers, and a guy who wants to be mayor.
Theme Park country music is the heartbeat of the country: Its discordant
rhythms energize a collision between old-time style and modern stuff that kids
like. There's a guitar and a gun, which Altman allows to illustrate the lack of
compassion arising from the culture war over Vietnam, and the power grab
set off by the American Dream.

ASHVILLE IS MY SECOND HOME. I'VE VISITED FREQUENTLY, ALWAYS AMAZED by how so much art exists in a place so small. Also, Robert Altman may be my favorite director, so distinguishing Nashville from *Nashville* isn't the simplest of tasks. When you visit Middle Tennessee for the first time, you usually make some kind of pilgrimage—to the Grand Ole Opry, the Country Music Hall of Fame, the communications building that looks like Batman, the Pancake Pantry where you can stand in line from six in the morning to get some sweet grease, Tootsie's Honky Tonk bar, the Loveless Café (whose biscuits are so good but so bad for you that they should probably be covered under a United Nations convention).

And then there's the Jack Daniel's distillery in nearby Lynchburg. If you can make it there, you'll make it anywhere, not least because the town is so hard to find (and inhabits the delicious irony that its county still outlaws the sale of alcohol within its borders). But once ensconced on the massive campus where every bottle of Jack's Tennessee sour mash has been produced for nearly a hundred and fifty years, you'll be guided by an old, dry-humored former distiller who'll regale you with tales of the history of the company. He especially loves to tell of the mistrust between Mr. Daniel and his nephew, the person still named as proprietor on the bottles—Lem Motlow—even though he's been dead since 1947. You'll hear a great story about how Mr. Daniel died from the gangrene that set in after he injured himself kicking the office safe whose combination he'd forgotten, a safe he was trying to open because he suspected young Lem was fiddling with the books. But that story's too long to tell here. Let it suffice to say that the punch line is, "There's never a reason to go into work early."

When you're driving back to Nashville, you might see a fruit cart by the side of the road, staffed by an elderly gent who looks like he lives by the side of the road. You might see little mottled blotches on the peaches at the top of the brown paper bag, and when you ask the man if there's something wrong with the peaches, he'll say, "No (and it will be a long "no," as if the word is composed of several syllables), *it's part of the design."* He'll smile, because life ain't perfect, so why would we expect peaches to be?

Nashville isn't perfect either, but *Nashville* might be. It's one of those films that knows it's a film, and is better for it. It takes place on the eve of the bicentennial and is all about selling—people selling the country to each other and to the world. It begins with a singer (played by Henry Gibson) cut from nationalistic cloth, paying musical tribute to the history of the country, but the only events he mentions are the wars. The fact that this song immediately segues into a gospel choir loudly demanding, "Do you believe in Jesus?" implies that Mr. Altman may have had a somewhat skeptical view of his country. That this choir is composed of a few dozen African Americans and Lily Tomlin also reminds us that Altman's criticism was always tempered by a good sense of irony. Gibson's most vicious criticism of one of his band members is to tell him that he needs to get his hair cut: "You don't belong in Nashville." Older Nashvegans might smile a wry smile and note that the city today is a place where everyone's hair needs to be cut, and everything is always in flux.

Altman portrays city politics as family feuds, cameras intrude on everyone's life, and there is mutual incomprehension between the patriotic agrarianism of Old Tennessee and the New Age youth. Cities like Nashville and Los Angeles have come to exist for the same reasons: everyone is trying to sell themselves, sell religion, sell happiness, and sell security by scapegoating political opponents. You recognize the faces, you recognize your own desire to make something of your life, and how easy it is to end up not listening to each other when you're only concerned about your future. Of course, in *Nashville*, this amount of ignorance eventually leads to a car crash, and the aftermath looks like an elephant's burial ground.

After you've eaten Nashville's deep fried food, listened to some bluegrass, and failed to purchase whiskey at the warehouse where it's distilled, you might travel to the Bongo Java café where, in 1997, the face of Mother

Teresa appeared in a cinnamon bun. Bongo exhibited the bun for a while in a glass case, its hipster-chic augmented to no end by being an early adopter of the ironic commercial intersection between the religious right and progressive culture. Of course, someone eventually stole the bun. But not before Mother Teresa had asked Bongo to donate profits from its merchandise to the kinds of causes she fought for. I saw the bun once and, you know, to be honest, it kinda did look like Mother Teresa. It also looked like *ET*. But it mostly looked like a cinnamon bun. Some things are better left less than what they're cracked up to be. Nashville doesn't need to be anything more than it is—a messy, vibrant, diverse city where people come to make art and commerce. Sometimes they get it right. It's got its theme park side, to be sure, and you can find the conveyor belt of music production without looking too hard. In the movie, the dangers of fame are revealed when a character decompensates on stage and another thinks she is loved just because a celebrity has slept with her. People will give up a lot of their soul for the sake of the dried-out mammon of the public eye. Then they learn the value of shredding their relationships in order to be seen.

You can enter Tennessee from eight other states—only Missouri equals the number of outsiders who immediately surround it. *Nashville* climaxes with a free concert at the Parthenon—a life-size replica of the ancient Greek monument, itself a kind of massive talisman to ward off enemies, and in Nashville an impressive building, but yet another part of America's invented tradition. The idea seems to be to make an Important Statement about the Greatness of the Country, but the stars singing on the Parthenon stage look tiny beside it and, of course, we know that the original Parthenon has long since fallen into ruin. No political culture lasts forever. When Elvis died in Memphis, the speed with which he had decayed was shocking. Al Gore didn't carry his own state in the 2000 election. The Cherokee nation of Oconostota is not what it once was. Why should the Anglo-Saxon America be any different? Imperfection is part of the *design*.

TEXAS

INDEPENDENCE

JAY WATSON (Station WFAA Dallas): And would you tell us your story please, sir?

ABRAHAM ZAPRUDER: I got out in, uh, about a half-hour earlier to get a good spot to shoot some pictures. And I found a spot, one of these concrete blocks they have down near that park, near the underpass. And I got on top there, there was another girl from my office, she was right behind me. And as I was shooting, as the President was coming down from Houston Street making his turn, it was about half-way down there, I heard a shot, and he slumped to the side, like this. Then I heard another shot or two, I couldn't say it was one or two, and I saw his head practically open up [places fingers of right hand to right side of head in a narrow cone, over his right ear], all blood and everything, and I kept on shooting. That's about all, I'm just sick, I can't . . .

WATSON: I think that pretty well expresses the entire feelings of the whole world.

ZAPRUDER: Terrible, terrible.

WATSON: You have the film in your camera, we'll try to get . . .

ZAPRUDER: Yes, I brought it on the studio, now.

WATSON: We'll try to get that processed and have it as soon as possible.

—Interview transcript from less than two hours after the assassination of President John F Kennedy, Dallas, November 22nd, 1963.

THE ZAPRUDER FILM, 1963. Directed by Abraham Zapruder. A real-life murder of a real-life king, ushering in an age of cynicism. We still don't know who did it.

THE SEARCHERS. 1954. Directed by John Ford, written by Frank S Nugent.
Ethan (John Wayne) returns late from the losing side of the Civil War to find
his niece Debbie kidnapped by Indians. He pursues, accompanied by his mixed-
ethnicity nephew (Jeffrey Hunter). There is no mercy for the Indians and no
respite for Ethan's soul. He returns Debbie, but walks away uncertain of how to
relate to his kin now that she has been "spoiled" by Native blood. The Searchers
regularly turns up on the best-of lists of self-selecting "serious" critics. A central question is whether or not it endorses its protagonist's racism or merely
represents it. Meanwhile, Ethan's love for his sister-in-law may be the greatest
unrequited affair of cinema history, matched only by his Texas descendants'
passion for the land.

**THE THREE BURIALS OF MELQUIADES ESTRADA, 2005. Directed by
Tommy Lee Jones, written by Guillermo Arriaga.** A man learns the meaning
of responsibility through facing the pain he has caused.

WHEN I WAS A KID, TEXAS WAS TWO THINGS—A HOME IMPROVEMENT STORE (think Lowe's, but smaller) and a song by the gravel-voiced North of England blues singer Chris Rea. Both of them stood for one thing, and one thing only: BIG. Rea sang of a place so large you could lose yourself there, safe from the threat of urban decay. The DIY store was of such epic dimensions, evoking the enormous storage facility where the government put the Lost Ark after Indy found it for them, that spending a Sunday afternoon there would satisfy the curiosity of even the most limited of childhood attention spans. This same hugeness was presumably what led Chris Rea to write a song about how he believed that the only place to which he could emigrate that would heal his anxiety caused by British motorway traffic jams would be the wide open spaces cradled by the Rio Grande. When I think of Texas now, I see a man chewing tobacco, photographed from behind, the camera almost tasting the sweat on his day-old stubble. He's wearing reflective sunglasses and carrying a pistol. He's looking at the rust-colored mountains in the distance, assuming that all the horizon holds for him is death, just like the rest of us, except he's pretty sure it won't come peaceful. We've already dipped our toes in the terrain of Cormac MacCarthy's *No Country for Old Men*, and we'll return to it soon, but first, there is the film all of us have seen. The most famous Texas film is not the one you're thinking of, but it may be the most-watched film mentioned in this book. It's only a few seconds long and not very well photographed, but it constitutes evidence beyond doubt that the deepest fascination of American cinema is with violence, and more specifically, murder. The monochromatic dissection of the film at the hands of scholars and conspiracy theorists alike has tended to focus on the forensic truth of who shot JFK rather than leading to a conversation about the meaning of violence in the world. But one day, people might look at Abraham Zapruder's home movie of the events of November 22nd, 1963 and wonder how human society existed for so long without destroying itself, given our taste for blood as entertainment.

Death lives in Movie Texas, its soil seeded with the blood of genocide and patriots. JFK happens to be only the best known victim of its revenge fantasy. But take a handful of Texas films at random and you'll see that the battle for the Lone Star soul is not yet won: There is more to this state than cattle and killing. *The Good, the Bad and the Ugly* allows its venal characters to get away with it; Welles in *Touch of Evil* was trying to tell, or remind, us something vital: that even bad men are capable of love; John Sayles' *Lone Star* wants us to forget the Alamo because too much blood has already been spilt over the dust and sand of this Free Republic; Lynch's *Wild at Heart* is more cynical, suggesting that the yellow brick road ends in violent conflagration; *Friday Night Lights* paints small town Texas life as dependent on impossible fantasies of the big time; and in *No Country for Old Men*, the Coen Brothers gave the state a whirl and came up with a nihilism neutralized by Gandhian non-violence.

Texas has everything.

★

SO ARCHETYPICAL IS JOHN WAYNE'S ETHAN EDWARDS IN *THE SEARCHERS* THAT he might have come from an ancient Greek drama. Edwards is a man unfree of trauma (his side lost the Civil War, but he wants to keep fighting). He hates otherness as if his own life depended on it (he can't deal with his nephew being one eighth Cherokee), and he believes that being an American is no less than what he sees in the mirror. And certainly no more.

John Wayne, of course, was big enough that no film could really contain him, while Ethan Edwards was so big that unlike his comrades he didn't come home after the war, wandering instead for three years. But his pilgrimage has further convinced him of what it means to be an American. His understanding of his ethnicity has been forged in a burned land, his certainty has been enshrined through the practice of a violence that he believes will cleanse the world.

For men like Ethan, his desire to surround himself only with the pure means that life on the open plains consists in leaving women behind to manage the farm while he goes to fight any other who happens to pass within a few hundred miles. He dislikes ambiguity, sneering about another character's attempts to forge a multi-faceted identity ("You answer a lot of descriptions") and, even though he would never admit to believing the Native story that you need to be able to see in the afterlife, he shoots out someone's eyes just to be sure they can't. He's a man who needs everything to be the same as it always was: Women know their place, white men know theirs, and you can't allow yourself to be distracted by nuance ("I figure a man's only good for one oath at a time").

He's so committed to suspicion of the other as a way of life that when he discovers his kidnapped niece has developed a kind of Stockholm syndrome with her Comanche captors, he wants to kill her because of her "impurity." He has sanctified his racism, praying to receive a spirit of violence despite the women's warnings not to "waste life in vengeance." But his sense of ethnic purity is an addiction. His life has been catechized by the fear of disorder, so it's not unreasonable for him to believe that a bloodline could be polluted just by touching the enemy. That he might kill Debbie for her own good perfectly exemplifies the axis around which the American version of the myth of redemptive violence has turned, and from which the country has not recovered in these continuing days of socially-constructed infidels and patriots alike.

The breach is so great (he fears Debbie might be having sex with a Comanche) that Ethan pronounces himself "without any blood kin." His religion is selfhood. He has been stunted by the Civil War. His America is himself. It's no wonder that Debbie doesn't want to be rescued. And yet, after all this, when it comes to it, Ethan cannot kill her any more than Abraham could kill Isaac. He fails the test of genetic puritanism, proving that there is a force more powerful than violence. "Let's go home," he says, but he can't enter the house he would otherwise think of as home. He's half-finished—his identity is hemorrhaging. And so, in the archetypal image of American individualism, the door closes on him, and leaves him behind.

This kind of character, some say, had not appeared before in movies—or at least not in the form of an identification figure for the audience. The revolutionary thing about *The Searchers* is that its antihero is played by America's surrogate. It messes with our paradigms, because John Wayne is not supposed to behave badly. The country was already broken open, but it took a cultural artifact like *The Searchers* to force the issue to consciousness, to bluntly show how America's civil religion is based on a historical lie: that genocide can be justified in the name of progress.

And it shouldn't be surprising that even the emperors of such progress are not immune. So it was on a cold autumn morning in November 1963, Abraham Zapruder made what turned out to be not only one of the most widely seen films in history, but one of the most honest—a work that circles back and forth to the moment it was shot, telegraphing our race's recursive addiction to, and terror of, violence. The Zapruder film has been part of my life for as long as I can remember. I probably first saw it in a high school history class, the shaky handheld camera, the colors garish, the open-top limo rounding the plaza corner, the approach, the wave, the hands going to the chest, the head exploding, Jackie running away, post-war innocence ending. Who knows what kind of Texan Abraham Zapruder was? A couple of hours after the assassination, he was on TV—natural enough for a witness to something so epochal. Within three days he had made $200,000 from the sale of the rights to *LIFE Magazine* (although he refused permission for the fatal shot to be shown, out of respect for the dead president). Natural enough as well, I suppose. Isn't that the American Dream? To, by your own ingenuity, make as much cash as you can? Zapruder's irony is that he made a film that people were originally not allowed to watch. The country had been blown wide open in plain sight, but closure must be brought. Kennedy's assassination became the secret murder at the heart of the American myth. The scapegoating of Oswald (as if he were the only person who ever wanted someone important dead) meant that the country could almost pretend that it hadn't happened. It was twelve years before the film was seen in public.

It can't be denied that murder as entertainment ails this country, this big country, this Texas—which used to be the biggest state until it wasn't anymore, its power dissolved with the stroke of a pen—this Big Country, which lets the keystones of American life occupy it: war, romance, myth, pioneer spirit, commerce, hospitality, arrogance, the fear to admit wrongdoing. In Rick Perry, Texas has a governor so intransigent that he won't rule out seceding from the Union. One of its poorest counties has the most expensive health care in the country. One of its most famous sons is known for the fact that he gave his name to a knife, another for lying to Congress about selling arms to Iran to fund an anti-democratic movement in Nicaragua, and another for pretending that he grew up there before starting one of the stupidest wars in history. But Terrence Malick is from Texas, and he makes some of the most poetic and life-affirming films; the civil rights bill was signed by Lyndon Johnson, also from Texas; *To Kill a Mockingbird* was adapted into one of the most humane of movies by Horton Foote, who was from Texas too.

And yet, does the independence of Texas imply a *refusal* to join? David Koresh. Mark Chapman. John Hinckley. Before they formed suicide cults, or killed John Lennon, or tried to assassinate President Reagan, they had all learned the ways of being free offered by the Texan plains. Did they want to emulate what they saw in the Zapruder film? Is the only difference between their fascination and ours that their fantasies crossed a line into practice? In his song "They Killed Him," Kris Kristofferson, a Texan, sang about how goodness seems to attract violence. It's a lament, grieving the repetitive venality that human beings exhibit when we confuse selfishness with moral power. Kris sings in a way that leaves you wondering if he thinks the spiral of violence will never end.

Yet there is another Texas film that answers the fears of Mr. Zapruder's home movie. *The Three Burials of Melquiades Estrada,* directed by Tommy Lee Jones, offers a vision of a man (played by Jones) called Pete Perkins who has reason to be angry, who might feel that violent revenge is not only justifiable but a duty, given the circumstances. Someone has shot his best friend and left him to die because he is Mexican—his otherness making him not worthy of compassion. Pete finds the perpetrator and rides him over the border, maybe to force him to apologize to his victim's family, and maybe to kill him. But by the time they arrive, the journey itself has been enough. The young killer has grown up. He has wept in regret and he is now prepared to become a human being. And so Pete lets him go. No one else dies, no one else suffers. Death is its own end. And Pete can go home, with the book closed, order restored, pain to grieve, but proving that you don't need to kill those who harm you. That you can be free without violence. That new chapters don't have to written in blood.

ꙊTAH

Re-birth

In an infinite and eternal universe, the point is, anything is possible.
—Stanley Kubrick

2001: A SPACE ODYSSEY, 1968. Directed by Stanley Kubrick, written by Arthur C Clarke. Monkeys invent violence; men kill each other, then create a computer to do it for them; one man — the astronaut David Bowman—is so nice that he can stop the computer. God likes him.

I'T'S BEEN SAID THAT IF YOU WERE TO BE ABLE TO TRANSMIT A MESSAGE TO A baby while still in the womb, letting it know that after nine months of wet comfort and warmth it would be expelled down a tunnel in which it would feel like it was dying, only to be greeted by blinding bright light and a strange group of people, one of whom would then sever the cord that attaches it to its mother, the baby might choose to stay put. We may not often think about the fact that it is a struggle to be born. The very fact that we are here is a testament to our survival of a pretty hairy journey. Indeed, being born might appear, to the subjective nearly delivered baby mind, to be the end of life as we know it. Birth is a kind of death. Each of us deserves more credit for just getting here in the first place than we may allow.

★

2001: A SPACE ODYSSEY MAY BE THE CLOSEST TO A RELIGIOUS LITURGY AS THE CINema has come. Apes. Monolith. Bones. Violence as a way of life. Exploration. Mutual suspicion among human beings. Love between family members and friends. Monolith. Noise. Violence as a way of life. More exploration. Bad computer. Violence as a way of life. Very bad computer. Shut down. More exploration. Invitation. Journey. Shattered Glass. Re-birth. Everything.

When David Bowman (I think we can assume his name is supposed to evoke both primal humanity and the repentant warrior known in the

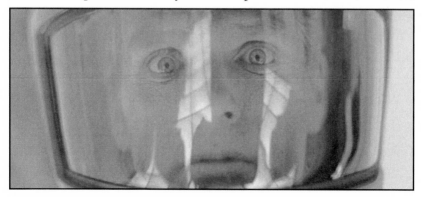

Bible as "friend of God") allows himself to be transported into his race's future, he is dying in much the same way as a caterpillar dies. It's inevitable. It's inevitable. It's inevitable. He knows it. But Some Thing tells him it's going to be OK. Now, I might be the first to admit that applying *OK* to the re-birth of the human race that climaxes *2001* is, at the very least, an under-statement (of the kind that Professor Floyd is faced with early in the movie when one of his colleagues hopes that his speech about the possible imminent destruction of the human race would be a "morale booster"). But I'm so overwhelmed by the experience of seeing the film again that it seems im-possible to know what the right word is. Evolution? Revolution? Redemption?

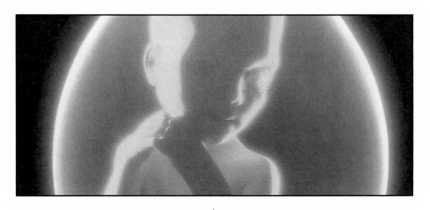

★

THESE WORDS ARE TOO SMALL, OR THEIR MEANING HAS BEEN LOST THROUGH over-use. Same with the kind of superlatives that we like to use to describe movies we like a lot ("It was a Masterpiece/Beat Film of the Decade/The. Best. Film. Ever!"). But my purpose here is not to encourage you to agree with me, or to be impressed with the fact that I can sometimes come up with nice words. I want you to watch the film. Or maybe I want to feel that my love for the film is somehow connected to it, as if such a thing were possible, since I wasn't even born when it was made. I'm running out of ways to say what I want to. So I'll stop. Instead of wasting your time with a defense of what I feel, let me risk reducing it to one statement:

I think that, in dealing with the most profound questions of our existence, *2001: A Space Odyssey* may be the most optimistic film ever made.

A film that can truly be said to have changed the world, it represents one of the moments when art took a great leap forward—no one had seen anything like this before its release in 1968. It covers themes as wide and varied as our relationship with technology, how relating through computer screens has changed us for the worse and the better, the journey toward emotional maturity, and the ultimate questions of our own existence.

The film traces the evolution of humanity from the dawn of human community and conflict to what Kubrick and Clarke suggest may be our destiny—to evolve into nothing less than the substance of love. In many ways, it is the story of the miracle that each human existence always is. It's an unusual story which doesn't bear literal analysis—it's far better just to experience this film as a meditative text, a fusion of sound and image that can fill your field of vision and stir your heart to consider just what Christian scriptures might mean when they speak of humans being made "a little lower than the angels."

What 'happens', for what it's worth, is this: An astronaut is chosen to travel through and beyond time, becoming the next phase of human evolution. He is child-like, pure love, totally free, and grace-filled. In the novel that accompanies the film, his first act appears to be the destruction of the world's nuclear weaponry. He's not sure what to do next, but, as the novel's last line has it, he "will think of something."

His journey toward this state of being nearly kills him—like the journey toward being born—feels like dying. There are no guarantees of what if anything will be on the other side. Everything is beautiful, but also a bit frightening. At the end of his faster than light journey, he is alone in a waiting room, for seconds or aeons before becoming what he is destined to be.

As far as I know, neither Kubrick nor Clarke claimed to be believers in God, but they also didn't care much for telling others how to interpret their work. I find *2001* to be the cinematic embodiment of a baby grasping toward the light, or an ancient sage imagining the journey toward afterlife. People who deal with the dying often tell of moments when the line between earthly existence and something Beyond is slightly blurred, as if the dying person is being somehow prepared for heaven. In this light, the idea of purgatory may be a healthy one—not as a "punishing post," but as a space of preparation for entering a state that, let's face it, is likely to be something rather different than anywhere you or I have been before.

2001 ends in Utah, although most of the audience won't realize this. The mountainous desertscape through which the protagonist speeds at the climax is supposed to be another planet. But the point is that there is a primal side to humanity that we must face if we are to emerge from the chrysalis that holds us as prisoners of our violent animal past. Utah, for many of its residents, is striving to be some kind of promised land—indeed, settlements were established there with the express purpose of bringing about the kingdom of God on earth. Even now the governance of the state may make it look more like a theocracy than anywhere else in the country. These days such lofty ideals have been reduced to making it slightly more difficult to buy alcohol in nightclubs and books on Sundays. But perhaps the equation of religious Puritanism with the freedom of human beings to unite with the Divine has always been a red herring. (The American knack for paradox is not hard to find in Utah either—while women were permitted to vote there sooner than anywhere else except Wyoming, the state has still not ratified the Equal Rights Amendment.)

2001 suggests that we are asleep until God speaks to us, and that being in God's presence is an enveloping experience—like going to the movies. We may have ideas about meaning, and we may want to be certain (one of the characters raises a perhaps unintentional laugh when he tries to predict the future, saying, "That's a completely reliable figure."), but they all pale beside the confrontation of life itself. A life of fear and love, in which we are invited to slow down and enter the center of Spirit, for the sake of . . . who knows? Utah's some distance from me, but wouldn't you be prepared to travel that far if you knew it would make you into a *human*?

At any rate, I wonder if the vision of life lived in the light of eternity that Utah was founded on requires us to take death more seriously, even to make a friend of it. Not in a morbid or self-serving sense—it is rather more subtle than that. There's something about death that is a lot less fearful than we make it, because if all of us have been born, then all of us know more of death than we might think. Perhaps what Utah tells us is that death shouldn't be so frightening after all—because it's already happened to each of us once before.

VERMONT

PSYCHOANALYSIS

SPELLBOUND, 1945. Directed by Alfred Hitchcock, written by Ben Hecht and Angus MacPhail. Gregory Peck and Ingrid Bergman define screen beauty in a story about psychoanalysis, which the film helpfully calls "the method by which modern science treats the emotional problems of the sane." They're both shrinks and they kinda like each other, if you know what I mean. But Greg's scared—there's something dark in his past that he can't get over, though he can't remember what. Thankfully, a ski trip jogs his memory—when he was a child, he accidentally knocked his younger brother into a rather unfortunate impalement on a fence. "Ah ha, *now* I understand" appears to be the revelation's import. He remembers, he smiles, and he gets on with his life. Analyze that. *Spellbound* is notable for two things—a dream sequence designed by Salvador Dali, and some of the most over-the-top psychoses ever committed to screen. Everyone's analyzing everyone else, everyone's in love with something, everyone is scared by the knock at the door. The Second World War has just ended, and so people are still nervous that it isn't really over. They intuit that nothing can be "just so" again, so they live in a state of fogged consciousness, an underground river of passion and terror streaming ever closer to the surface. If only they could find out what went wrong. If only they knew their original sin, they could confess it.

O   UR SUBJECT IS A MAN IN EARLY MIDDLE-AGE, DARK-HAIRED AND BEAUTIFUL, of the kind who got all the girls when he was young, and whom no challenger could get past, even if he did not intend to challenge. He is a Romantic who only wants to think the best of people. And yet, he is Troubled. With a decisive capital "T." He is so Troubled that he uses bad expository dialogue to tell us that he can't remember why he is Troubled. He has moved to Vermont, which is not a bad idea if you want to get well from the inside and out. (There are probably more Western converts to Buddhism there than anywhere else, and despite being the home of Ben & Jerry's Ice Cream, it's considered the healthiest state in the country. And presumably being the biggest exporter of maple syrup means there's much less left in Vermont to keep the locals lethargic.)

Spellbound is an innuendo—the characters never actually take their clothes off, but they say things like:

"I had a perfect hand, I would have beaten the pants off you."

"There's nothing wrong with me that a nice kiss wouldn't cure."

"Do not complicate this with the usual female contradictions."

Also, all the men in the film are philanderers or smutty or prurient or amnesiac. The hotel Greg and Inge visit has a "house detective"—no one is interested in what's going on in front of their faces: They want to see behind the door. Doors and entrances are explicitly portrayed as phallic receivers—train tunnels in particular (a motif to which Hitchcock would return a decade later, when Cary and Eva were leaving South Dakota). And they do things like take a book called *Labyrinth of the Guilt Complex* to bed instead of the well-dressed man who is hiding in the hallway. Its early scenes take place in what would have then been called a "sanatorium," a laboratory for people that evokes *Fantastic Voyage*, the 1966 science fiction adventure movie in which a team of investigators is miniaturized inside a diplomat's body. *Spellbound* has the same aim: It's trying to get inside a man's head to uncover what is locking him up. Its opening scrawl has it that "once the complexes that have been disturbing the patient are uncovered and interpreted, the illness and confusion disappear . . . and the devils of unreason are driven from the human soul." Simple as that. Who knew just how American Freud was?

And so it probes. It takes its protagonist on a quest for the lost fragment, going underground to hide from the authorities, visiting an "old friendly expert" who once was the teacher of the hero's female accomplice (thereby creating a movie cliché that lasts longer than Woody Allen's time in psychoanalysis), trying to find out who the killer is (for Hitchcock, there's always a killer), but not without finding time for an interlude involving skiing while wearing a three-piece suit (along with everything else it happens to be, *Spellbound* is one of the funniest of Hitchcock's movies). The characters are afraid that they are on the verge of collapse, scared to look in the mirror in case they find out who they are. They know that they are not who they say they are—but is anyone?

Gregory Peck freaks out when he sees straight lines because they look like the railings that killed his brother. Like Gregory, I am easily frightened by loud noises at three o'clock in the morning. Like Gregory, I once had a therapist (who helped me save my life); he told me with a smile that as a young man a traumatic experience left him unable to eat bacon for three years—the smell reminded him of something awful. He might have enjoyed *Spellbound*, but so might anyone because these fear-eruptions are, of course, common to us all, bacon or no bacon. The desire to go back to a time when we were not scared is universal. Hitchcock's example is yearning for the purity of snow, the sled tracks, the life of the mind that is buried in our child-self. This speaks. It is said that today's primary use of Freud's original work, now basically either discredited or improved on, is in film analysis because films represent our dreams of ourselves. What then, do we make of a film *about* a dream? Is it a dream of one man's past or of a nation's psyche?

Of all the places in the United States that I have visited, Vermont is where I'd most like to return. It's green, it has great ice cream, the constitution helpfully guarantees the right to walk on unfenced land without being shot, it was where laughing gas was invented, its junior senator is a Democratic Socialist, there John Irving writes his remarkable books about how human beings might learn to forgive each other, and it has a political movement that favors becoming the eleventh province of Canada. You feel safe in Vermont. The trees are like a womb, which appears to be what we all need. When Gregory Peck remembers the childhood trauma that has hamstrung his soul, he is fixed. He becomes the *father* of his inner child rather than its victim; his mature voice is now louder than his fear. Is it possible that Vermont, fully American, fully open, could be the country's rightful father? Does the fact that a substantial number of its citizens want to abandon the US and move north suggest a kind of parental despair? Everything's fine for Gregory once he acknowledges and comes to terms with the fact that he killed his brother—he faces the truth, and the truth sets him free. America's myth of itself, what it might consider its "march to progress," inhibits it from looking back, or so it would like to think. Maybe closer to the truth is the word of one of Hitchcock's scientists:

"The human being doesn't want to know the truth about himself because he's afraid it will make him sick. So he makes himself sicker trying to forget."

America is thus spellbound by its own myth. Even Vermonters might be likely to pretend that all is rosy in the garden of liberalism, gently sweeping under the rug the memory of how Brigham Young hated Vermont so much that he helped invent a religion to escape from it; or of Ethan Allen and his Green Mountain Boys—a paramilitary organization set up to keep migrants out of the state. Hitchcock would endorse this analysis, which he puts in one of his character's mouths:

"Old people cause the most trouble in the world. They are always worried about what is going to happen tomorrow after they are gone. That is why they have wars, because old people have nothing better to do."

And yet, his film is not ultimately without hope (in fact, given that this statement is made by a character who is himself old, it's clearly not the whole truth). It begins with Shakespeare's adage that "the fault is not in our stars, but in ourselves." Hitchcock, born at the turn of the 20th century, the working class son of a London greengrocer, transplanted to the new world around the time Hitler was trying to take the old world over, is asking the same question any ex-pat would ask: "Can you see what I see?" He knows the dark side of human behavior, and how our tendency to lead unexamined lives can be as much a national sport as an individual one. The killer in *Spellbound* exposes the end of that particular journey when he turns the gun on himself. Hitchcock closes in on the weapon and shoots the audience. To invert one of his contemporaries, this then would be the end of our not searching—not a whimper, but a bang. Hitchcock wants us to play the other hand. The hand that Robert Frost, who would spend the last forty-three summers of his life teaching in Vermont, beckons in his most famous poem. What should we do when "two roads diverge?" How do lives of quiet desperation become examined lives? If the country I'm asking to adopt me is to be more like Gregory Peck than his professor, it will find the answer in Vermont. It will find it in Bill W., son of East Dorset, 2nd Lieutenant in the First World War Coast artillery, and the co-founder of Alcoholics Anonymous. Twelve steps. The first of which is Frost's. How do you choose the road less taken?

Step 1: We admit we are powerless—that our lives have become unmanageable.

What would Hitchcock's wise old man say to a traveler on the unbeaten path? Probably what he says to Ingrid Bergman about the best a person can hope for in this life:

"I wish you have babies and no phobias."

I wish America only had babies, and no phobias. There must be places where this is already close to the truth. Places where people are still dreaming.

VIRGINIA

NEW WORLDS

We shall make a new start. A fresh beginning. Here the blessings of the earth are bestowed upon all. None need grow poor. Here there is good ground for all, and no cost but one's labor. We shall build a true commonwealth, hard work and self-reliance our virtues. We shall have no landlords to rack us with high rents or extort the fruit of our labor. We'll all live under the same law; no one will be above any other . . . Men shall not make each other their spoil.
—Capt. John Smith, at the start.

How much they err, that think every one which has been at Virginia understands or knows what Virginia is.
—Capt. John Smith, a little bit later.

THE NEW WORLD, 2004. Directed and written by Terrence Malick. The English colonize, the natives resist. Captain Smith loves Pocahontas. She gives him fever. The nation begins.

THE SILENCE OF THE LAMBS, 1991. Directed by Jonathan Demme, written by Ted Tally. Extremely polite mad man teaches young woman how to find things.

VIRGINIA WAS MY FAVORITE SMELL. WHEN I WAS A KID, MY GRANDFATHER Charles (or Michael, depending on what mood my grandmother was in with him at the time. Long story.) used to take big damp wedges of tobacco, stuff them in one of his twelve or fifteen pipes, and puff-puff-puff to his heart's (and my nostrils') content. The tobacco came in green and yellow packages with a logo on the front shaped like an arch opening onto a heavenly pasture. Golden Virginia. And so, Virginia will always be, for me, something that looks back, associated with an old man, an old chair, and an old smoke. My grandfather, of course, is part of the terrain of my origin story. His seed fertilized the existence of my mother. If you want to understand me, you'd need to talk to him. You'd need to hear his song.

The New World opens, as Terrence Malick's huge canvas poetic sketches always do, with a visual song, unveiling images of people experiencing nature as if they had been there before the cameras rolled, and will stay there long after the final "Cut" has been called. A voiceover invites the Great Spirit to sing the story of how things came to be—we, humanity, are the field of corn growing under the arms of Mother Earth. It is Pocahontas speaking and, since this is a Malick film, not only is she unaccompanied by a friendly Disneyfied cartoon gerbil, he wants her to speak for *all* of us. We see the original blessing of a naked man and a naked woman gliding underwater, at one with themselves, with each other, with the earth: This is Malick's vision of what America could have been, and could be still.

★

HE MAY THEREFORE BE ACCUSED OF BEING AS NAÏVE AS I AM, BUT HE KNOWS something very profound: that *how* we tell the story shapes how we feel about the world. The sanctuary of our common memory stores the tools for how we behave. As the saying goes, if the tools we think we have are all hammers, then pretty much everything starts to look like a nail, so it is that the only words in the playbook are angry, then everything starts to look like a fight. Malick's trying to give us a different dictionary. Instead of conquest by the culturally superior, his story is of natives who are wise and happy, no one goes hungry, and they are rightly angered by the encroachment of belligerent strangers. Us.

The first decision the new arrivals make is to build a wall around themselves as protection from those who may have legitimate reasons to attack ("In the morning we will chop down every tree within a mile of the moorage."), and to hoard the fruits of their plunder. From this behavior, Virginians have developed a habit. They once moved their capital to another city because they were afraid it would be attacked. We have developed a habit of this—economic ingenuity being determined by how much can be taken from the land. But Malick is saying that nature has enough for us all. The country is not a machine, nor its inhabitants cogs. The people who colonized America were here to steward, not to exploit. They were here to swim with the stream. They were here not to be afraid, but to experience awe. But four hundred years ago these English settlers, driven by (among other things) a twisted vision of Christianity, ravaged the earth and collapsed the world.

Long before Captain Smith was memorialized by Peggy Lee, he was a prisoner on the crossing from England. His first sight of the land was through a rectangular peep hole in the side of the boat. He could have been watching a film. When his companions made landing, they were in the kind of armor that made them look like astronauts on the ground. It was not long until he became the first head of the colony, and you could say that in going from prisoner to president, Captain John Smith's story is the original American Dream. Men in the colonies, of course, are worried about their political stature; they get by standing on top of others. The first thing they do to make friends with the people they call "the savages" is to offer them gunpowder, an "article that might interest you." This, to a people of whom Smith says, "Greed, slander, envy, and forgiveness have never been heard.

They have no jealousy, no sense of possession." It's not long before the spiral of an eye for an eye gives way to winner takes all. And forget the wisdom uttered by a settler: "Treasure excuses vulgarity; makes the ignoble, noble." And so, in another film that starts in Virginia but ends up elsewhere, *The Silence of the Lambs*, the American obsession with violence turns a sadistic cannibal into a folk hero. The audience's pleasure at Hannibal Lecter sticking it to the man at the end of his movie looks a little bit like the paradox subtly touched on in *The New World*—that Christian colonization could give birth to genocide, that weapons could be given as tokens of friendship, that priests could be executioners.

★

COLONIZATION TURNS INTO INSANITY. MAD MEN WANDER FREE IN THE CAMP, evoking audience memory's of the primitivized Kurtz acolytes in *Apocalypse Now*. Back in *The New World*, the actor John Savage seems to be playing the same character he embodied in *The Deer Hunter*, an insane war veteran, with glossolalia, cursing and the end of days dripping from his salivating lips. Not that the natives are all sweetness and light—of course they turn out to have their history of violence too (and *The New World* does nothing to disprove the theory that, if a film needs an angry Native American, Wes Studi's bound to play him.)

When Queen Elizabeth II visited Jamestown in 2007, it was hard not to wonder whether she would meet the descendants of the colonized as well as the colonizers. Brits and Yanks have kind of reconciled themselves with each other. Hitler helped with that, I suppose. But there is no reconciliation with the indigenous people. Pocahontas was a one-off. Wanna know the colors of *her* wind? The red and yellow lights of slot machines in reservation casinos, granted to the ancient peoples of this land by those who laughably think they now own it.

It'd break her heart. For by the end of her life, the most famous American woman entwined herself with the white man. Love has been given to them, as love can only be a gift. And the gift exchange of love between human beings, for Malick, may be the most important thing—perhaps the *only* important thing. As Pocahontas is buried in England (the ironic destination for so many conservative American tourists, so committed to "freedom" that they forget from whom they were fleeing to get to the Promised Land; a freedom, lest *we* forget, defined by Virginia resident Patrick Henry as something worth dying for), and the pilgrim boat sets off for the new world once more—this place where people could start again, where the potential exists for strangers to become friends rather than to kill each other, where an agreeable compromise between nature and humans can occur in which neither party loses because both realize that love is the only thing that matters—we ask, can America go back to being Virginia? What's stopping it? Couldn't the CIA and the Pentagon be moved somewhere else? Don't you *want* your Virginia to look like Pocahontas, or Patch Adams, or Ella Fitzgerald? What's stopping America from looking back? What are we afraid of *seeing*?

WASHINGTON

Business

MCCABE AND MRS MILLER, 1971. Directed by Robert Altman, written by Altman and Brian McKay, from Edmund Naughton's novel. Whiskey drinker tries to make his fortune in a desperate Western town; hangs out with an opium-addicted madam. It all goes to hell.

THERE'S A STORY IN PETER BISKIND'S BIOGRAPHY OF WARREN BEATTY ABOUT the atmosphere on the set of *McCabe and Mrs Miller*, Robert Altman's astonishing critique of the myth of American progress and the literally cutthroat ways of business in the Old West (and the New West too, I suppose). It was freewheeling, like Altman's scripts, and it was the '70s, so everyone was having a good time, the booze and other substances in ready supply. The crew were doing their level best to capture a story about a man we first see stumbling through brown rain (to Leonard Cohen's "Stranger Song," making it one of the most compelling opening scenes of any film), trying to make a name and a stash for himself, evoking every question you've ever asked about the meaning of wealth. Altman's camera is like a fly treading air, and this time it's buzzing round pioneers who have found there's not much pioneering to be done when all you can see is bad weather and alcohol. And so it came to pass that on this set that a party was thrown. A party to which Jack Nicholson was invited and during which the stars of the film, Warren Beatty and Julie Christie, may have found themselves falling in love. A party outside which Jack stood, "staring balefully at Beatty, whom he'd never met before. 'He's the right height for a movie star,' he said. 'I'm too short.'" And so even movie sets are part of the fantasy—their participants can just as easily pull the wool over their own eyes as ours.

McCabe and Mrs Miller sees life in general and Washington (the only state named after a president) in particular as a poker game, as a hustle. Business is a task for whores. Altman thinks we're all selfish, ultimately unsentimental beings who will always jump on other people's hopes if we can make some cash. This is what makes America, where people cut new life out of the rocks, where Western towns were built on murder, where just over a century ago nobody could really say that they knew where they were going because the map hadn't been drawn yet. The implication seems to be that you can't do business the American way without people dying. This might be a bit pessimistic, but let's face it, you smiled a wry smile when you read that, didn't you?

Washington, which calls itself the evergreen state, is the only one other than Hawaii to have had a volcanic eruption in my lifetime, and it has a soft spot in my heart because ninety percent of the country's raspberries originate there. America's contemporary economy would be unthinkable without Washington—if it fell into the sea and took Microsoft, Amazon, and Starbucks with it, would there even be a contemporary American economy? *McCabe and Mrs Miller* wants us to remember where this economy came from, to visualize the role that religious ritual plays in taking people to where their community feels like it needs to be, to face the fact that so many of us are compelled by the fear of death to behave in the strangest ways. It does this by way of some of the most beautiful images and pathos-colonized characters I've ever seen. *McCabe and Mrs Miller*, two pioneers who don't know where they're going, and don't know where they've been, who may be street smart but are not wise enough to figure out that until people stop killing for freedom, they're never going to be free.

WEST VIRGINIA

THE ONLY PEOPLE WHO KNOW
HOW TO DEFEAT EVIL ARE
GRANDMOTHERS

It's a hard world for little things.
—Rachel Cooper (Lillian Gish)

THE NIGHT OF THE HUNTER, 1955. Directed by Charles Laughton, written by James Agee. Thought by many to be one of the most frightening films ever made, *The Night of the Hunter* also happens to be one of the most poetic and hopeful. Recently released psychopath Harry Powell chases children whom he believes hold cash in amounts beyond his—or the audience's—dreams. Shelly Winters begins to enact a prophecy that she will later fulfill in *Lolita* by marrying absolutely the wrong guy for the second time in a row. The well-worn path of the love/hate tattoo on the hands of the demonic Robert Mitchum represents his relationship with Lillian Gish, who here bears as much relation to a goddess as a grandmother.

℘REACHERS IN AMERICAN FICTION ARE USUALLY NOT TO BE TRUSTED—ELMER
Gantry might steal from you, the priest in Clint Eastwood's *Mystic River*
might kidnap you, Robert Duvall's Sonny in *The Apostle* might kill you—but
they'd all tumble like jelly before the witness of Harry Powell. Mitchum
plays him as a kind of Frankenstein-meets-lumbering-thief hybrid, a fake
man of the cloth who feels called to erase sexual sin by killing the women
he lusts over. He's an archetype alright. (An exception to prove the rule
might be Danny Radnor in John Sayles' *Matewan*, another West Virginia
preacher, but one who fuses his faith with concern for social justice to help
spark a union revolt against unjust labor practices.)

As for cinematic grandmothers, there's the sweet and wise one in
Parenthood who calms Steve Martin down by telling him to get used to life as
a rollercoaster, there's the sharp one in *Driving Miss Daisy*, and there's Lillian
Gish in *The Night of the Hunter*. She stands guard over the film's children, and
while the question of whether or not she will win is moot, this being the
1950s, the question of how she will do it is what compels us to keep watching.

This is an art film about the power of the word. Powell is threatening
because of the way he talks. Despite having a gun, Grandma Lillian defeats
evil by telling Powell he isn't welcome in her house, young John gives his
word—an unbreakable bond—to his dad at the start of the movie, and the
wound in the film arises as much from what people say (other kids mocking
our protagonists, the children of an executed man) as what they do. It takes
place during the Great Depression, so the robbery that starts the movie is
nothing more sinister than one inevitable outcome of poverty. Children are
having to grow up very fast and their voices are as worthy of attention as
any other, and perhaps more, for as the scriptural quotation referenced in
the film has it, "a little child shall lead them." One of the executioners says
he wishes he was back working in the mines of West Virginia where life,
ironically, was cleaner. People are tainted by their poverty, tainted still more
by their greed. Powell is fascinating because he is obsessed with dirty cash,

can't wait to get his hands on it, and will kill to steal it. But he also convinces himself that he's pure enough to judge the intimate hopes of others.

It's a film of light and shadow falling in the Appalachian mountains, and subtlety is not invited to this particular party. Hymns become threats, there is nothing standing between love and hate, and having faith in family or in the safety of grandmother's arms is impossible in the face of complex thought. God is reduced to an interventionist who fails to act, and the amazing beauty of the West Virginia landscape evokes the fantasies of childhood, of the land of Oz, of the River Jordan. It wants to imagine a world that darkness can't touch. Because West Virginia has seen its share of darkness—despite its poverty, its territory has been contested by other states and mining companies ever since industrialists discovered what could be taken from beneath its soil. The fact that the transcendence of evil by good in *The Night of the Hunter* depends on oration is no coincidence, for sometimes residents may feel that words are all they've got, evidenced by their tendency to invoke divine help when merely referring to the name of their state ("West by God Virginia").

Grandma Lillian's words are a comfort to me, even over half a century after this film was made. The films I've watched to explore the American obsession with its shadow side tempt me to imagine the existence of a monster around every corner. But, Lillian Gish cannot be divorced from her place in film history. When she was younger than I am now, she played in silent movies the object of male desire, then later she portrayed feisty heroines, and now in her crowning achievement, she enacts love itself to answer the obsession with blood-letting in American popular culture.

When you're young, you're afraid of dying; strange then, that some of our most nurturing relationships come from people who are themselves close to death. Maybe this implies that what our grandmothers taught us about death is true: that being close to death is also being close to love. Powell thinks that he is love and hate embodied in one person, but he really doesn't know himself at all. Grandma Lillian, on the other hand, close to death and therefore unafraid, knows that her persistence will transcend his cruelty. Grandma Lillian teaches us to sing to make ourselves less afraid. We fear that the authorities won't protect us, but Grandma Lillian is a "strong tree with branches for many birds." She knows that pain is a part of life—she has lost the love of her own son, but this wound has opened her to loving anyone who needs it. She understands the difference between money and contentment. She believes that innocence trumps cynicism. She has seen that "children are Man at his strongest. They abide.' Her hymn will win.

And I can't help thinking that the man with the biggest lungs in popular music, and another son of West Virginia, certainly wasn't thinking of Lillian Gish when he wrote a song that names the place each of us wants to fold ourselves into when we are afraid—though she reminds me of this place, a place that has the power to heal the state, the country, and the world. Bill Withers says that if he gets to heaven he'll look for Grandma's hands. Me too.

WISCONSIN

SUCCESS

AMERICAN MOVIE, 1999. Directed by Chris Smith. Documentary about a poor guy struggling to make his film, and his life, in the cold of rural Wisconsin.

Everyone wants to make a movie. Mark Borchardt wants it more than most, and in the documentary *American Movie*, the most "movie" of all the movies in this book, we observe his monumental struggle to get it done. You may never casually dismiss a film again after seeing just how difficult it is to get your work on the screen. More than that, the poverty-induced fantasies of fame on display in *American Movie* are so resonant that you may never be able to mock the tribe so trivially disregarded as "white trash."

It's a portrait of an American family, and an American disappointment, a microcosm of the Dream that goes something like this:

Kid has idea: "I wanna make movies and be famous." The movies live in the part of his brain where magic is one step away from the madness and fear of failure.

Kid decides what kind of movie he wants to make—a horror movie, a terrifying movie, a movie about death. (Sociologists may look on and wonder why the preoccupation with horror seems to be a disproportionate domain of the poor.)

Kid gathers friends and family to make the movie. His crotchety skin-flint uncle throws in some cash and always complains while doing it, his best friend (whose gentleness appears to derive from a head injury) assists him, his mother bakes cookies. (Aspiring film-makers take note: You need to work with what you have before anyone will give you anything.)

Kid faces setbacks—the camera won't work, the actors won't work, the props won't work, the weather won't work. (Psychologists stand, open-mouthed in awe at the determination to get the damn thing made.)

Kid never gives up, to the point where he lets a stranger film him breaking down and falling apart. (For familial angst, *American Movie* is more realistic than *American Beauty*. For the struggle to make capitalism work to your advantage, *American Movie* is better than *The Godfather*. It's more honest than either.)

There is desperation in making art as there is desperation in building

345

a nation. Here Wisconsin seems to have been only half-built, putting the structure in place was exhausting enough without finding something meaningful to pour into it. In *American Movie*, Mark explains his dream with the succinctness of Socrates:

"Doesn't everyone want to be somewhere they're not?"

This is not a discordant thing to hear from the mouth of a man who has spent his most recent years vacuum-cleaning a cemetery. More than any other character I've seen on this journey, Mark Borchardt represents the loneliness of the working man and the failure of the American Dream to deliver satisfaction to the vast majority of its people. But the film doesn't mock him—indeed, with its honorable engagement with his life, *American Movie* reveals him to be a philosopher king. He knows that all around him is "rust and decay," but he also is in touch enough with his soul to declare, almost as an act of war with the powers that conspire to keep him down, that "within rust and decay there is warmth." Mark Borchardt is here the quintessential American, embodying what might be the country's most beautiful trait: a wide eyed optimism in the face of monumental odds that somehow gets shit done.

Wisconsin has its happy middle class liberal heartland in Madison (where *The Onion* is produced), you get some nice cheese there, and Milwaukee has always sounded like one of the most interesting places on earth just because of its name. Alas the state is also known for the self-loathing projected rage of Joe McCarthy. And in *American Movie*, it's a bare, sparse, cold place—a state where individual desire is displaced onto the successes of national sports stars because it has nowhere local to go. It's a place that, as Mark Borchardt says about his youth, "there wasn't college or religion, there was drinking." It's a sad, chilled, creaking place. But it's still America, and so it still has a cinematic imagination. People believe that they are here to fight, and to fight to win, even though they know they will probably lose. But for the people of Wisconsin, when you fall this way, you just pick yourself up, dust yourself off, yell cut, re-set the markers, and shoot the scene all over again.

WYOMING

COWBOY JUSTICE

UNFORGIVEN, 1992. Directed by Clint Eastwood, written by David Webb Peoples. William Munny doesn't have enough of it, and when called upon to avenge the scarring of a prostitute in the Old West, he finds his dormant demons don't need much help to be resurrected. He embodies the movie's title.

HEAVEN'S GATE, 1980. Directed and written by Michael Cimino. Business kills immigrants in Johnston County. The immigrants fight back. An eye for an eye leaves everyone blind. The land stumbles toward being a nation.

BROKEBACK MOUNTAIN, 2005. Directed by Ang Lee, written by James Schamus. Two cowboys give voice to their sexuality in the 1960s; one of them does not survive, but their love lasts forever.

UNFORGIVEN, HEAVEN'S GATE, AND *BROKEBACK MOUNTAIN,* THE REVISIONIST Westerns to end all revisionist Westerns, are also far more than that—the economic and psychological roots of violence are laid bare, and the only possible antidote is a re-imagining of community that depends not on who is excluded, but on how much others are welcomed.

At the beginning of *Unforgiven,* Clint Eastwood appears as a solitary figure, digging for something on his sparse farmland. Perhaps it is his sense of humor, for in this kind of film, Clint rarely does more than grunt. He is poor amidst the astonishing landscape that nestles the town of Big Whiskey, Wyoming, a state whose mountain-framed plateau is a reminder that nature can be both cruel and generous, and of how the American national ego does, at the end of the day, have a point. But those critics who suggest that the extraordinary American natural beauty will last much longer than the American people because of their culture's excessive addiction to violence, well, *they* have a point too.

Between 9/11 and the day that the H1N1 swine flu virus appeared here in May 2009, 120,000 people were killed by gunfire in the US—120,000 people in seven and a half years. Within a couple of days of the swine flu's arrival, it was reported on National Public Radio that a billion dollars had been spent to prevent an American sneezing pandemic. One national emergency that kills 13,000 people a year but appears to be considered business as usual gave way to another that killed a few hundred, yet managed to capture the public imagination. It's not just novelty versus monotony. It's flu versus murder. *Unforgiven* is about this national obsession, with people reputed only for the murders they've committed, where children look to killers for their cues ("I ain't killed as many as you because of my youth," says the kid who tries to emulate Eastwood's character), where the only way a man suffering loss can think of to help a wounded woman is to kill the people who harmed her.

The sexual politics of *Unforgiven* dovetail with those in *Brokeback Mountain*—both films take characters usually portrayed as weak (women, gay and bisexual men) and make them into something heroic. But even their courage can't save them from the economic web that compels people in the American Western myth to participate in violence for the sake of survival. Munny, whose name of course rhymes with the reason for his killing, lives in western Kansas, but the action takes place in Wyoming, the least populous state in the Union, where it's easy to stand out. Now, if Mr. Munny had watched any movies, he would know that crossing state lines in a film is almost always a bad idea. Just ask Thelma and Louise's car dealer, or Clark Griswold's dog. But he's gotta do what he's gotta do—his kids are starving, some suffering needs avenging, and he knows how to do the shooting. Deeper than this, and why *Unforgiven* should be required study material for God's psychoanalyst when she comes to give cognitive therapy to the United States, is the terrain of Munny's wounded soul. We learn at the beginning that he loved a woman and she stopped him from killing, but she is now dead and he is not healed. His injury combines with his sense of economic scarcity to produce murder.

"It's a hell of a thing, killing a man," says Munny, the night hours before the murders to come slipping too slowly away. "You take away all he's got and all he's ever gonna have." The kid who looks up to him, having just been bloodied by his first kill, tries to justify himself to himself with the ancient, well-worn, but still ridiculous philosophical formulation, "Well, I guess they had it coming," to which Munny can respond only in the limited terms with which *he* sees the world: "We *all* have it coming, kid." Munny's afraid ("When I'm hurting, I want to make someone else hurt") and he *becomes* Death in order to conquer his fear. Even the cry of Munny's antagonist, "I don't deserve to die like this. I was building a house" (what could be more American than that?) fails to elicit mercy from this dark angel.

Clint Eastwood's early films weren't known for psychological nuance[8]. Shoot first and don't even *think* about the questions was Dirty Harry's mantra. But *Unforgiven* can be seen as an apology for America's wounding of others—a long, hard look at the shadow side. "Deserve's got nothing to do with it," says Munny, before shooting Gene Hackman's sheriff's teeth through the back of his head, and you can read this as either nihilism or an invitation to empathy. In the myth of *Unforgiven*'s America, *nobody* gets what they deserve, which would make all equally worthy of our empathy, our pity, and our anger.

The film's title may be pessimistic, but it's worth bearing in mind that the word at least implies that forgiveness is possible. Surely this is what Munny's late wife had gifted him, and which made him temporarily sane. We glimpse this sanity in one of the film's rare tender moments when he turns down free sex from one of the prostitutes because he is faithful to his grief. Still he never forgave himself. He knows violence to be the only recourse that sorrow permits and he feels unable to do anything different when the opportunity is presented. Who knows what would have happened if Munny, or the country of money, had learned to self-acceptance, weakness and all? Who knows why we so often ascribe greatness to killers? Munny had love and humanity, but it disappeared when he went into town where people

---

8   *High Plains Drifter* may be an exception - it understands revenge, and proffers respect to Native Americans well before it was fashionable.

would pay him—in respect and coins and greatness to his manhood—to kill. He is one side of the American archetype—a pioneer who will kill you if you get in his way. Question is, if his way transcends all others, will there be a civilization left to remember what we once were?

This civilization is what is *being built* in *Heaven's Gate*, a film that bankrupted a studio and whose box office failure has largely concealed from the public the most amazing light ever committed to film. The fact that it opens declaring its director and writer as not only author, but *owner* (this is *"Michael Cimino's* Heaven's Gate") tells you everything: Its story and the reality of its filming are metaphors for what went wrong with America from the start. It's one thing to flee religious persecution in the hopes of building a new, free promised land, it's quite another to see your life story as an epic in which the only dramatic momentum comes from the desire to make a quick buck.

We embark from Harvard, where the presidential address, given by a preacher (announcing Cimino's intent to etch *Heaven's Gate* in the panorama of Cinematic Being by being played by Joseph Cotten), ordains cultural imperialism: "It is not great wealth alone that builds the library; it is to diffuse a high learning and culture among a people; it is the contact of the cultivated mind with the uncultivated." The class orator, played by John Hurt, speaks of a world in which everything is just fine as it is, which, of course, for the professional class in the 1860s, it *was*. These men were about to take the land—the intelligentsia grabbing fields and taking human lives, just as Pol Pot gathered his thoughts in Paris, and the more recent bloody Iraq misadventure began partly at Yale. To the audience it is some kind of sick but obvious joke for a white American pilgrim descendant to tell a recently pogrommed Eastern European Jew to "go back where you came from," while the desperation and powerlessness of the population movements that built this nation are confronted as if they were something out of *Schindler's List*.

And so we have Wyoming, where the tax rates are among the lowest in the Union, from where both the torture advocate Dick Cheney and the gay martyr Matthew Shepard hail, where the land is so beautiful it makes you feel like crying because the emotional resonance of being at home in the presence or absence of God sometimes can't be expressed any other way. Wyoming, where Jackson Pollock was born to splash paint in dynamic vibrancy, where the carpenter-pilot Harrison Ford carves tables and flies small planes, and where Buffalo Bill learned to sell Western culture back to itself, creating the town of Cody for that very purpose. Because of Buffalo Bill, you could say that Wyoming was where American celebrity was born. Bill knew the power of an over-sell, and he made the country his own. He could learn something from Cimino/Cotten's Harvard president who despite inviting imperialist ambition, managed to evoke humility too, speaking of a rather different way to imagine America's founding, and perhaps an answer to the crises in America's future:

"Do you wish to write better than you can? We must *endeavor* to speak to the best of our ability, but we must speak *according* to our ability."

NEW JERSEY

My First America

ON THE WATERFRONT, 1954. Directed by Elia Kazan, written by Budd Schulberg. Every time an injustice happens, that's a crucifixion. Every time a person acts like a human, that's a resurrection.

AH, NEW JERSEY, YOU CROSSROADS OF THE REVOLUTION; YOU GARDEN STATE; you butt of everyone's jokes, even though you have the second highest median income in the US; you bringer-of-Springsteen; you who only one hundred and eighty million years ago bordered North Africa; you, the only state with a direct flight to my home town; you who abolished the death penalty earlier than most; you, where the Sopranos run a successful waste management business and Thomas Edison claimed to have invented the movies before the French; where Sinatra learned to sing, Martha Stewart learned to cook, and I learned American.

At age eighteen, I found myself in the wiry harshness of Camden, the fifth poorest and perhaps most dangerous city in free America, where an epidemic of white flight in the 1960s gave birth to a marginal space which few on the outside seem to want to notice. And yet the American paradox erupted in Camden in 1970 when twenty-eight people put their lives on the line to protest the violence of the state by breaking into a draft board office and witnessing an alternative to the insanity of the Vietnam War. A decade and a half later, some non-violent activists showed up to work on programs to supplement the limited educational opportunities that were the legacy of suburbia's erection. The programs are still there and kids are graduating, not just from high school, but also from college. Now these graduates are coming back to the city to build something new. People who live in Jersey go to the shore for their vacation; people who live in Camden are lucky to afford one. It's therefore no wonder that Budd Schulberg used Jersey as the setting for one of the most powerful American films about social injustice.

I once talked to Schulberg on the phone. A mutual friend put us in touch in the Fall of 2003—I was eager to put on an event to mark the 50th anniversary of the quintessential New Jersey film, *On the Waterfront*, and innocent, enthusiastic, grasping, and annoying film fan that I was, I figured I should just call up the screenwriter and see if he wanted to come to a poetry club on Bleecker Street to talk about it while we showed clips. He was ninety-years-old when I called and if he had felt significantly older by the time the call was over, I couldn't blame him. Grace and brevity don't always come easily to me. It's even harder than usual when I'm talking to someone whose identity—although he was just an ordinary guy, and Schulberg would have been at pains to remind people of that fact—had become mutated and mingled with memories and experience. "I coulda been a contender" is, of course, now a cliché, but that's not Schulberg's fault. Clichés don't start out that way—they're just something someone else writes first.

Now, who knows what kind of man was Budd Schulberg? We know that he wrote *On the Waterfront*. We know that his life span was such that he was able to collaborate with both F. Scott Fitzgerald (on a film called *Winter Carnival*) and Ben Stiller (who may turn *What Makes Sammy Run* into a movie). We know that he established the Watts Writers Workshop in the aftermath of the civil unrest. We know he named names after he himself had been named as a Party member. We know that he made documentaries for the army. We know that he's in the Boxing Hall of Fame. And I know that, a few years ago, even though my plans for the poetry club event didn't get beyond the idea stage, on the phone, at the age of ninety, he was gracious, sweet-natured, generous, and patient with a northern Irish film critic who thought— presumably like many others— that he had some special magic, just because he carved a cinematic myth into stone. Rest in Peace.

As for me, I'm going to watch *On the Waterfront* today. Five of its principals have died in the past few years, a fact which only makes it seem more important: Rod Steiger, Marlon Brando, Elia Kazan, Karl Malden, Schulberg. It may not be a subtle film, it may have come from all kinds of ambivalent or complicated motivation (a film that justifies ratting on your colleagues), its dialogue may sound more theatrical than realistic . . . It may be all these things, but, and I don't know how much this should count for anything other than the fact that it's true, every time I see it, it moves me.

On the Waterfront is a simple story in which Brando's character Terry has to discern whether to stand up for what he believes by refusing to give in to the corrupt oppression of gangsters who control the New York docks, knowing that it may cost his mob flunkey brother if he does so. Terry is broken on the wheels of circumstance, his dignity stripped by not being able to follow through on the only natural talent he believes he had—boxing—because his brother's job depends on Terry throwing a fight. He's a man let down by his own choices, himself being the one guy he should have been able to trust, and ultimately he feels abandoned by the whole world. He feels that he embodies failure, although his priest (played by Karl Malden), who understands the difference between success and honor, says that "Every time the mob puts the squeeze on someone that's a crucifixion; and those who keep silent about it are as guilty as the centurion."

When Terry agrees to testify against the people who might kill him, *On the Waterfront* is dealing with the sacrifice that is often required for us to be of any use in this world. When he risks honesty, to do the right thing, his peers initially only stand by and watch. At this point, *On the Waterfront* is about how easy it is to get into bed with evil. Like many clichés, it's true: All it takes for evil to prosper is for good people to do nothing; or, as one character puts it, "I don't know nothing, I've not seen nothing, and I ain't saying nothing."

That kind of silence, of course, kills. Human beings everywhere are capable of terrorizing others. But it takes a huge psychological leap to be able to kill another human being, or even to just deliberately hurt them. You have to pretend that the other person is less of a self than you are.

You have to wipe the slate clean before you can break it.

Human beings become broken slates because we have made it too easy to erase any sense of unique dignity from others, which begins by distorting our own sense of self. We know that some of the stories we tell teach us to devalue and dehumanize self and others because of who they are, or who we think we are. But human beings are also capable of crossing boundaries, loving people who are different, and forgiving those who have hurt them. I imagine that Budd Schulberg knew this, and that it isn't a far stretch to also guess that he knew that dehumanizing someone is not the path to take if you really want to be a person, to contend as a human being, to welcome and accept everyone without cramming others into ideological boxes. Schulberg knew that if we devalue the humanity of others, we cannot be fully human ourselves.

If he wanted to root these thoughts even more firmly in New Jersey, he could evoke another of the state's sons whose voice echoes a century after his death. Walt Whitman knew bodies and desire, knew spirits and broken things, knew Jersey. He would know that today the humanity displayed by the Camden 28, by the folks who struggle to get by in that most dangerous city, and by those who love dangerously is the best sign that America really can be a free land for a brave people. He wrote a poem about an alien that makes me think of the person I was at eighteen, landing in Philadelphia, crossing the Delaware River, arriving on Rudderow Avenue, meeting friends I would know for the rest of my life, and seeing an American underbelly that felt strangely more safe and welcoming than the mansions of Beverly Hills or an Upper West Side penthouse ever could. His poem is about a stranger, maybe an immigrant, maybe the new guy in town, and I quote it here from *Leaves of Grass* because it evokes the feeling I have when I think about New Jersey, and how my dreams of America, which had only been cinematic until I finally visited, were to be made flesh.

"To a Stranger"

Passing stranger! you do not know how longingly I look upon you,
You must be he I was seeking, or she I was seeking, (it comes to me, as of a dream,)
I have somewhere surely lived a life of joy with you,
All I recall'd as we flit by each other, fluid, affectionate, chaste, matured,
You grew up with me, were a boy with me, or a girl with me,

*I ate with you, and slept with you—your body has become not yours only, nor left
my body mine only,*

*You give me the pleasure of your eyes, face, flesh, as we pass—you take of my
beard, breast, hands, in return,*

*I am not to speak to you—I am to think of you when I sit alone, or wake at night
alone,*

I am to wait—I do not doubt I am to meet you again,
I am to see to it that I do not lose you.

★

How I long for the part of me that was prepared to dream as if no one
was watching, how this journey through American cinema, now winding
down, is leaving me unsettled, the echoes of previously dormant persua-
sion sounding, the sinews of the tree of memory gently wrapping around
my body so that I would stand still long enough to hear the voice calling to
me, the one that called me when I was four and watching *The Black Hole*,
when I was thirteen and not watching *Bull Durham*, when I was fourteen and
watching *Field of Dreams*, when I was twenty-four and watching *Magnolia*,
when I was thirty and watching, and thirty-five and watching, and now,
still watching. The voice is trying to persuade me to stay. It's trying to
persuade me to realize that the movies aren't responsible for my journey.
It's trying to persuade me to understand something new about home. It's
trying to persuade me to dream. And so I'm dreaming of the New Jersey I
knew when I was young enough still to dream, to dream of what Whitman
wrote in "To a Stranger". He may not have known what he was seeking,
but he found it. He surely did know that love emerges in the unlikeliest of
places, like the docks in Hoboken, or Camden urban decay; he knew that
the human heart, and the heart of America, is fragile. He could demand
America answer him, or he could just be grateful that it was. Whatever the

case, he knew that only he was responsible to decide what kind of man he would be. What kind of nation he would shape. Jersey.

Magic comes fleeting; forget to pay attention, and you'll miss it.

Jersey.

Where I first came to America and started to learn that the nation contains multitudes. Whitman ends "To a Stranger" like a love letter, and he speaks for me. He seems to want me to know that this place is a gift, but it won't reveal itself as such unless I learn to look for it.

ΦOSTSCRIPT

You Should Stay to the End of the Credits

It's the question that drives you.
—Morpheus, *The Matrix*

Nobody's perfect.
—Joe E. Brown, *Some Like it Hot*

THE MOST REAL PLACES FREQUENTLY AREN'T. THEY'RE PLACES I'VE SEEN DANC-ing on a white screen, animated by dusty light in a darkened room. They're places I've been to without leaving the (dis)comfort of a plush red seat with no legroom. They're places that seem bigger than real life.

These places exist, because In The Beginning, the Creator, in the form of two French engineers down on their luck, perhaps not sure what to do with their lives, had an idea. On a winter's night in the early 1890s, it occurred to them that what the world of the mid-Industrial Revolution needed most was the opportunity to watch pictures dance with light and dust. The well-being of the planet could be nurtured by thirty-foot high images of men with guns, women with perfectly fake breasts, and young men having sex with cherry pies. That was the gift of the Lumiere Brothers. If you visit the cemetery where they're buried, you can find their grave easily—it's the one with the neatly tilled soil. They've turned over in shame so many times that their plot always looks freshly dug.

Despite the sometimes embarrassing nature of their legacy, when I reflect on what makes me human, or at least what makes me feel human— because, God knows, there's enough out there that tries to kill any sentient notion of experiential human-ness—I find my thoughts turn, more often than not, to the movies.

I think my soul finds rest when the curtain goes up in the way that, for some people, watching football on television can make them feel at home in themselves. I often feel whole when I'm in a cinema, partly, I think, because it connects me with the innocence of childhood, and partly because, for the two hours or so that I'm in that space, nothing else can touch me. One of the characters in *Death of a Salesman* lives by the shibboleth "attention must be paid;" a call so powerful it can kill. Sometimes it feels that the films I'm watching are paying attention to *me*, they're reading *me*, they're showing me who I am.

And every once in a while, someone on the screen says or does something that makes me feel understood, as when Donnie Smith in *Magnolia* cries, "I really do have love to give, I just don't know where to put it." Or when Gene Hackman's master thief in David Mamet's *Heist* explains how he gets away with it:

"You're a pretty smart fella."

"Not that smart."

"How'd you figure it out?"

"I imagined someone smarter than me. Then I tried to think, 'What would *he* do?'"

Or when I watch *The Wizard of Oz* in late December and am reminded that my fears are just an old man behind a curtain who only has the power I give him. And if the notion of using a fairy tale wizard as a psychological tool strikes you as odd, I guess I'd say that I have long believed the way cinema portrays life doesn't have to be real so long as it's not *fake*.

But my reasons for believing film to be worthy of investing my precious time are more than psychotherapeutic—they're sociological, and perhaps even prophetic. Arthur Miller, author of *Death of a Salesman*, was described by *Time Magazine* upon his death as a "slayer of false values," and the best cinematic art does just that. Chuck Palahniuk says that he wrote the section in *Fight Club* about IKEA catalogues as postmodern porn because he wanted to satirize his own superficiality—his book is about his attempts to break free from mediocrity. So is this one. You know by now whether or not it has succeeded. And you also know that the films I give a damn about are the ones that give a damn about me, or at least about people generally, and the struggle to be human in a technophiliac world, driven by the forces of the military-industrial-entertainment complex.

★

MARTIN SCORSESE FAMOUSLY SPENT EARLY YEARS IN A MOVIE THEATER BECAUSE his asthma prevented him from doing much else. I did it because I didn't like playing school rugby, and that's the only other thing that was available on Saturdays. I wonder now as I write whether or not I would have been any good at rugby had Marty McFly not gone back to the future in such a compelling fashion. It was the first movie I saw more than once at the cinema, and on the day my primary school exam results were issued, I chose to see it a third time rather than take a day trip to the seaside. That kind of commitment is a bit like the smoker who can't afford to buy you a drink, but can always find enough money for another pack. Friends and lovers alike have found my willingness to drop everything in favor of the movies endearing, at least the first time round, although the charm of considering cinema more important than real life soon wears off.

But that's only because the world is made up of two kinds of people— those who get movies, and those who get something else. The first kind can sit in the enclosed darkened room at any time of day and get excited when the lights go down, no matter what is about to appear on screen. We travel halfway around the world to visit film festivals and see movies that will be released at home in a few months anyway. We pay good money to go to Berlin for a morning just to see the statue the angels perch on in *Wings of Desire*, we fall into ourselves with delirium when we catch a glimpse of Isabella Rossellini on the street, we stay up late to watch pictures we've only vaguely heard of because our fellow cinematic nerds have said the cinematographer has A Wonderful Eye, or that the movie influenced the mid-wave of the post-apocalyptic Mongolian agricultural documentary movement, or perhaps merely because someone told us the director's dog has a great bark.

★

FOR WHAT IT'S WORTH, THIS IS WHAT I THINK ABOUT THE POWER OF CINEMA: It makes us imagine something bigger than us; a representation of the best selves which we think we might be capable of embodying. Cinema is a kind of memory, because what we see when we're watching is the sculpted detritus of someone else's dream. What we're experiencing at the movies may feel brand new, but it's already happened to someone else. What has happened is profound enough that that someone devoted a year or more of their life to turning it into image and sound, marshaling up to a thousand or more someone elses to produce a plasticky reel or a digital file that will be transformed by projected light into a dream in which the rest of us may wake up.

I think about the magic of cinema, the God's-eye view we have of those on screen, and how, when I once met a Big Star, I felt weird because he wasn't as tall as he should be. Given that that would be around eighteen feet, I shouldn't have been surprised, but I suppose I am still pretty naïve at heart.

I think of *Magnolia* and wonder at its capacity for squeezing in what is wrong with modern North American middle-class life, and how the opportunity for redemption cannot be engineered, but must simply be received.

I think of a hundred heroic films that made me feel like anything was possible, or romantic comedies that taught me something about love, or dramas that helped explain the meaning of life.

I think of *Jean de Florette* and *Manon des Sources* and how they begin as innocuous dramas about a dispute between neighbors, but conclude with you being terrified for the characters, and you want them to love and not destroy each other because they make you think about how knowing one extra piece of information about a person can change everything. The fearful miracle is that it can make you love instead of killing them.

I think about how I'd prefer the magic of cinema to stay where it used to be—in the half-hidden caverns of my heart. I wish that I didn't have to force myself to become innocent every time I see a movie. I sometimes long for the time when there was no difference between my beliefs and Hollywood's vision about what is possible. I sometimes wish for the day when I didn't have to try to compel myself into the frame of mind that believed in the possibility of hope.

I think about going to see *Basquiat* in an art house in Kansas City on a day in the summer of 1996 when it appeared that only single men were allowed in. Thirteen of us, sitting alone, dotted around the theater, enraptured by the imagery that told of this broken artist and member of Andy Warhol's Factory during the Reagan era. The film ends with the telling of a medieval myth about a prince locked in a tower by his evil relatives. To alert the local peasantry to his predicament, he bangs his crown off the wall, but they hear this only as music. It is an image with the potential to become the definition of cliché, but to us, it spoke only of the way we sometimes feel about the world and our secrets: lonely, a little self-absorbed, to be sure, because we think we are trapped in one of the most distressing of prisons—from which we are not sure how to get our truth out. As Henryk Gorecki's *Symphony of Sorrowful Songs* reached its long crescendo and the prince banged his head harder, a guy in the front row flung his arms in the air, and held them there, as if this was a worship service. And it was worship, of a kind—worship of the God, or the Reality so many of us still want to believe in or hope for, and perhaps also of the extraordinary creative urge of which humans are sometimes capable.

★

TODAY, I'M THINKING ABOUT MIA FARROW, BECAUSE I'VE BEEN WATCHING HER experience the miracle of fantasizing herself into a movie, playing the put upon wife of Danny Aiello in Woody Allen's Great Depression picture *The Purple Rose of Cairo*. That film begins with the words, "I'm in heaven," because it's about how the movies can grant us a measure of happiness when life on earth is difficult. Mia's character watches the same film every day, falling in love with Jeff Daniels's dashing hero until he steps out of the screen for a whirlwind romance that ends when the corporation that produced the film forces him back onto the other side. Other than perhaps Jonathan Caouette's *Tarnation*, no film has better captured the way movies "mutate into our memories," as the critic Molly Haskell says—how looking up from our lives into the dream of cinema can be a respite from whatever sorrows have mounted through whatever dreary Monday we're living through. "It's not me, it's the movies" is the most comprehensible excuse I can think of for selling myself to a celluloid version of my own dreams.

Richard Dreyfuss says that everyone wants to be in the movies—*Purple Rose* goes a step further by telling a story in which the movies want to be in us. We prefer our heroes to be like Indy or Han because they're not like us: They succeed, they have closure, they can be in fights and not suffer realistically, they always have something extravagantly witty to say, and they always look good. Fictional characters have to behave consistently, otherwise we won't believe them, and the American Dream of what reality is depends on our suspending what we know to be true—that Hollywood is a venal business whose dominant purpose is to steal from us. Hollywood is afraid of only one thing, and it's not the failure to make great art. The only thing the film industry is scared of is losing its place as the monopolizer of the American soul. Hollywood has so dominated US popular culture in my lifetime that it may well be legitimate to ask that if America fell in the forest, and there were no cinema screen to project it on, did America ever really happen?

★

I'M PRETTY MUCH OBSESSED WITH THE MOVIES—THIS MUCH YOU KNOW. MY EGO mingles with the ids on screen. My real life dreams are shaped by the fictional ones I've seen. Like Jeff Daniels in *The Purple Rose of Cairo*, I sometimes imagine that God is the writer of whatever film I happen to be watching. But I know, at the end of the day, that I am just an ordinary person. And the movies that don't like ordinary won't let me in. They will always ultimately betray me, unless I can continue to learn appropriate boundaries between my life and the movie world. I'd rather be the real me than the movie me, anyway. I'm sure Harrison Ford (an actor, a carpenter) feels the same way. Perhaps that's why he lives in Wyoming and making tables instead of in Brentwood having them waited on. At the end of *Purple Rose*, Mia Farrow chooses her real life over the imaginary one. But she keeps going to the movies—Fred Astaire this week, Errol Flynn the next, Joan Crawford the week after. She'll find her solace and fund her imagination there, because that's what the movies are for, and that's what she needs them to do.

★

Nikos Kazantzakis, the author of *The Last Temptation*, later made into Martin Scorsese's most explicitly religious movie, once wrote words that name my current state of mind: "I believe in a world which does not exist, but by believing in it, I create it. We call 'non-existent' whatever we have not desired with sufficient strength."

The movies, dreams of desire, teach us the limits of our own possibility. And that's the reason my journey round these cinematic states has to end where it began. In the possible. Where I am. In North Carolina, with a man playing baseball and trying to make a life.

Susan Sarandon speaks the last words of *Bull Durham*, cementing the mystical notions with which the film has been replete. Quoting, or re-writing, Walt Whitman, she says:

"I see great things in baseball. It's our game, the American game. It will repair our losses and be a blessing to us."

For me, this has become the truth about the movies, too. Towns like the Durham of *Bull Durham* that still live in the imagined past, where men get their identity from being ordinary, where something as mundane as how fast you can throw a ball, can make people think you have been singled out for attention by God, where people chart their lives through the ups and downs of local sporting fixtures, and there's not much to worry about except what to cook for dinner and how to make sure you have enough candles to enjoy your bath—these imaginary towns offer the hope that something like real human community is still possible, in America, in northern Ireland, wherever. Even though we don't really believe these towns exist, the dream might be enough to help us build one that does. Baseball is the American constant—Whitman said so, the PBS film-maker Ken Burns made an epic documentary series to underline his belief that it was true, and Terrence Mann at the end of *Field of Dreams* suggests that sitting on the bleachers for an afternoon might be enough to save the human race from its own grief. But Durham hadn't, in reality, made my life better. In fact, after my experience of the threat of violence and a system unable to handle it without simply adding fuel to the fire, I was probably more afraid than ever. Not to put too fine a point on it, the vision of America presented in *Bull Durham* had not fleshed itself out. Yet.

My experience of Durham isn't the whole story of Durham—neither, of course, is *Bull Durham*. But both are part of the truth. It dawned on me, being exposed to the breadth of America through watching a movie from each state, that if North Carolina was a mystery to me even when it was staring me in the face, I could hardly expect that my perceptions of the rest of the country would be accurate. Those perceptions should not, I suppose, have surprised me. I found what we always find when we look for greener grass. I found that most places in America are pretty good. They've got problems, like the rest of us, and they've got miracles, like the rest of us. There is something attractive everywhere, and also something that makes me uneasy. I had to acknowledge that nowhere was going to offer itself as the perfect home. And why should it? I was lost in America, and I know that there's only one thing to do when you're lost.

I re-traced my steps and watched *Bull Durham* one more time.

And you know what? It was pretty good. This exchange in particular stopped me in my tracks:

ANNIE: I think that in a former life I was Catherine the Great or Francis of Assisi.

CRASH: How come in former lifetimes everybody's somebody famous? How come nobody ever says they were Joe Schmo?

★

AND THAT'S WHAT THIS FILM IS ABOUT. IN FACT, THAT'S WHAT EVERY HONEST film is about. It's about how being Joe Schmo, or Crash Davis, or [INSERT YOUR NAME HERE] is the answer to the quest for happiness. The magic happens in the everyday. The dream is about being happy where you are, or more than that, *being* who you are. And given that who you experience yourself to be depends on how you remember your past, the dream of the movies in which so much of your memory is embedded has something to say about how to create your future. I struggled to live in Durham partly because I was remembering badly. I think I was remembering the dream as being unreachable, or deliverable only unto people who looked or acted like Brad or Tom or Julia or Cary or Channing. I was remembering the wrong dream.

Bill Withers once said that if you're going to live the American Dream, "It's alright to head for wonderful. But to get to wonderful you'll have to pass through alright; and when you get to alright, take a look around." Because alright might look like home. As I write this, I've moved several times since I first arrived in North Carolina. I've spent the better part of a year living in a cinematic dream factory with the hope that I might be able to persuade myself there actually is some place in America perfect for me and mine. It is a silly hope. There may be no place like it, but home isn't really a physical location. You can have all the house in the world without ever finding home. You can have all the material goods in the world without ever being rich. You can live in Beverly Hills without ever visiting America.

★

I KNOW THAT, TO SOME READERS, THE AMERICA DISCUSSED IN THIS BOOK WILL not look like the America in Budweiser ads, or State of the Union speeches, or Uncle Sam finger-pointing posters, or even books by Mark Twain. No, the Cinematic States of America is sometimes—how shall I put this?—a bit of an asshole. But it's also sometimes a saint. Its physical landscape can encompass not just the technical prowess and urban blight of Detroit, but the imperial tack of Disney World alongside the natural glory of the Grand Canyon and the creative marvel of the Empire State Building too. Its representative people can be painted along a continuum that includes not just Dick Cheney and Kim Kardashian, but also Dorothy Day and Dr. King. Its totems are not restricted merely to international belligerence and domestic arrogance, but just as much—and maybe even more—the desire to share its goodness with others and live free amidst beauty.

It's a 300 million person paradox. If there's one thing its recent history tells us, it's that the American empire is declining. But if there's one thing that living here has taught me, it's that if it can accept this reality with humility, it might just figure out its gift to the world. Because it will have learned to remember things the way they were, rather than how we might have wished them to be. It is teaching me something that might make me a whole person—that there's nothing wrong with having a dream, but if you want your dream to come true, you need to work for it. And then you need to give it away. It's the only way to enjoy it. And you'll never get it if your finger is pointed toward others, blaming them for why you don't have it yet.

So, here we are. At the end. Or at the end of the beginning. I didn't know what to expect when I started this journey. It really was a sincere attempt to understand my adopted country, in the hope that I might find a way to stay here. I ended up finding out something about myself. America's not the asshole. I'm the asshole. But sometimes I'm a saint. I can have my American Dream; but if it's to be worthy of the name, I need to work for it. And if that work is to *work*, I need to remind myself of a cinematic truth: that the American Dream never belonged to me in the first place. It was someone else's dream. I didn't invent it, I don't own it. I get to be in relationship with it, to be sure. And even then, the dance of orientation toward a dream depends on at least two partners stepping up. Whitman's passing stranger is an invitation to the poet to ensure his part of the bargain of relationship. Camden's where Whitman started; me too. I think my American Dream is simple. I am to see to it that I do not lose you.

ȺCKNOWLEDGMENTS

This book was originally a film—on a flight to New Zealand in October 2007, an idea appeared in my neck-pillowless head, fully formed, and ready to go. I would make a documentary film about America, traveling across the country, meeting interesting people, screening the iconic film from their particular state, and interviewing them about how they feel represented therein. So I'd meet with civil war re-enactors in Georgia to discuss *Gone with the Wind*, lifeguards in Massachusetts to talk about *Jaws*, and members of the Kansas chapter of Little People of America to explore *The Wizard of Oz* (it's rather unsurprising that many folk with dwarfism have an ambivalent relationship with that film). The challenges of squeezing fifty states into a feature length running time pushed me in the direction of writing this book instead; maybe one day some of us will get together and make the film, and if that's the case, it will be partly because of the encouragement and help I am grateful to have received from the following people.

Erin Parish gave unwavering support to a potentially quixotic endeavor.

She was there at the start of this project, advised me, supported its develop-
ment, patiently read and listened to early drafts, and never ceased to be available to listen to Ennio Morricone's L'estasi Dell'oro when I needed a boost.

My friend Jett Loe has sustained working with me for seven years on
www.thefilmtalk.com, over the course of which he has frequently astonishing insight into what movies mean, why they matter, and their craft. He
helps me see things differently every time we talk.

Amazingly enough, people I greatly admire, including Monte Hellman,
David Thomson, Glenn Kenny, Frank Schaeffer, Dan Siegel, Loretta Roome,
Lelia Doolan, Wendy Grisham, Tom Burstyn, Trace Murphy, and Elvis
Mitchell all said kind things at key moments that allowed me to believe
the project was worth pursuing. My agent Kathy Helmers cares about my
writing and the health of my soul, and her friendship is more important to
me than her professional advice. Given that her professional advice is among
the wisest I've ever received, I'm deeply grateful to her.

Scott Teems gave me more comprehensive notes on a close reading of
the text than any writer has reason to expect. I don't see him very often, but
it's easy to consider him a true friend. He's a great filmmaker too.

Colin Fraser Wishart, Karen Moore, Dave Wilcox, Nance Pettit, Bart
Campolo, Will Otto, David LaMotte, Mike Morrell, Jasmin Morrell, Jacob
Kuntz, Rachel Swan, Tim Tyson, Mike King, Barry Taylor, Lesley Gaspar,
Milton Brasher-Cunningham, Paul Fromberg, Denison Witmer (without
whom I never may have known that *Fight Club* is set in Delaware), Phyllis
Tickle, Brian McLaren, Rodrigo Dorfman, Mark Scandrette, Scott Bass,
Ian Cron, Nick Roosevelt, Tony Jones, Kevin Davis, Valerie Davis, Steve
Knight and Holly Roach read or listened to parts of the manuscript. Their
comments always made it better.

Mike and Rosemary Riddell never cease to help me believe in the
power of telling stories.

No one I know cares more about revealing the breadth of the magic of movies, and no one I know who works in the industry cares less about celebrity than my friend and mentor Mark Cousins.

Jason Lehel and John Gordon inspire me with their approach to filmmaking, and helped nudge me toward turning this idea into something that could be printed. Their film *Gaia* is a magnificent work of art, and has the power to help heal weary souls.

Caleb Seeling and Jordan Green have been both hands-on and friendly publishers. Their kindness and enthusiasm have kept me going, and the shared task of editing the manuscript was far more pleasurable than anything otherwise called "cutting" should be.

I'm blessed with friends like Don Shriver, Peggy Shriver, Carl McColman, Cathleen Falsani, Ched Myers, Elaine Enns, Will Crawley, David Dark, Tom Wills, Geoff Little, Jared Williams, Jeff Ham, Ken Morefield, Andrew Johnson, Kristine Fleck, Laurel Meath, Linda Alvarez, Mark McCleary, Trevor Henderson, Michelle LeBaron, Terry Hogg, Gerrie Dwyer Hogg, Clare Dwyer Hogg, and Lisa Dwyer Hogg, Rob Johnston, Pete Rollins, Roy Samuelson, Linda Sack, Scott Bass, June Keener Wink, Shannon McNally Ham, Rosa Lee Harden, Steve Berry, Tamara Feightner, Greg Feightner, my fairy godmother Karla Yaconelli, Michael Open, Alistair Spence, Tim King, Tisha Speelman, and Todd Fadel, all of whom encouraged the journey of this book. Brian Ammons stopped me throwing in the towel, told me the truth, and stuck with me when I got a case or two of "writer's ego".

When I was younger my mum and dad, Iain and Fay Higgins, allowed me the space to watch a few hundred movies; they may have thought my time would be better spent elsewhere. For *The Black Hole, One Flew Over the Cuckoo's Nest, Field of Dreams, Forrest Gump* and *Buena Vista Social Club*, I thank them. And for *The Goonies, Gandhi,* and *Back to the Future*. And that's just for starters.

My brother and sister, Brian and Caryll, love movies too, and I love them for how we can talk about them—Brian, I think, loves movies more than any of us. He makes them as well. Look out for him. He's good.

★

FOR A DECADE BETWEEN THEM, JOHN O'DONOHUE AND WALTER WINK GAVE of their hearts and time to speak into the life of an often morose northern Irish writer. They both moved onto their next chapters during the writing of this book. I am deeply grateful to have known them, and I miss them every day.

THIN BLUE SMOKE

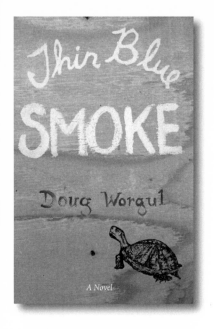

More than gorgeous prose and fully developed characters, this novel offers us catharsis.
—MATTHEW QUICK, AUTHOR OF *THE SILVER LININGS PLAYBOOK*

A powerful novel worthy to be shelved alongside Buechner and Flannery O' Connor.
— *ENGLEWOOD REVIEW OF BOOKS*

This was, without a doubt, the novel which captivated me the most, that I couldn't put down, that I wanted to talk about.
—BYRON BORGER, HEARTS & MINDS BOOKS

AVAILABLE IN PAPERBACK AND EBOOK

 IF YOU LOVE GREAT STORIES . . .

LET THE BIRDS DRINK IN PEACE

From the mind of ROBERT GARNER MCBREARTY

Winner of the PUSHCART PRIZE *and the* SHERWOOD ANDERSON FICTION AWARD

A superb mix of dark and comic, intervowen seamlessly into the fabric of his fiction . . . McBrearty is a master stylist.
—*PRAIRIE SCHOONER*

What threads through McBrearty's work is a humaneness toward his characters and a gental, sometimes sad irony . . . as adept at moving the reader as he is at making one laugh.
—*CHICAGO TRIBUNE*

AVAILABLE IN PAPERBACK AND EBOOK